SALAL

LISTENING FOR THE NORTHWEST UNDERSTORY

LAURIE RICOU

NeWest Press

Library and Archives Canada Cataloguing in Publication

Ricou, Laurence, 1944-
Salal: listening for the Northwest Understory / Laurie Ricou.

Includes bibliographical references and index.
ISBN 978-1-897126-22-6

I. Salal. 2. Salal--Social aspects. I. Title.

SB413.E7R52 2007   635.9'3366   C2007-902161-I

Editor for the Board: Smaro Kamboureli
Text editor: Carol Berger
Cover and interior design: Natalie Olsen
Author photo: Dominique Yupangco
Back cover image: Margaret Butschler
Research associate: Maia Joseph

NeWest Press acknowledges the support of the Canada Council for the Arts, the Alberta Foundation for the Arts, and the Edmonton Arts Council for our publishing program. We also acknowledge the financial support of the Government of Canada through the Book Publishing Industry Development Program (BPIDP) for our publishing activities.

NeWest Press

201.8540.109 Street
Edmonton, Alberta T6G IE6
(780) 432-9427
www.newestpress.com

NeWest Press is committed to protecting the environment and to the responsible use of natural resources. This book is printed on recycled and ancient-forest-friendly paper.

PRINTED AND BOUND IN CANADA

I 2 3 4 5 10 09 08 07

TABLE OF CONTENTS

ix ILLUSTRATIONS

1 LISTENING: A PREFACE

9 MULLING: AN INTRODUCTION

15 INTERVIEWING

19 GUIDING

23 NAMING

33 NURTURING

45 DEPENDING

61 ARRANGING

65 GARDENING

69 PICKING

81 COLLECTING

89 GETTING NATIVE

99 GATHERING

103 WORKING

115 INHABITING

119 SOURCING

125 CONTAINERING

135 RAMBLING

145 BOTANIZING

155 MOSTLY SHINING

159 BROWSING

165 STORYING

169 GLEANING

179 SALAL-SEEING

187 SUCKING TIDE

199 SALALMAN@HOTMAIL.COM

209 NOTES

223 BIBLIOGRAPHY

251 INDEX

259 ACKNOWLEDGEMENTS

ILLUSTRATIONS

5	figure 1	Salal Café
10	figure 2	Salal in blossom
21	figure 3	Salal in sunlight
25	figure 4	*Wood Interior*
27	figure 5	"Berries"
34	figure 6	Tom Wilkins's nursery truck
36	figure 7	Pots of salal ready for market
39	figure 8	Propagation house
43	figure 9	Pots of salal
50	figure 10	John Tappeiner
77	figure 11	Bales of salal "shorts"
82	figure 12	Sample of *Gaultheria shallon*
116	figure 13	Salal rooted on tree trunk
120	figure 14	Sourcing Northwest
126	figure 15	Rick Ross unloading boxed salal
134	figure 16	Processing room
149	figure 17	Stalk and leaves of the Shallon
152	figure 18	Botanical painting
174	figure 19	Seed package
180	figure 20	*Hopkins Landing, Howe Sound*
181	figure 21	*Tree Study*
183	figure 22	*A Rushing Sea of Undergrowth*
188	figure 23	Judy Christensen and Beth Slater
189	figure 24	Judy Christensen and Beth Slater
190	figure 25	Volkswagen as salal transporter
204	figure 26	Advertisement
267	figure 27	"Salal: An Idyll for Orchestra, opus 71."

[A] bit of red madrona around the edges, patches of pipsissewa and kinnikinnick, and endless acreage of glossy-leaved salal. Impenetrable, salal gives the impression of one endless, interconnected plant, up and down the Northwest coast.

· Robert Michael Pyle

Wintergreen: Rambles in a Ravaged Land

LISTENING: A PREFACE

> To live in a storied world is to know that ... each land,
> each valley, each wild community of plants and animals and
> soils has its particular style of intelligence.... Each ecology
> has its own psyche and the local people buy into their
> imaginations, to the psyche of their place, by letting the
> land dream its tales through them.

> · **David Abram** *The Spell of the Sensuous*

Salal. Its leaves glisten green, even where it's black-green in the gray-est greyness of a North Pacific Coast winter. Its salmon-white flowers dance easily at the end of red stems. Relatively few people recognize the plant, but it has surely beautified most of their homes. Its wine-dark berries don't burst on the tongue so much as they crumble — but their taste will twist your mouth into a smile.[1]

Here's how salal is described in a modest guidebook:

> *Gaultheria shallon*
>
> *Heather family,* ERICACEAE
>
> **SHRUB** 1–5 feet high, sometimes straggling.
>
> **LEAVES** oval, 1–4 inches long, evergreen.
>
> **FLOWERS** white to pink, urn-shaped, five-toothed, on a loosely flowered stem. (Smith *et al.* 66)

I

When I am asked why I wrote this book, what compelled it, my first answer is that I don't know why. Or, I *didn't* know why. I wanted to do something different. I wanted to write something that would resonate with the "storied ... intelligence" of a particular community, with the dream of habitat, of living at once simply (with one bush) and complexly (within and amidst all that plant's connections) in place. As in these two opening paragraphs, the measured observation of the compact guidebook would mingle with the impressionistic response of letting the land dream.

I was interested, simply, in where salal might lead. What if I tried to listen to "the animate earth" (Abram 291)? To the ways in which salal speaks? What would I hear? And, because I have been teaching poetry and fiction for almost 40 years, I wondered if there might be "literature" of salal. Still, mostly, I just went looking — foraging perhaps — watching and listening for nourishment, wherever it might be uncovered.

The method of the book rests in a question: could a regional culture be found by focusing on a single, native, uncharismatic species? Following what Lucy Lippard called the "lure of the local," I wanted — singularly, obsessively — to be alert to as many references to salal as I could. I have not included all that I found, but I've included a surprising many. Sometimes I comment on the significance of an allusion, but I am also happy just to provide little more than a glance and a list, because each instance provides another example of someone else paying attention to the local.

I chose salal for its unnoticed implicit localness, but I also liked the paradox of its potential globalness. The salal-region, and the centre of my attention, would be that Pacific coastal slope stretching from mid-California to Alaska marked by a species-distribution map for *Gaultheria shallon*. However, regional blinkering is challenged and complicated when salal plantations are being established in Colombia, and bouquets incorporating salal can be bought from a street-corner vendor in Antwerp.

But before words on pages, before facts about salal, I wanted the stories of people who live closely with salal. In letters, usually sent by conventional post, I described my project and asked people to respond if they shared my interest and were willing to contribute. Many, of course, never replied. Some were churlish: one nursery owner advised that she was often asked to do other people's work for them — but she was just too busy. So, no systematic field work or ethnography is involved or implied. My tellers are those who were willing. I think they are at once representative and wholly unique.

Although a single author's assimilation and retelling might have made the book easier to read, I decided during my first interviews that the salal-tellers should "talk" with a minimum of mediation. I wanted the voices to be heard in their own distinctiveness. They appear in an alternate typeface, and with very little of the question-and-answer primness often found in printed interviews. This format attempts to disperse authority, allowing the integrity and specialness of different actors with concerns, commitments, and interests very different from mine.

As I look back on this book, the finding and the surprise continue to please me, and to explain to me why I have resisted much conventional structure, spatial or chronological or thematic. Those "-ing" words in the Table of Contents propose that we pay attention to salal as continuing: a process, a complex of connections going on. That, I hope, is the endless, interconnected, somehow ecological form. In the sequence of sections is a trace of growing: early attention to gathering and distributing salal seeds, then to professionals and others nurturing seeds and tiny plants in nurseries and gardens, to salal's place in the forest, then to those picking, gathering, marketing, shipping and displaying salal. Display leads to some wondering about salal as dreamed and imagined. This cycle is interrupted at the end of the book with the story of a native plant man who retains salal as a nickname, even as he turns to a different profession.

Another possible form and two motives, in retrospect, also seem crucial. First, that the book might be a travel book. Then, that I want its narrow focus to speak a form of respect, and that the book should be grounded in hope — that it might grow hope.

Salal does report on some literal travels. Explicitly or implicitly it records visits to the Vancouver neighbourhood of Strathcona, to Pacific Spirit Park at Vancouver's western edge, and to the agricultural zones of the suburban city of Surrey, BC; to Courtenay and Victoria, BC, on Vancouver Island; to Ketchikan, Alaska; to Calgary, Alberta, and San Antonio, Texas; to Portland, Corvallis, Eugene and Astoria,

Oregon; to Olympia, Washington; to Inside Passage Seeds and Sourcing Northwest. It remembers looking for salal in London, England, and Paris, France, and talking about the plant in Saarbrucken, Germany, and Pamplona, Spain.

Yet, in its attention to the habitat of a single species, this travel book stays home, wanders "the nations of spruce and hemlock,/head-high salal and the thorny devil's club" (180). These lines are from Tess Gallagher's "Simple Sonatina." The poem continues from this specific cluster of flora to celebrate, elegiacally,

> That country I could speak with intimately
> in myself, country Whitman honored, teeming
> and lustrous, country I crossed and recrossed
> like a thrown-out child until anywhere
> wasn't home. (1987, 180)

Readers will understand "country" in these lines in various ways. For me, looking for the dimension of travel book, it conveys the sense of being at home in multiplicity, head-high in a teeming and lustrous undergrowth.

Salal spreads by rhizomes — that is, by the robust growth of a network of underground stems. It also spreads by seed, especially on decaying cedars. I have met it on a carved café sign on the main street of Port Townsend, Washington (figure 1); as the name of a 50-metre-long non-road on Saturna Island, BC; growing rather raggedly on the median strip of Pearl Street in Tacoma, Washington; blossoming in September at the administrative entrance to the Vancouver Aquarium; and proudly announcing a local commitment from a small pot on the bar at Shallon Winery in Astoria, Oregon.

In my own unsystematic tracking of the plant's range north, I am pleased that on the rock-strewn fractured shores of Nigei Island, BC, salal seems to cling to the cliff face, surrounded by weeping, stringy moss. Clumps are everywhere, but only occasional on the tops of small rock outcrops and islets, where it's clearly been seeded by birds. When I walk into the forest even 20 metres, the salal, under closed hemlock canopy, disappears. A large, twisted tree trunk and part of its root system rests on the beach, and in its crevices tiny salal plants, maybe

figure 1

Salal Café.
PORT TOWNSEND, WA

second-year growth, almost look as if they took root in the moss. Near the northern tip of Vancouver Island, along the boardwalks at Telegraph Cove, someone has planted some rhodies, but the salal is crowding them and outpacing their growth. At Baranof Springs on Baranof Island, Alaska, I cannot locate any salal, although it's used as a landscape plant around the Federal Building in Ketchikan. In Sitka, where sustained winter frost is likely, no salal is to be seen.

During a short day's searching in February 2004, I am not able to find salal growing in California's Pfeiffer Big Sur State Park or vicinity. However, many books say it grows this far south. In fact, if you were to depend on the *Encyclopedia Britannica* (15th Edition), you might think *Gaultheria shallon* grew *only* in California forests. Salal's range also extends further inland than its reputation as a coastal plant might suggest. In British Columbia's West Kootenays, salal apparently grows near the east shore of Kootenay Lake in a "'coastal refugium' ... hundreds of kilometres away from [the plant's] centre of abundance on the coast" (Gayton 85).[2]

In my wanderings through books, I also keep spotting salal. So, in what may be Canada's first eco-terrorist novel, Brian Brett's *Coyote: A Mystery,* the winding driveway leading down to the last resort at the far end of the fictional Artemis Island is "salal-lined" (153). Or in the saucy ironies of Jonathan Raban's rain-soaked Seattle in his novel *Waxwings,* where green sprouts and swarms and sags and chokes, where things rot fast and grow fast (207), the "ungovernable greenery" consists of two unspecific plants ("bramble, vine") and one named: "salal" (21). As it does so often, the salal forms "dense tangles" (171), and its mission, allied with that of its sarcastic author, is to obscure the city's pretensions to being civilized (21).

The Pacific Northwest is often conceived as an exaggerated landscape. Huge cedars and a huge logging industry. Hulking mountains, a string of volcanoes poised to erupt, fractured vertiginous geoscapes. Somewhere beneath, continental plates shift relentlessly. A grandiose mining industry moves to match or master the geology. More biomass. More rain. Feeling new, and uncomfortable, amid all this hyperbole, we kneel down, look close up, regard the little things. Looking at the bush and berries and blight might tell us as much about our uncomfortable feel for place as do stories of wood wars and gold rush.

The Nlakapamux writer Shirley Sterling tells us about her grandmother in the woods: "She would sprinkle sugar into holes in the ground when she pulled out tiger lily roots, then cover the hole over so as to leave the earth in the same condition as she found it. She said that when you take something from the ground you must leave something. She thanked the plant" (42). I have tried to attend to such elementary, but — in a world of missiles and instant-messaging — unusual gratitude. Much of the experience of writing this book has involved the discomfort of realizing how remote from me is the cultural history of respect for the spirit of a rock and the living animate soul of a shrub. Nonetheless, I thank the plant.

The hope that I seek to nurture I can express compactly by paraphrasing the philosopher of ecological ethics Kathleen Dean Moore, whom I heard speak at the University of Oregon in June 2005. When people begin to look, she insisted, they begin to see. And when they begin to see, they begin to care. To which, I would add, when they begin to listen ... The attitude, I believe, animates the sophistication and savvy so variably found in the people I have met in writing this book. Their hope, again expressed in terms I borrow from Dean Moore's address, closes the distance between what is and what ought to be.

MULLING: AN INTRODUCTION

We always learn something in a thicket.

· Jarold Ramsey "In the Thicket" *Love in an Earthquake*

Forget about the condor, the snow leopard, and
the panda.... Find some little musquash, guib,
or buzzing thingamajig that nobody else thinks
about. Care about it. Adopt it. See that it gets
what it needs — its space, its food, clean air and
pure water. Succeed in that, and the condor,
snow leopard, and panda will be okay too.

· John Cody *Wings of Paradise*[1]

The musquash I've picked out is salal. Or *shalal* as it's sometimes, and
maybe more correctly, pronounced (if it's noticed or pronounced at all).
When I whisper the word *salal*, even in the presence of people who have
lived on the North Pacific Coast for 30 years, I often draw a blank. I
sometimes think nobody else thinks about it.

Certainly my little musquash does not offer the same sustained narrative as follows the salmon, or the explicit iconography that identifies
the Pacific Northwest with cedar or slug. Perhaps salal's everywhereness

9

at the beach's edge, or on the rainforest floor, makes it possible to overlook. Still, its very commonplace fecundity also compels attention. Novelist Jack Hodgins takes notice, and often uses salal as localizing detail. So does the Saanich poet Philip Kevin Paul. So does Timothy Taylor, celebrating local foodstuffs in his novel *Stanley Park.*

Symbolic or defining shrubs readily identify places and cultures: chaparral, for instance, derives from the Spanish word for evergreen scrub oak, and describes a region dense with tough shrubs and stunted trees. Maquis, mesquite, sagebrush, tumbleweed, wolf willow: all these have more symbolic purchase and popular presence than salal. All speak one way or another of toughness, survival, resistance. Each carries an aura of romance. This book perhaps initiates — or better, uncovers — a parallel mythology for *Gaultheria shallon.*[2]

Robert Michael Pyle's book *Wintergreen* mulls variations of the colour green for 300 pages.[3] Or perhaps, as his title implies, the absence of green is Pyle's topic. Not the absence of colour, but the absence of a vocabulary that can begin to evoke the range and diversity and nuance of green that defines all seasons in the Willapa Hills of southwest Washington, and, hence, in the extended winter-green place he calls the Maritime Northwest (4).

This third morning of October is the second morning this fall we've had fog, and it lingers as I sit trying to write about green, even near noon. Fog catches your breath, but the honest eye will acknowledge that green still pervades. It emerges. It hides. And any catalogue of analogues (avocado? broccoli? pea soup? butter lettuce?) can't satisfy either the variety of green, or the shimmer of that increasingly low-angle sun that the weather report assures us is shining in our cloudless sky.

figure 2

Salal in blossom.
MAYNE ISLAND, BC

Pyle tries to write about what "touches our inner circuits" (225). It's a risky business, and inclined to redundant lushness: "Green, and greener, is as it should be" (239). But because he tries to explain his passion by reference to a more austere boyhood, his book makes me wonder how I came to this ... a book on salal. To this ... stopping on the way home to pick a few berries from the salal thicket that runs along an abandoned Canadian Pacific Railway line just down the street. Colour there too amidst the misted wintergreen: the micro bruises of those now retracting and shrivelled berries, but especially the way the red and pink of the spring blossoms seem to endure in the end of a branch, in the burgundy cups of the calyxes at the base of each flower that remain after the birds have eaten off the berry, in the cranberry hue of the stem mingled with white-green, and in the near-black fur-dust of the fruit.

Unlike Pyle, who attributes his attentiveness to a Colorado childhood, I cannot think of much in Brandon, Manitoba, my boyhood home, that prepared me for this. Other than crocuses and a vague sense of maples, I can't recall many plant names. Wolf willow I love — but I learned that from Wallace Stegner's book. Wolf Cubs and Boy Scouts were supposed to prepare us for the outdoor life, but for all the struggles of irrigating Bell tents and tying reef knots, we didn't learn much local flora and fauna from Lord Baden-Powell. He was more interested in luring us to the imperial ventures of India or Africa than teaching us how to tell flax from barley. No, I think I began to learn such distinctions when I went to teach in Lethbridge, Alberta. My colleague Bill Latta and then writer-in-residence Bob Kroetsch often stopped to point and look. And as we tried to start a new university there in the coulees, we knew we had to pay attention to what we had there in order to make something there.

That impulse quickened in the Maritime Northwest, especially because, as Pyle himself keeps saying, there's so much green here (or there), "endless acreage of glossy-leaved salal," and so many greens that challenge you to name them. Still, I'm no Pyle — professionally trained as a forester, self-taught as the Northwest's leading lepidopterist, married to a botanical artist. Rather, I am a literature professor keen on field trips and soccer, essentially a book-man trusting he can get to know the world through language. The conviction extends to trusting

And no one
Asks out of politeness why I stare at nothing
As if it were really here.
David Wagoner
"Into the Nameless Places"
In Broken Country

the play in language. Where Pyle teaches us to identify salamander, I also want to know what a salalamander might be.

Okay, it's not going to be easy to find the cross between darting amphibian and fronding shrub. Looking for the salalamander may be to stare at nothing. But coining a word from salal, and then asking where that imaginary thing touches our inner cicuits, does follow my own travels as an English teacher and lover of poetry who once studied how literature represents region, and now is writing with a plant as a starting point. The travel is random and slightly ludic, like inventing a salalamander.

At first, it seems an absurd comparison, but David Abram's comments on hermeneutics and the Torah show the path from salal into its habitat: "an organic, open-ended process to be entered into, an evolving being to be confronted and engaged" (244). Although it says relatively little about *plants*, Abram's *The Spell of the Sensuous* is a crucially relevant book about the language of the non-human world. Entering into this process includes the story of the journey that takes this English professor from image hunting and archiving to native plant as *text*.

Three square miles clearcut

...

No birdsong. Not one note

...

Among the living: a bent huckleberry,
A patch of salal, a wasp,
And now, making a mistake about me,
Two brown-and-black butterflies landing
For a moment on my boot.
David Wagoner
"Report from a Forest Logged by
the Weyerhaeuser Company"
Traveling Light

Mulling a salal-place is rather stunningly and surprisingly reinforced at the end of *The Spell of the Sensuous* when Abram locates the writing of the book amidst the flora and fauna of the North Pacific Coast surrounded by Douglas-fir, madrone, fog and ferns (262). As he comes to the end of the book, to provide a counter to the book's global scope, to signal his "interaction" with the "local," he describes "the moist earth of a half-logged island off the northwest coast of North America" (266), and devotes three paragraphs to its "texture and color" (267). This enormously influential book ends with a story of the intelligence of a half-logged, moist-earth region: Abram's visionary, ecstatic celebration and advocacy of the synaesthetically *oral* comes from the air and smells of salal habitat. Maybe David Abram is the shaman of the printing-press, and *The Spell of the Sensuous* sings his spirit quest, his search for a spirit helper, a totem.

Michael Cohen's *A Garden of Bristlecones*, entirely devoted to one totemic conifer species, provided me with an early model for imagining place through a single plant. Michael Pollan's *The Botany of Desire* immersed me in the psyche of four plants. Then I read Graham Harvey's *The Forgiveness of Nature: The Story of Grass.* Robin Kimmerer's *Gathering Moss: A Natural and Cultural History of Mosses* deftly teaches that new (often big) words increase our ability to see. At the video store, we can now rent a film version of the narrative guidebook, *Adaptation* — a Charlie Kaufman film based on Susan Orlean's book *The Orchid Thief*—and mull a renegade environmentalist's singular obsession with a singular plant, a narrow yet enabling focus that "whittles the world down to a more manageable size. It makes the world seem not huge and empty but full of possibility" (Orlean 109).[4] In a teasing, fascinating exercise of mind and art form, the film wonders reflexively what it is to make a film out of a flower, about a flower. I think the film decides it can't be done. Or does it?

INTERVIEWING

The only oneness that's interesting
is the oneness of a mosaic of diversities,
which is the nature of the ecosystem as well.
 We live in a time when people need to
be taught to pay attention to the specific before
their insistence on oneness can have meaning.

· Gary Snyder "Interview"

The real place doesn't come with postcards
or a map, just the fine details accumulating
for miles, and for years, and then the big
story comes up on you from behind.

· Kim Stafford *Lochsa Road*

What is it to want to make a book out of an ordinary shrub — not about the seductive shiver of the orchid, but an unremarked, straggling, loosely flowered member of the Ericaceae/heather family? Certainly, such a book should go beyond the pondering of printed words. I wanted to listen to people whose lives and often livelihoods were connected to salal in sustained ways.

Commenting on the writing process in his book *The Muses Among Us*, poet and essayist Kim Stafford proposes that "coherence is born of random abundance" (31). Take down the bits and fragments that interest you, he says. Be open, too, to the talk and the words that don't interest you right now — but may when they are read or re-read in a different context, on another day. This project is the least systematic I have ever pursued, and as I look at the Table of Contents I recognize its un-cohering. Still, beginning with the notion of writing a book titled *Salal* and coming back to a singular species in every paragraph might be the craziest of systematizings, the most limiting of systems. But it doesn't seem that way: keeping an eye out for the small, the unremarked, the generally unnoticed and the understory seems to provoke both randomness and abundance rather than hide them.

The other hoped-for coherence lies in habitat — in the proposition that defining place and drawing boundaries by the range and growth habits of a single species is a way of "sourcing Northwest," a history and culture that links California to Alaska, and that finds home — as do the distressed mariners in Ivan Doig's novel *The Sea Runners* — in a nurse log crowned in *Gaultheria shallon,* speaking of wine and ceremony and occasion. It lies, too, in understanding how this region connects to all the places that salal is now grown or sold.

I determined early on that paying attention to just one form of life would make a oneness of diversities. That premise explains why I interviewed just a few pickers, a few propagators, and but one wholesale florist. I did not want to enumerate prices or shipment quantities, or analyze patterns of training, or calculate average years in the business. Rather, I wanted to listen to salal stories. I particularly wanted to honour the under-stories — to celebrate unnoticed people caring in different ways for their environment.

Allowing for a mosaic of diversities meant that I was not going to try to provide ethnographic interpretation. I transcribed tapes, edited them mainly to remove repetition, rearranged the sequence only rarely, and generally avoided much intervening. In some sense, the presentation is distorting — it leaves out a measure of dialogue. But the measure is slight: in most of the interviews in the book, I had to ask very few questions. My interventions tended to consist of encouraging "Uh-huhs" and a surprised "Oh really." In lightly editing the interviews and sometimes reordering them, I have not recorded every alteration from the original. Ellipses, where they occur, indicate pace, silence and extended pauses rather than omissions.

People talked — and for the most part I listened. When it came time to incorporate the talking in the book, I opted to stand aside and let the reader listen to a wonderful "cast of characters" (as one early reader described them). Hence, my interview with wholesale florist Ernie Myer ends with his final comment, before we spoke good-byes and thank yous. I am not quite sure what to make of his warning — "Gotta watch out for cougars and bears" — but I can better suggest Ernie's character and the tenor of the interview by avoiding comment and encouraging the reader to lean forward, listening.

The verb "interview" often implies a formality of questioning and evaluating, but it also incorporates betweenness, coming to us from the French verb "entrevoir," often translated as "to glimpse." In interviewing salal pickers, distributors, growers, and researchers, and then in writing those up for publication, I have hoped for a glimpse. What stories do the salal-makers think are worth telling? Or embellishing? Or making up? I believe that stories, however partial, "give evidence … of the unique power of particular bioregions, the unique ways in which different ecologies call upon the human community" (Abram 182). I also know that the real place is just the fine details accumulating. Leave the big story to come up on us from behind.

The characters and stories here are integral to the region or landscape of salal. The salal storymakers are the subjects of their own stories. As for published poets and novelists, I don't seclude them in separate sections. They keep coming in to help, and push, and turn over, and just to play and imagine. And the process — it's the nature of the ecosystem — I like to think is reciprocal.

GUIDING

Where shall we walk?
· **David Wagoner "A Guide to Dungeness Spit"**
The Nesting Ground

What is it about guidebooks? I browse ten of them this grey morning when I'm not going anywhere, just to remind myself of the necessities of this traveller's essential. The guidebook aspires both to simplicity and accuracy, ease of use and thoroughness. Words and illustrations are interdependent, equally important. It should be organized. And explicitly or implicitly it's a book intended to accompany you outside your dry and cozy study, beyond that lazy armchair with that afghan wrapped around your feet. It's supposed to be with you "in the field" — to help you identify, to provide you with names. So, why is it that I am almost always without a guidebook in the "field"?

I know I'm not alone. Maybe in an odd way we fear displaying a book that might name its reader: as tourist, as outsider, as beginner. If I stand in the streets of Salamanca or Seoul, or on the sand of Long Beach with guidebook open, and, worse, reading from it aloud to a companion, I feel furtive, vulnerable. Or unjustifiably smug — if I'm watching someone else doing the guidebook thing. So, if I have any book with me, on the beach or the streets of Siena, it's more likely to be a novel or a book of essays than a guidebook. I want to know, I need the names — but something there is that does not love a guide.

Maybe a need for story and essay, as much as information, lies behind my reading (in my armchair) guidebook after guidebook entry on salal. The guidebook not for walking with, but for wandering in. The guidebook for browsing through. Many guidebooks, despite my summary of the genre, indulge in a technical and specialized vocabulary. I like this aspect: I like to stop and explore vocabulary. I learn that "urceolate" is a shape. The diminutive of the Latin urceus, "a little pitcher," designates a corolla hollow and contracted near the mouth. By analogy, the flower could be on the altar; it is ready to pour a precious liquid. James and Belinda Harris's *Plant Identification Terminology: An Illustrated Glossary,* a title I would not have glanced at two years ago, now becomes a book to settle down with. Poet and essayist Don McKay finds part of the lure of the guidebook in "the pleasures of system to which us big brains are addicted" (84). In an eloquently attentive essay titled "The Bushtits' Nest" — which, incidentally, traces connecting to the Pacific Coast after a move from New Brunswick — he also honours the poetry:

> field guides and reference books usually convey information in terse asyntactical bursts of fact and like to think of themselves as clinically awe-free. But the pose is pretty thin, and wears through entirely in their frequent recourse to metaphor… [T]hat move into mini-poem, far from being an aberration, is often the point of greatest descriptive accuracy,… the point that's likely to stick in memory. (85)

But think also on the more familiar vocabulary. In describing salal leaves, guide-writers divide fairly equally between "shining" and "glossy." They seem to confirm Robert Michael Pyle's lament in *Wintergreen* that we have almost no vocabulary for the green that stays all winter. Most describers resign themselves to an indeterminate "dark." Two metaphors dominate our guides to salal: however "showy" or "handsome" the foliage, almost every guidebook tells us the leaves are "leathery." And given the option of "bells" or "urns" to describe those urceolate corollas (whether "hanging" or "drooping" or "pendant" or "nodding"), four out of five books opt for the urn.

figure 3

Salal in sunlight.
SAVARY ISLAND, BC
Photo credit:
Janet Giltrow

On a spongy path in West Vancouver's Lighthouse Park, these guide-book clichés would likely prompt me to touch or to photograph. At my desk, they provoke delight at something like an implied holism. We seem to want to understand salal leaves as somehow treated, and trans-formed, so that they will not decay. And the leathery plant is breathable, is clothing, is animal. Unlike most other vessels, containers and vases, the urn has a long association with the dead, with ancient beauty, with human artifact: it holds the human body within a narrowing and then expanding form as it morphs back to the living world. Ashes to ashes, dust to a new salal blossom.

To wander sideways, thus, from the topic of guidebook to writing the connection between "shining" shrub, the surface where animal meets world, and the achievement of human art work, is to signal not only our resistance to being guided, but my sense of this narrative as a whole. Here is the problem: if we want to know salal, or seaweed or sow's ear, language, with all its agility, will not quite satisfy. Leathery helps, but it's also inadequate.

Thirty salal entries from 30 different guidebooks provide a pretty good case study for the samenesses and differences in a genre. But even a stack of 30 could not make the guidebook the Pacific Northwest ur-book — at least not in the way Bob Kroetsch showed us the seed catalogue as the prairie's foundational genre. It might be more provocative to thinking about wintergreen region to acknowledge that the guidebook is crucial because it impedes rather than facilitates travel. You set out to get somewhere, but you don't go very far before you're kneeling down to examine some lichen or mushroom or shrublet, and you have to look it up, and you get distracted, and then distracted again. Many of the stories that have resonated in the region — Ivan Doig's *Winter Brothers*, Malcolm Lowry's *October Ferry to Gabriola*, Richard Hugo's river poems, Daphne Marlatt's great estuary poem *Steveston* — tell of travels that don't go anywhere.

My unease with the guidebook is, of course, an unease with a book titled *Salal*, a guidebook perhaps more suitable for the sofa and the study than for the pocket of a Taiga® Gore-Tex® jacket with Velcro® fasteners. If the guidebook is one model (and certainly source and base) of this book — it should identify this plant, and teach its names — then it must be a guide such as the poet David Wagoner prepares for Dungeness Spit, one that pivots on a solitary and unanswered question: "Where shall we walk?" But the appreciation of intricate connection to place might require more specific and ample guidebooks than are conveniently portable — ones that push description to the aesthetics of arranging flowers against foliage, ones that reveal how many metres of rhizomes might be spreading beneath that glistening shrub.

NAMING

Every old cedar that falls, the damp earth,
the crushed salal, speak to me too.
I keep trying to say this.

· Mavis Jones "Controversy"

The Island mountains were a high blue jagged wall all
down one side of the world, with nothing beyond them but
ocean and Japan. You thought you might know the name
of something you saw — flower or bush, twice the size
you were used to — and discovered that you didn't.

· Jack Hodgins *Broken Ground*

An essential aspect of travel is the rest that makes motion, change,
and successive encounters meaningful. The traveller seeks both novelty
and interlude, a stop to reflect on where you are, how far you've come,
what you've learned so far. This is such a moment, a pause into naming.

Anne Rayner, a doctoral student who lived on Gabriola Island, BC,
first told me to pay attention to salal. It's everywhere, she urged, unspec-
tacular, impressive, thoroughly native. Often, it provides a livelihood
for those who would like to live harmless on the earth; it travels to

florist shops in many countries. Salal seemed to urge thinking locally while inevitably and ethically living globally.

Good students are always good teachers, and I knew that Anne, who had trusted many pages of her diary to me, was onto something. But Anne surely intuited that there was another attraction inside the green and growing and gathering. That salal — the word salal — wanted listening to.

SOFT CURRENTS

In writing about the paintings whose titles he borrows, poet John Barton in the book *West of Darkness* imagines Emily Carr drawing herself in words. As she paints, Emily speaks as "I." This I/eye, although the thickness and sprawl of paint might blur them, clearly recognizes plants by their specific names — and especially notices salal, which Barton's Carr names three times. The most resonant instance sounds in *"Wood Interior,"*[1] where Barton goes beyond the sea-of-salal idea to acknowledge Carr's recognition of a plant language, if only in a whisper:

> Boughs swim around me like astonished fish.
> Salal
> in soft currents whispers
> delight in my ear. (81)

Currents, whether in wire or water, ripple with forces difficult to see but strongly evident in their effects. Pursuing salal often has something clandestine about it: Barton's — or Emily's — "current," by extending to the slightly redundant "in my ear," emphasizes some secret language. Salal makes a private utterance, as if confiding softly to the insider, jealously excluding the outsider.

That whisper wants listening to. Salal. A sibilant, followed by two looping liquids. Two long flat a's separating the consonants, yet also integral to their sounding. The name makes its own micro-poem:

> SAL
> AL

Two monosyllabic characters, two partners, rhyming in love. Sometimes, the name urges silence with an opening *shhh* —. And the delight
in my ear is that tongue-twister that a character named "Small" (Emily
Carr's child alter ego) might savour and sing over and over. This shrub
could be the region's salalvation, poet Bill New told me. The berries
make me salalivate, I said. [2]

DZA̲'WEST (COAST TSIMSHIAN)

Al Purdy's poem "Say the Names" is a paradoxically ecstatic lament urging that in sounding a name such as Similkameen or Lillooet, we might listen to difference, and overhear our deep self, and dream. Salal, too, is a name "that ride[s] the wind" (579). In it you hear the voice of the first people who picked its fruit.[3] Only a relatively few Northwest Coast native plants are known by common names, and still fewer by Latin binomials, derived from native languages. Salal is rooted rhizomatically,[4] ecologically, economically — but also, from the Chinookan *klkwu-shalu* via Chinook Jargon, linguistically[5] (Harris and Hrubant 223).

In Coast Tsimshian, the word for *Gaultheria shallon is dza̲'west,* a term that translates roughly as "laughing berries."[6] Most guidebooks describe salal as a shrub, with berries dark and mealy, edible but not particularly palatable. I don't know why salal should produce smiling berries. I can only speculate. I did find one suggestion that the laugh is the big purple stain around an eater's mouth — but I want to hear more. I keep trying to say this. On the pre-contact (that is, the first and primary) North Pacific Coast, things behave differently. Salal, when it is noticed at all, is now known mainly for its leaf, or its invasiveness, but for the Tsimshian it is primarily a source of food. And the food welcomes, with invitation, with approval: prompts a smile. Different cultures at different times in different places tell us to read the surroundings differently. Saying the names — well, trying to say them … it's very difficult for an English speaker to reshape tongue and glottis and cheek to say even one Coast Tsimshian word fluently — convincingly saying the names connects us to place, but not simply. Saying connects us to the differences rooting themselves supportively, like mycorrhizal fungi, in our own place.

THAT WHICH WILL NOT BE NAMED

If I was asked to recommend a congenial and provocative work of theory as companion to this book, it would be difficult to find a happier choice than Neil Evernden's *The Social Creation of Nature.* Evernden wonders how we mean what we mean by "nature," and he teases out the implications of that intricate conundrum within such concepts as conservation, preservation, and ecology — precious concepts to most people who would buy or read a book about salal. In his cogent and compact epilogue, Evernden reminds us again, as he has in many ways throughout the book, of the limits of naming: "that which will not be named cannot be controlled" (132).

Laughing berries. A translation of a Coast Tsimshian name, and surely an inevitably limited one, draws us paradoxically to what "cannot be controlled." *One* name might give us control. Trying to get to know this name exposes us, I think, to what Evernden terms, and honours, as "the uncertainties of strangeness" (129). In the word laughing, and in its concealed metaphor, we might glimpse "the wild other" (131), the plant that cannot be controlled — and a culture's hopes and possibilities beyond naming.

figure 5

"Berries" (detail)
The Great Marpole Midden
(1994/07)

VANCOUVER, BC
by Christos Dikeakos

Part of Dikeakos's Sites and Place Names Project, this colour photograph is viewed through an etched sheet of glass that remembers — in English and Hunqum'i'num (a Coast Salish language) — the names of native plants no longer found at the site.

Printed with the permission of the artist

LAUGHING BERRIES

I often teach courses on the concept of habitat by asking my literature students to focus on a single species of flora or fauna. About midway through the course we listen to an audio tape, *Coyote and Rock, and Other Lushootseed Stories,* by the elder Vi Hilbert — especially to her gentle and wondering retelling of how the world came to have language. The Creator was flying across the continent distributing here and there languages, more or less whimsically. And when he came to the West Coast, he was so overwhelmed by its soft beauty that he decided to stop and stay. Whereupon, he promptly flung up all the many many languages he still carried with him and allowed them to settle, in all their numerous variety, on the peoples of the Northwest.

I don't know your metaphors.
I don't know what your thinking is....
It's still very confusing to me, sometimes,
when I look at your culture.
It sometimes seems pretty strange ... but I
understand the reverse of that is also true.

Jeannette Armstrong

"Words"

Telling It: Women and Language
Across Cultures

Amidst such plenitude, a long list of names for salal might be compiled. I do not try for comprehensiveness here, but instead offer a small selection that suggests geographical range and difference in vocabulary. Some of the words, to me, seem pretty strange. Such strangeness in words is, as Jeannette Armstrong suggests, a challenge to understanding across cultures — and a caution to acknowledge where a different understanding might be beyond our knowing.

Salal (berries) answer to *sk'idgaan* in Haida. That's the Skidegate dialect. In the Masset dialect, the word is *sk'idaan.* Another name also exists in Skidegate: *taan gaanga.* This second term comes with a translation — "black-bear berries" — that conveys a season and ecological niche, and is easily remembered in alliterative and assonantal harmonies. Several hundred kilometres south of Haida Gwaii, on the northwestern tip of the Olympic Peninsula, the Qwiqwidicciat word for salal used by the Makah people is *sala'xbupt.* The term in this language belonging to the Southern Nootkan branch of the Wakashan language family is apparently connected to the English term for the plant. But among the Quileute people, living further south on the Peninsula at the mouth of the Quillayute River, the term for salal in the Quileute language (part of the Chimakuan language family) is the very different *ko'o·'d.* [7]

One of the best sources I have found in which to read a bit about these words and ways of thinking is a patient and careful PhD thesis by Brian Compton, "Upper North Wakashan and Southern Tsimshian Ethnobotany." In some 500 pages, Compton brings together much of what is known and recorded about plants among the first peoples of the central and north British Columbia coast. Compton compiles, for example, 15 salal words in the two closely related languages of the Hanaksiala (Henaaksiala) and Haisla people, as well as terms for salal in the Oweekyala language of the Oweekeno people, and in the South Tsimshian language of the Kitasoo people.[8]

When Compton reflects on nomenclature, he keeps coming back to berries. Laughing berries, these might be. Some of the languages he considers do not even have a separate single term equivalent to

The Heiltsuk lexicon consists of bracken, great trees, multitudinous fish, and giant brown bears. The ecosystem is their mythology, and the stories, their syntax.
Susan Zwinger
The Last Wild Edge

the English word "plant." But the Oweekyala, Hanaksiala, Haisla, and Southern Tsimshian languages all provide separate botanical categories, of varying exclusivity, for berries. That is, the naming system, and hence "what your thinking is," is founded on function or use. The word that translates "salal" in Hanaksiala and Haisla, *nk̓ʷ ƚ*, refers to salal *berries* — almost the reverse of what we assume in English, where there is a whole plant called salal, which sometimes has berries.[9] As Compton sums up, in a rather anodyne phrase to refer to the extinction of languages and their active speakers, these language features, "despite substantial botanical lexical loss,... emphasize the significance of recognizing 'berry' as a valid life-form category" (469).

Sometimes laughing, in connection with trying to speak another language, is a sign not of pleasure or amusement, but discomfort. Naming salal often implies unrealized possibilities and reminders of the obligation to be open to another way of thinking, a different system of knowing. Berry as a life-form category means you can use berry to tell time. Coast Tsimshian recognizes the "moon when some kind of late berries ripen," a specific reference to salal (401). In Oweekyala, one period of the year, roughly September, is *tsakulstsAm*, "moon when there are no more berries" (371).

"A place is a story happening many times," Kim Stafford tells us in his contemplation of Franz Boas's work on Kwakwa̱ka'wakw place names (1987, 11). A life-form category keeps growing itself over and over, making its story of harvest and nurture and ceremony. *Nànak̓ʷasu*, which speaks "place where salal berries are picked" in Haisla (240), could be a name to name the North Pacific Coast. It could be a name for this book.

Taking the Names Down from the Hill is the title of Philip Kevin Paul's first book of poetry. It won the BC Book Prize for poetry in 2003. As his title seems to tell us, Kevin Paul is committed to the mystery of naming: many of the poems translate terms from his own Saanich language, SENĆOŦEN.[10] But translating here means taking the names down, as from the highest shelf, and re-examining them, listening to them in a contemporary setting. Kevin Paul makes poetry not by locating the "closest equivalent" term in English, but by translating as story, by a growing of connections.

In Kevin Paul's poem "What We Call Life," names themselves compound and overlap to possess salal. HELI, S'HELI, and SOX,HELI are the titles of the poem's three sections. These build a story of *alive* and *lively* (HELI) and *life* (S'HELI) into *personal belief* (SOX,HELI). Salal, in Kevin Paul's book, is food for deer, then concealment and protection. Then, in SOX,HELI, Kevin Paul stories the personal belief that has accumulated in the book through his mother's love for salal berries. I assume "SOX,HELI" is not a strict translation of salal, but salal emerges as love and sweetness delivering a promise of "harvest" and "jest" (2003, 89).

"What We Call Life" is an intricate reflection on many aspects of translation. Kevin Paul wonders about what his six-year-old nephew calls things, and then worries where he will find power if he cannot speak "our language." He aches for the "presence of ancient beings" in both his languages. He hopes that poems, his chosen form of language, will speak to his mother and his nephew.

To realize the translation, in the third section of the poem he tells his most straightforward and extended story:

> ... the story of
> my mother's love for salal berries. She believed
> their power was so sacred it could *only* be belittled
> by words, so we went out at daybreak so she could
> show me how to harvest and prepare them properly.
> Then, by the dream-light of false dawn, she taught me
> the pathway of words: morning, harvest, goodness, salal ...
> Having never attempted a salal berry pie, we waited
> nervously at tea and cribbage for the pie to cool.
> The pie wasn't that good. But we ate it knowing
> the plants had given their *gift,* and it was healthy
> to preserve this belief about a harvest and keep it
> alive in the family. Feeling silly enough to allow
> the edges of our mouths to become purple all around,
> she taught me the proper uses of the harvest words. (89)

Mother's salal pie doesn't taste "that good," but learning the "pathway of words" teaches a simplicity of what is compressed beyond and outside language, including the "sacred" power of salal berries, that "could *only* be belittled/by words" (89). Naming, I have noted, is one of those points in our travels when we stop moving — the interlude to assess what we still need to learn. Kevin Paul's poem, foregrounding his own language, is a reminder of the limits of translation.

In an essay titled "The Sweetly Neglected," Kevin Paul honours the "oral" — and questions the accompanying term "tradition." At the essay's heart, he remembers the teaching of plants in a passage that is a welcome guide along the pathway of the word salal:

> I remember the names of salal, because Grandpa told me. I remember
> the names in his voice. When the berries are full and ripe, he reminds
> me they are good for skin ailments and that their roots will help keep
> my teeth healthy. My father reminds me that salal bush is the best
> material for a hunting blind, since the leaves retain their colour long

after the plant has been picked. My father also gave me a vision of the fat trees in the old forests when only salal and sword fern could survive in what modest amounts of light the dense trees let through. How many times he described the forests of his childhood, nearly disbelieving it himself when he exclaimed, "You could see for miles!"

But it was my mother who gave me the attitude for walking among trees. It was for her severe eczema that we rose at dawn to go out and harvest salal berries. She also helped me grow the best spirit to carry with me into harvest. One cup of tea after the other until my fidgeting ceased, while false dawn thinned into morning, she watched her quieting son. With my most serious mind I watched her forget me, while she rolled dewdrops back and forth on a salal leaf, amused by something living deep inside her. It's something she never spoke of. (2004, 13–14)

"In the era of the true Saanich"—by which Kevin Paul means the time of a wholly oral mapping of place — he notes that "naming required the once habitual respect and love, along with an uncommon courtesy to that being named" (15). For Kevin Paul, "the danger inherent in the *literization* of a language is in storing information — valuable information — in an inanimate source" (2005, np). "Proper use" of words, of the word salal, embeds uncommon courtesy and an alertness for the store of information in an animate source.

NURTURING

It is the nature of roots to nose into cracks.

· Aldo Leopold *Sand County Almanac*

Growing salal has become a (small) big business. Landscaping with native plants has become environmental necessity, or fashionably necessary. As a resolute non-gardener, I am very much a visitor to the process and business of propagating. Trying to follow it took me to nurseries surrounded by cedar and hemlock, to rural spaces in big cities. It also took me beyond the reaches of Seattle, Portland, Vancouver, the commercial centres of the Northwest, where I realized how urban my worldview is. My own impatience in the garden is an obstacle to learning about a patient art.

WOODBROOK

When I get out of the car at Woodbrook Nursery on Bainbridge Island, Washington, no one comes to greet me.[1] A cube van — as I have since learned to name it — is parked in front of the building, and behind it is Ingrid Wachtler unloading. Before we can sit down to talk, she drives the truck to the other end of the lot and returns astride a small John Deere yard tractor dragging two wooden palettes, also to be unloaded.

She drives this toy machine with hot-rodder enthusiasm, tires spinning on the loose gravel.

We sit on the verandah of a bungalow-sized office and storehouse, shaded from the record-breaking heat. It's 26° or 27° Celsius at 10:30 AM. Ingrid is dressed in blue and talks in an efficient, matter-of-fact manner, bursting every so often into near-frantic and loving laughter. She's generous, kindly, but she approaches native plants with more market savvy than mission. When we start to wander around the large site to see salal in the various stages of its growing, she points and walks on ahead of me to another spot without a pause, suppressing the sense that somewhere she has a business to run, and many plants to care for in this unusual heat. So, she does everything to look after me, but isn't ready to linger long — she keeps reminding herself about getting to the weeding.

Maybe the untold story here explains how an electrical engineer comes to be a dynamo of native plant sales. Or, the middle-woman, refusing to consider trying to grow salal from seed, then trading her young plants to a landscaper to do the roadside work. The arrival of Tom Wilkins is a happy coincidence. Tom bubbles with enthusiasm for growing salal from seed, and shows off his literary sensibility, enthusing about the palindrome on the side of his truck: "The Kinnikinnik Connection," the motto for the Wilkins nursery (figure 6). Only later, I come to know him as salalman.

figure 6

Tom Wilkins's nursery truck. BAINBRIDGE ISLAND, WA

NATS NURSERY

When I arrive at the rows of greenhouses in rural Surrey, BC, two or three minutes before 10:00 AM on a July morning, owner Rod Nataros is out in the nursery. He's summoned in by phone, I think. The small reception area has no place to sit, but a coffee pot hums and, for diversion, a bulletin board filled with snapshots of family and company outings, a large Mercator projection of the world with the Pacific at its centre, and a poster of Northwest native wildflowers — salal included.

When Rod comes in, and ushers me into his office, I sense a slight strain in the air; he asks me almost immediately for my business card, and when I say "I'm just learning, it's in the car — in my briefcase," he asks if I can go and get it. Then, when I return, he says he's been snooping through the file folder I left on the table, trying, no doubt, to figure out what I could possibly be after.

Despite an unpromising start, our conversation turns warm, extending well beyond the 30 minutes he tells me at the outset he has to spare. I have learned always to present a calling card: whatever my fantasies about careful and caring cultivation, "nursery" here obviously means "business."

Rod leans back in his chair as if he's not very hurried. His voice is soft, sometimes fuzzy; only parts are audible on my tape recording. Yet there's no doubting his enthusiasm, especially when he several times points out the environmental niceties: better to plant seed and grow and replant, than to root up and transplant a shrub growing in the wild. At one point, he sums up his work as "environmental enhancement". If there's a story here, this may be its theme: a family guy, educated at the Christian university Trinity Western in Langley, BC, commits to restoring the garden.

When I allude to rumours of money laundering in the picking and wholesaling of florist greens, Rod says he's been hearing such stories for years. The first group that he connects to these rumours is Koreans, rather than the Vietnamese I am becoming used to hearing about.

He says he plants 350,000 salal seedlings a year, probably his second biggest seller after *Cornus canadensis* — bunchberry. Days later, when I check this name in Nancy Turner's *Food Plants of the Coastal First Peoples,* I find the Sechelt name for bunchberry means "the one that pretends to be salal" (71).

Rod speaks about various projects his company has been involved in. One landscaping project required some 10,000 salal plants. He spoke of sending five-gallon containers of salal, a seldom heard of size, so that his buyer could have instant landscaping.

Rod keeps repeating that salal is difficult to establish. And he marvels that some customers think that since plants are "native" they don't need watering. But once established, he confirms, salal thrives and is hardy. The difficulty in establishing salal partly explains why salal plantations seem rare, or rarely successful. So Rod's account of marketing small plants to Colombian intrigues.

❧ We ship through a fellow in Florida who ships it to Colombia, so we don't directly ship it to Colombia. Technically, we do, because it goes from us to Colombia, but it stops in Florida and it's in bond, and then it goes to the Florida guy's client. We don't know his client. We've worked with the Colombian government, and as soon as you mention to our agency here in Canada, CIDA, that you're shipping to Colombia — ohmygoodness the paperwork. But we've been able to work it out and it's been fairly smooth. We've seen less trade this year, 2004, than in 2003, but they're getting it into production, it's starting to happen.

"So," I muse, "they plant salal in plantations, harvest it and sell it back into Florida?" [2]

figure 7
Pots of salal ready for market.
NATS NURSERY, SURREY, BC

❧ Yes, in Colombia, where the cost of labour is quite low. As I understand, the location where it's being grown is very similar to the Ucluelet area. It's a little bit more like Costa Rica with the hills, all the slopes of coffee. But the climate is similar. Lots of humidity, rain all the time, 60 to 70 degrees, not real cold, not real hot. And that's where salal excels. It doesn't like the real heat. In Oregon, right, where it's real hot, or in any local planting in the Lower Mainland this summer, when it's been real hot, it's done poorly. The people in the south of Florida can't grow it very well because it's too dry, too warm. It just doesn't like that 90 degrees.

When I ask about unique methods of nurturing, Rod does not think, contrary to expectations I developed from our telephone contact, that there is much unique they do in the way of seed nurturing. They do put multiple plants in a set, so that customers can divide them and get more for the same shipped weight, although he points out that this generosity carries risk of increased disease damage.

When we part, he gives me book titles and contact names, and invites me back when the "propagator" is in. Propagator, I decide, is a nice term that suggests an advocate for salal, and a vocation that will sway public opinion.

PROPAGATING

So, I return to NATS Nursery a month later: unfortunately, the salal planting has already been completed, but Vanessa Adams will talk me through the details, with illustrations. She certainly does so … with gusto. It is all I can do to slow her down for explanations.

Vanessa is hurried (not impatient), slightly anxious, and obviously well learned in her craft. She is rather private about technical matters, so when I ask her to explain 0.5 and 1.0 fertilizer ratios, she just knows what it should be, but cannot describe the ingredients in a way that this visitor can quite grasp. Vanessa has the intuition of a great gardener, and I am hard to teach.

My encounter teaches another form of humility: Vanessa has a huge fund of knowledge, but it's different, and differently expressed, than the book-stuff I'm used to. She keeps coming back to add more details.

After our interview ends and I am off taking photographs, she returns to tell me that salal seeds need no chemical treatment or soaking to promote germination. Still later, she notes proudly that because salal requires less light per day to germinate than most other plants, she can grow it from seed in winter with no artificial light needed. Again, I think, *wintergreen:* a genuine winter native low-light plant.

Vanessa loves her job: she wants to make things grow, and knows a lot about how to do it. When I leave her, she's sitting in front of a full tray of 72 plugs, taking salal-cuttings, dipping the ends in rooting compound (which looks like very fine ash), and making a hole in each plug with a pencil. The cuttings come from a very young plant — a wee filament or thread of stem — with the lower leaves pulled off to create extra nodes where roots might emerge.

In this exacting process is a delicate beginning: the story is starting to grow. From seed to germination to seedling to transplanting to market. But Vanessa's story is more interesting for its tempo. I constantly sense, maybe especially in her pace of speech, and her movement from site to site, the need to maximize growth rate. Among ground covers, salal has particular appeal for Vanessa because she has the talent to get it to grow quickly. A *propagator* truly. The sooner she can get the seed to germinate, and transplant it, and get it out of there, the better. Rod and the world will like it.

At the time I met with Vanessa, I had been reading Carol Shields's novel *Unless.* It creates a poetics based on that single word, a syntax not quite of avoidance, but one venturing an apology that paradoxically refuses to apologize. Shields quietly but insistently links the unless-ness of being female (daughter, mother, artist) to botany. So I can't help understanding Vanessa, whom I've barely met, through Shields's eloquence on seed: "[Flowers] were miraculously encoded from the beginning.... They sprouted, then opened out in a studious and careful program of increments. Now, that was astonishing, all those compressed unfoldings and burstings, but no one said so" (148).

> *"Sense of place" as a political force, a cultural allegiance, a way of daily life, a combative alternative to the industrial juggernaut that treats watersheds, people, soil, and forest as liquid inventory, strikes me as being as necessary to human beings as water or soil itself.*
>
> **David James Duncan**
> ***My Story as Told by Water***

SEEDLING AND PLUG

A few months later, still intrigued at the scope of commercial growing of salal, I revisit NATS to see their all-new facilities, located further south and east, and isolated on a dead-end road. To enter the much more elaborate propagation house at the new site, you step through an anti-bacterial, anti-fungal footbath. The soaked mats are one means of curbing the spread of Sudden Oak Death, a fungus-like pathogen known to affect nursery plants. Inside, the building feels like a hockey arena built entirely of glass (figure 8). Vanessa has moved to another job, so Angela Anderson, the nursery's new native plant manager, walks me again through the steps of propagation, beginning by holding up a bag of seed.

❧ From 10 kilograms of fruit, you get half a kilogram of seed. They're very small seeds. So that's not an enormous yield, but we have somebody with a secret spot where there's excellent fruit and he can pick fast and pick bagloads. Much like the harvest of the leaves, people have their picking sites for seeds too. There's a lot of people who pick fruit and seeds for seed sellers. And so they're out there gathering as well.

figure 8

Propagation house at NATS Nursery.
SURREY, BC
Photo credit:
Andrea Martinello,
NATS Nursery

As we salute the precious secret seed, Angela introduces John Mill, who cleans the seed and has a long history of extracting seed from conifer cones. He and Angela used to work at PRT Reid Collins Nursery in Aldergrove, BC, doing cone and native seed processing. They now work together with native plant seeds at NATS.

❧ John's brother has actually been out collecting for us. We keep the berries that come in in the cooler here, and when John gets a chance he extracts seeds.

We put the berries in a big blender. It's not so much a concern for the salal, but for some of the seeds you don't want the blade to be too sharp — it'll actually shatter the seeds. So this is perfect — it's a nice dough hook. It's dulled. That's perfect; it'll still break up the fruit. If it's something really juicy like salal, you probably don't have to add water. If it gets too gummy, you just add a bit of water to let it blend properly. And then it's just a matter of seeds sinking, floating off pulp, using sieves, finding different ways to clean the fruit — the seed — as best you can. Different methods for all the different kinds of seeds. There are actually some seeds that float in certain species, which makes it a bit harder, but the salal's pretty good at sinking below the blade here. And then you just lay it out to dry for a couple of days. There are some years, depending on weather, when you might not get a good crop, so it's best in a good year to get as much seed as you can. We ran into a problem with *Mahonia nervosa*, the Oregon-grape, last year: it was a drought year, and nobody had seed. So we've got a lot now so we can cover a bad year. We can store the seed for several years as long as it's below 4 degrees and it's dried.

Angela and I move into the main greenhouse, a bright, large space solely devoted to propagating.

❧ We have an Argus control system in here. There's a sensor box up there, so we can vent based on humidity and temperature. And we have heating underneath the benches, so that we can heat each section at a different temperature based on the soil temperature. We have a good facility. The ferns are doing really well, the salal's doing really well, so we're really pleased with it. Nice, clean and new, and well ventilated.

Salal needs a pH that's quite acidic, and we've found the water we have here is about a 7½; I was testing some of the plugs, and they were at 8. They can't take up iron, so you see iron deficiency when that happens. We've corrected the pH now.

We don't have any freshly seeded salal at the moment. We have to sow it on the surface, because it needs light. And we want four to six seedlings in one of these plugs. So, we aim for up to eight or ten seeds — that's ideally what you want. Parminder Brar, our propagator, sprinkles the seed by hand, and she's very fast. She does a good job when you consider the size of the seeds. This crop is ready to go: you don't want to hold the plugs much longer than about five months. [At this stage, the plants are about 5 centimetres high with five or six leaves on each.]

The initial part of the germination is the really slow part. They take about three weeks to start germinating. In that time you have to make sure your surface stays moist enough for the germination. At the same time, we're trying not to grow moss, because we grow the seeds on straight peat. And that way you can control the nutrition, and you keep an acid environment.

Moss is a problem in the industry with anyone who grows plugs that take a while. If it's something that turns over in six weeks, it's probably not a problem. This moss here has stayed small enough that the plants have overgrown it and it's not an issue. We have more trouble in something that stays shorter, and the moss ends up blooming, and getting the same height as your plant. Salal plantings stay quite tiny for a while, and that's when you might get a problem. Once they reach about a centimetre, though, they really start growing.

We do fertilize, but growing salal in straight peat means you have more control. We don't have a soil mixture — there's no perlite in it, or added sawdust or anything. It's just peat moss. My history of growing is with PRT [Pacific Regeneration Technologies], where they primarily grow conifers. And I did the native plant program, so I had to work with whatever they worked with. I grew everything I had in peat. You can control fertilizer very precisely in it.

You can fertilize at a high rate, like 100 parts per million nitrogen, and then water the next time. I prefer to use a lower level of nitrogen, but use it every time. Parminder tells me that she doesn't fertilize at all, at first — just gradually. After a month, when they have tiny leaves, then she starts fertilizing. She uses 50 parts per million, once a week.

Generally, we use a 12−2−14, and then we have to supplement with a magnesium sulfate because there's no sulfur in that mix, and that can lead to paling of the leaves.

Our control system allows us three methods of fertilizing. We can fertilize from overhead, because we can switch the system. There are two sources here, so we can switch it to plain water or fertilizer, and we have injectors out there. We can also do it by hose — this side is water and this side is feed, so we can actually hand-water if we don't want to water the whole bay. And the other method involves a dosamatic, a separate apparatus that you attach your hose to if you're going to supplement with something and you don't have room to mix it in your main injector tanks. For instance, I gave these plants acid-treated water to bring the pH down, and I did it with the dosamatic — I just treated the area I wanted.

These four-month-old plants could get shipped out if they're purchased. Or we could stick the plug into a four-inch pot, or we might take two plugs and put them into a gallon pot, and grow them until you have a finished product. We won't divide a plug up. We want several plants, because you want a bushy product.

This is a 128-cavity plastic tray. We also grow them in 72-cavity trays: in those, each plug is a little larger. You can grow your plant a little bigger; it'll have a longer shelf life.

Manju Khaley there is getting an order ready. She would do the same for the salal. She's collecting *Gaultheria procumbens* right now. She's taking out the largest, most mature ones for an order. It's a little early for this crop, but a lot of the customers want it now, because they're going to transplant it. It'll grow great once it's transplanted.

I would say salal is probably number one in terms of volume and sales among the natives that we grow. *Procumbens* is a good ground cover, but it's not native to our area — it's native to the East Coast. *Arctostaphylos uva-ursi* [kinnikinnick] has the potential of being number two. Again, we grow that one from seed. We can grow it from cuttings, as well, but a seed product is really nice.

We don't grow salal from cuttings. I've heard stories of people trying to transplant salal and having no luck whatsoever. Kind of like transplanting an arbutus. . . . It really is easy to grow salal from seed. And seed is relatively plentiful, in our area anyway. With any kind of crop, it's always cheaper to grow from seed than from cuttings, for the most part. Labour-wise, there's less handling, so that's the way you go. Plus, genetic diversity: growing from seed versus from cuttings, you don't end up with a monoculture of one clone. Being a native plant nursery, I think that is relatively important.

"So, you have a new facility," I observe. "It's bigger, more high tech. Is the interest in native plants really increasing in the marketplace and among the general public?"

❧ That's been my impression. There are a lot of people growing ground covers, so if we can grow native plants, there are certainly staples like salal and kinnikinnick as well as willows and other plants for restoration. But there's also room for some of the more ornamental ones that people just don't know about and aren't available. Even some of our native asters — the ones that are right along the road here, with the purple flowers, look great. So there's a lot of room for natives in the garden. With the recent environmental movement, people have this concept that native plants are better. People have a misconception that they won't suffer any of the diseases that your purchased hybrids will. Of course they will. But also there might be some that are more adapted to the weather with drought tolerance and that sort of thing. And I don't think that people have to plant their whole yard with natives either. A lot of the showy ones are shade lovers, and they blend very well with plants like hostas and such. So incorporate some into your garden.

Listening to Vanessa and then Angela helped me learn the discipline of nurturing. In their work, I watched their attention to a plant emerging from an almost invisible seed. The honesty of their craft consisted of the careful learning of pH measures, dosamatics, and parts per million of nitrogen. Reading the transcript of Angela's guided tour, I realized that in this case the culture of salal extended to something resembling a manual for the cultivation of salal. Angela's craft and talk, however technical, teach an understanding of the most literal meaning of culture.

figure 9

Pots of salal.
WOODBROOK
NURSERY,
BAINBRIDGE
ISLAND, WA

DEPENDING

Ecosystems are not only more complicated than we think, they are more complicated than we can think.

· Jack Ward Thomas

Cindy Prescott is a professor of forestry specializing in forest nutrition at the University of British Columbia, and the coordinator of a now 15-year-long forest-management study whose imposing title, the Salal Cedar Hemlock Integrated Research Program, itself proposes complicated ecological connecting. Cindy has been my willing teacher over six or seven years. Although we meet for lunch on the university campus, her enthusiasm transports me to her primary research site on the northeast coast of Vancouver Island, BC (between the towns of Port Hardy and Port McNeill), a particularly moist part of the Coastal Western Hemlock ecological zone that receives 190 centimetres of precipitation annually.

When we meet for the fourth time in May 2006, Cindy reports on new perspectives gained from her group's long-term trials. Their research has focused primarily on explaining the poor growth of western redcedar, western hemlock, and other trees on recently forested, salal-thick sites. Over the years, their views of salal ecology have changed greatly, as Cindy explains:

❧ When you and I first talked, we were still viewing salal as a serious competitor that was severely limiting the productivity and growth rate of harvestable tree seedlings at newly planted sites. The cutovers [areas of forest clearcut of all useable timber] were showing a lot of little yellow trees, so we thought salal might be taking up a lot of nutrients and starving the trees. It was a pretty logical conclusion at the time.

But then we put in these long-term trials — a lot of them are more than 10 years old now. We've been able to compare removing the salal — using herbicides or mechanical means — with doing other things, like adding nutrients. In the long run, we're finding there is very little gain from getting rid of salal.

Where we added nutrients we got better growth from trees — but simultaneously we saw huge response from salal. So we changed the focus to its *not* being so much a problem.

Then, we had the hypothesis, based on the behaviours of another ericaceous shrub, that salal was actually binding up the nitrogen, keeping it from nourishing the trees. This had been suggested in the biggest science magazine, *Nature*. But that's all a bit of a myth as well.

Then we tried to replicate a previous experiment done in Quebec. We put tons of straw knee-high on the forest floor to smother the competing growth. We got a huge growth response, but it didn't kill the salal. We were able to get good response from the trees without actually getting rid of salal — in fact, while encouraging the salal.

So, instead of being negative on salal, we began to think the reason these sites are poor is the same reason they have salal. We've tested many hypotheses, but now we think maybe the sites are nutrient-poor because they're just too wet. That could set off all sorts of things with the microbes that are there.

It's weird how sites just a few metres apart are so different. It's been quite a mystery.

Cindy is a conscientiously rigorous scientist who is repeatedly bemused at her discipline's, and her personal, lack of certainty. The combination makes her a persuasive teacher. The sense of elation she exudes when she doesn't "get it" helps a non-scientist to get it. Listening to Cindy I realize that it might be compatible with salal ecology to incorporate many questions and leave most of them, ultimately, unanswered.

LOW DOWN

On a fine Sunday morning in June 2004, I sit in the forward lounge of the *Nautilus Explorer* as we cruise into Hakai Strait. It's as close to a perfect day as we could have — warm, a cloudless sky, sea barely rippled. Yet, even in ideal conditions, the vista is blurred. One, two, three, four, five, is that six? islands in retreating shades not of green, but of brown, then blue-grey receding to grey and white. And I know I'm describing the North Pacific Coast the way many other writers, painters, and photographers have taught me to describe it. Seen through this misted lens, a native plant that's always green and thrives in relatively low light could become symbolic.

Writing salal requires stopping to think about what escapes our notice. In contemplating the ecology of salal, the *low down* becomes exhilarating. By virtue of its massive and robust rhizomatous system, salal's special ecological property is that in almost every case it does not yield when disturbed by fire or by what foresters call "brushing" and "screefing" — that is, some form of mowing, or scraping of the forest floor (Boateng and Comeau 9, 7); rather, it comes back more vigorously.

To think salal ecology, and its complications, I begin from the ground up. Salal prefers well-drained, dry sites and does especially well in acid and sandy soils (Van Dersal 135). Dense and intricate threads of fungus, known as mycorrhizae, increase the efficiency of the root system. Mycorrhizal fungi assist many plants: scientists are still trying to determine whether a unique mycorrhizal fungus contributes to the vigorous growth of salal (Xia and Berch, Natar and Berch). Cindy observes:

❧ We had some very crude ideas not long ago that salal had one kind of mycorrhizal fungus, and that the adjacent trees had different forms. But we now have new molecular methods for analyzing types of fungi. What we've found is quite contrary to expectations. Salal, cedar, and hemlock all have a range of very different mycorrhizae, and they actually share the same fungi. So, rather than explaining antagonism, we found compatibility.

The North Pacific Coast gardener's question is also the forester's: not "How do you grow?" but "How do you stop the growing?" Salal doesn't want to give up its native habitat easily. Where climax or old-growth forests are cut, salal seems to survive the single grip harvesters and log skidders, and any burning, to re-sprout from rhizomes and establish dominance. (As forest management practices change, salal is more likely to be harvested for greens, although picking is not likely to destroy it.) To forest workers slogging up steep slopes to re-establish cedar and hemlock seedlings, salal, the ultimate North Pacific Coast native species, is an obstacle and invader.

Although gardening books reiterate salal's preference for well-drained, acid soil, an article on Burns Bog, a 70-square-kilometre wetland preserve in southwestern BC between the Fraser River and Boundary Bay, observes that salal marks the springiness of the soil: when you jump up and down on the bogland, you make the salal bush jiggle. So, dry sites are no necessity: salal's ubiquity might be explained by its ability to thrive in moderately moist, to dry, to super-saturated soil (Harvey 2000, 23). Recall that plant nurseries often start salal seedlings in pure peat moss. In Camosun Bog, a small preserve just metres from residential Vancouver where conservationist "boggers" struggle to re-establish sphagnum moss thread by thread, salal is again a worrying invader. And salal's opportunistic volunteering in stumps and driftwood also shows the suitability of sponge habitat. Cindy enthuses about the plant's ecological amplitude: it flourishes in a whole range of moisture conditions.

UNDERBRUSH

Anne Marriott's rainforest-undergrowth poem, "Underbrush," recounts trying to create a "human passage *in*" (42, my emphasis). Along with devil's club, salal is a key impediment, but one, placed in parentheses, that is "not so dramatic": "Just the old salal that knots and twines" (42). Affectionate familiarity and impenetrability of salal commingle. How to find a passage *in?* Maybe just identifying, even creating, the knots and twines finds the inside passage. Marriott questions the human need to make a passage through.

Oregon State University Professor David Huffman, reporting on the salal growth process in the understory, celebrates salal's exceedingly vigorous rhizomatous propagation or "vegetative expansion" (i.e., distinct from new starts); he notes, by contrast, a rather modest propagation by seed. Much in the article "Regeneration of Salal" (Huffman *et al.*) confirms that salal is a *very* strong competitor for nutrients and moisture. I wonder if there are measures of these things: for instance, does salal take up more available nutrients (such as nitrogen) than, say, huckleberry or Oregon-grape? Cindy proposes that salal takes up less: it thrives by needing less.

Salal seeds are tiny. It takes 7687 of them to make a gram (Huffman 49). They especially like rotting wood to germinate in. The seedlings do not take at all well on the forest floor itself (47). But, of course, those underground rhizomes more than compensate. Huffman and colleagues report that they have measured a single-season rhizome extension as long as 94 centimetres. And, even more astonishing, they have measured 218 metres of rhizomes, occupying an area of 29 square metres, from one clonal fragment (42).

In *On the Line*, philosophers Gilles Deleuze and Félix Guattari overlap and reverse their way through a proposal that *book* is a rhizome. In a teasing assertion bound to appeal to someone writing about the understory, they announce, "We are tired of the tree" (33). And they go on to refuse the "whole arborescent culture" in favour of the rhizomatic: "only underground stems and aerial roots, the adventitious and the rhizome are truly beautiful, loving, or political" (33). They note that the rhizome "connects any point with any other point," and that it is "made not of units, but of dimensions, or rather of shifting directions" (77). To a

When a seedling regenerates, and leaves come up and roots go down, eventually, right at the surface of the ground, it will start to produce stems that run underneath the ground. They're not roots, they're stems. And as the rhizomes begin to develop, if you pulled them out of the ground and stood them upright, they wouldn't look any different from aerial stems. Or if you took an aerial stem and buried it, it wouldn't look any different from a rhizome. So they're interchangeable. They put out this network of aerial stems and underground stems.

And as the rhizomes – these underground stems – develop, they give rise to more aerial stems. Then you have this big mat of interconnected stems. A clone – they're all the same genetic material.

If you walk through a patch of salal, it probably started from one or two seeds. An individual clone can get quite big: it can spread from here over to the wall.

If you have some windthrow, or clearing, then the underground stems will start to grow and throw up aerial stems. They'll grow right through a decomposed log.

John Tappeiner
Department of Forest Resources
Oregon State University

writer struggling to grasp how salal spreads or is rooted, and who takes special glee in a photo of a forestry professor clutching an armful of rhizomes (figure 10), the possibility of the book-rhizome has special allure. A book — I'd like to think they're talking about this book — is "an arrangement, it exists only in connection with other arrangements" (3). The rhizome, the rhizomatous salal, proceeds by "variation, expansion, conquest, capture, sticking" (78).

Forest scientists tell us that salal's own most congenial habitat is "thinned stands." However, the rhizome biomass and density (the below-ground growth) is highest in clearcut sites, and clearcuts are also where salal seedlings emerge earliest (Huffman 45). Evidently canopy, understory, and even underground story thrive in interdepending patterns. But conclusions turn speculative in their very particularity. That salal persists in various settings is perhaps more crucial. Total biomass (i.e., both above and below ground) seems to be the same in clearcut

figure 10

John Tappeiner with a bundle of salal rhizomes — one of his teaching aids.
FORESTRY BUILDING, OREGON STATE UNIVERSITY, CORVALLIS, OR

and thinned stands (45), although in low light the total biomass falls
—yet maintains vigour.

In *The Egg and I*, her memoir of trying to farm on the Olympic Peninsula, Betty MacDonald includes salal among a small group of "low-class
squatters" reclaiming a burned-over ravine (101). Salal bushes "slap" her
"in the face" when she is carrying an armload of cedar shakes (60),
and "obliterate" abandoned homes (193). The forest ecologist defines
the same dense habitat and prolific habits by identifying three key attributes of salal: the plant's ability to continually produce new aerial stems
(that is, the uneven age structure of new stems helps to maintain steady
renewal [Huffman 49]), the ability of a clonal fragment of salal to
occupy a large area (20 + square metres) (49), and salal's ability to grow
in conditions of relatively low light.

TWINES

Allelopathy is the process by which one
plant produces biochemicals that give it
a competitive advantage over other plants
in the same ecological niche. Salal is often thought to be allelopathic, creating
its own micro-ecology to outcompete
other species (Messier 289). To me the
term seems alien, and when I strive to
pronounce the word my tongue seems
to stick to my teeth on the third syllable.
But, when I mention in conversation the
possibility that the leachate from salal
leaves encourages more robust growth of

*Being a member of the Heather family
(like rhododendrons), salal has this huge
ability to absorb surface nutrients. It may
have long rhizomes, but those are right at
the surface. It has an extensive system of
side roots that just takes everything that
comes down. They had a project on the
North Island where they added fertilizer,
and they found 80 percent of the
fertilizer was taken up by salal.*
Rick Ross
Western Evergreens

salal, the word allelopathic rolls off Forest Shomer's tongue effortlessly,
perhaps reflecting his experience on the Noxious Weed Control Board.

Just as we might over-read or over-interpret habitat relations, so we
might be too enamoured of allelopathic behaviour. Cindy, and many
other researchers, once thought it might explain salal's prolificness.[1]
But, she warns me on another occasion, if you can't calculate the rate
at which a plant produces a certain agent, then you can't really prove

allelopathy. Any chemical agent produced, she notes, will inhibit growth of nearby species if it occurs in high enough concentrations.

But absence of definitive proof may be the ecological principle Cindy is teaching. From the Greek *allel-*, allelopathy is a redundant formation incorporating both *állos* meaning "other" and the genitive plural of *állos*, *allelōn*, meaning "of others." So, within allelopathy lies some reflexive concept of the "other of others" or, as one dictionary summarizes, "of one another." This tautology points to a species depending, as it were, on its own depending — an idea appealing to poet and to biochemist alike.

LOW LIGHT

Scientists measure meticulously. They measure the stems of salal for height and diameter; they oven-dry the leaves and weigh them. Usually they are looking to give advice to forest managers — to determine in what environment trees are most likely to get the moisture and nutrients to accelerate their growth. Other times, they may want to increase salal growth to ensure that deer have ample winter forage.

Measurement is a little baffling: try to imagine 7687 seeds, or a team of researchers digging and pulling and snipping and stretching and measuring and adding and recording every stem and root. Two hundred and eighteen metres of information, but no way to tell if the clonal fragment just to the south, unexcavated, might not be twice the length. There's some precise undecidability here that somewhere remembers the suspended uncertainty of a good poem.

Yet, I am pleased — despite my questions about measuring — that the LI-COR Biosciences Corporation manufactures "plant canopy analyzers," making it possible for diligent and patient field workers at Cape Creek on the Oregon Coast to record (20 readings per site) what they term "percent sky" (Huffman 40). Shaded salal is often better salal. Better, in the sense that the florist would prefer larger leaves and fewer blemishes. Appropriate for the misted, raincoast über-species (under, actually) — the best green is found in the grey. Science both proves and disproves this bit of regional chauvinism: salal presence declines sharply in a climax forest with closed canopy; however, as I've noted, salal will survive in exceedingly low light conditions — one to two percent sky (48). After clearcutting, those rhizomes grow like crazy: "Salal initially invests a large fraction of available photoassimilate into below-ground growth following disturbance, and this may facilitate persistence of salal through the stem exclusion stage of forest stand development" (49). But, as a forest begins to mature and available light decreases, more nutrients are assigned to stem and leaf growth (49). The change in growth, form, and redistribution of biomass in response to light is crucial: salal will grow even in full sun, will thrive in slight shade, and will only be eradicated by very low light.

Salal in low light has bigger and darker leaves, and fewer flowers — and, hence, lower reproductive capacity from seed (Vales 73, 74). So, to think of interdependencies, we appreciate how the understory plant depends on the overstory plant to provide its optimum growing conditions. Yet, we also note how salal governs itself, shifting its balances to take advantage of whatever light and moisture conditions it finds.

ABUNDANCE

Tracing an ecology must consider the plant's own inherent habits and its relations. What habitat does it provide for other life forms? What lives in and under salal? We know that salal leaves and berries feed the Columbia black-tailed deer, wren tit, Roosevelt elk (Olympic wapiti), blue grouse, brown mountain beaver, sooty grouse, Olympic black bear, band-tailed pigeon, Townsend's chipmunk, spruce grouse, and Douglas squirrel. Ruffed grouse, black bear, white-footed vole, red squirrel, and Norway rat feed on the buds and blossoms.[2]

The birds "exhibit" on the Royal BC Museum website, which draws largely on information in *The Birds of British Columbia* (Campbell *et al.*), associates the habitat of several birds with salal, including the winter wren, rufous hummingbird, Bewick's wren, and Swainson's thrush. Only the hummingbird is explicitly identified as nesting in salal (eight percent of its nests were found in the plant). I wonder if other birds also nest in salal, or live near it and just feed off the plant. How to connect flora and fauna through shared preference for "edge habitat" in a salal thicket, as the birds exhibit suggests? Or maybe, as Cindy hints, I overdefine habitat. If all these birds are in a cedar-hemlock forest, or observed in salal, we cannot conclude that they absolutely need it and depend on it for survival. Perhaps it or they just happen to be there. It depends.

The association of species in a particular habitat, some linearity of connect and depend, would be syntax in the word world. Conventions, some would say rules, decide what words live in what relation to other words, and how closely. In what set of associations, what semantic field, do we find salal? In David Guterson's novel *Our Lady of the Forest,* the connections might be: Oregon-grape — mushroom — salal — mystic — vision — erotic. More grounded written associations, only partly based on observation, would include "pines and cedars and tangles of salal bushes and brown-barked manzanita bushes" in a photo-essay titled *The Northwest Coast* (Williams 1973, 155); "a screen of cedars, hemlock and salal bushes" concealing the Japanese bunkhouse in Amanda Hale's novel *Sounding the Blood* (182–83); or the "struggling shore pines, wind-swept Sitka spruce, dense thickets of head-high salal brush" defining the saltwater ocean beach variant of the Coast Forest Zone in a Washington State park pamphlet.

Such clustering of species in literary or guidebook descriptions seldom extends to the strawberry-root weevils or butterflies that more immediately depend on salal ("Special Forest Products"). The Brown Elfin butterfly, *Incisalia augustinus,* lives on many plants, especially Ericaceae, and including salal: "single, greenish eggs" are laid "at the base of or in the flower buds;" "larva feeds on the flower and developing fruit" (Guppy and Shepard 214–15; Green and Huang). The larva pupates after a month, about mid June, and lies dormant on the ground among the dead plant material until the following spring. I have yet to see this butterfly in flight, but the next best thing is to read Robert Michael Pyle's attentively observed descriptions: "they pursued one another in tight circles.... One departed, was followed by the other and they soon returned together. Continually in flight for five minutes, in frantic pursuit" (1974, 51). Pyle uses eleven colour words, from orange to violet to dark chocolate, to describe the butterfly's subtle palette (2002, 214). Elfin, from elf, designates the butterfly's size, but also "flight habits that make them seem to magically appear and disappear" (Guppy and Shepard 214). They will "dart at chips of bark," Pyle explains, a habit that provides "a great way to find them in their extensive palaces of salal" (Pyle 1984, 136).

On some leaves of salal, "blotchy dime-sized patches [appear,] resembling white tissue paper, or splashes of thinned paint" (Dirks-Edmunds 1999, 65). These are evidence of the feeding of the larva of the salal leaf miner, a moth which gets its name, *Cameraria gaultheriella*, from its host. This tiny creature enters through the openings in the leaf and feeds on its inner soft-cell layer, leaving the outer "skin," the epidermal layer, intact. In turn, leaf miner larvae provide food for tiny wasp-like chalcids — no name yet, according to my source — two millimetres long. A dark leaf beetle, *Timarcha intricata* (known as the salal beetle [Dirks-Edmunds 1947, 252]), also thrives on the plant. And undoubtedly is fed *upon.* So, at least three species uniquely depend on this single plant (Dirks-Edmunds 1999, 65–68). Yet another insect, the grey weevil, can apparently cause "severe damage" to salal leaves (Boateng and Comeau 8).

Still, salal is relatively resistant to insects. Many salal leaves, whole plants, are perfect. Harvesters depend on it. What does this mean? Do the small numbers of insects feeding on salal simply confirm that the leaves are tough, difficult to chew? Alan Bown, a biologist at Brock University, has found that plants produce defensive chemicals within seconds of an insect lighting on their leaves ("Research Shorts" 7). Does salal exude more defensive chemical than other plants? If so, why isn't the leaf miner deterred?

A parasite, the small groundcone or Vancouver groundcone (*Boschniakia hookeri*), grows on salal roots (McConnaughey 71). It is quite rare, flowers in a tight cluster of what look like closed crocuses, and also grows on kinnikinnick and evergreen huckleberry. But where does groundcone fit ecologically? How does it affect salal? Is it, in turn, food for something else? As a report from the Washington Department of Natural Resources advises, more information is still needed.

Gardeners and nursery catalogues describe salal as disease resistant. But in the patches I regularly visit, many leaves are spotted brown or black — the result, presumably, of salal fungus (*Phyllostica gaultheriae*) (Vance *et al.* 70) or of leaf spot fungus (*Mycosphaerella gaultheriae*) (Boateng and Comeau 3). Of course, salal might be relatively disease and insect resistant, and still be subject to stress, especially in urban environments. Following Michael Pollan's challenge in *The Botany of Desire*, we need to ask not "what is salal to me?," but "what am I to salal?" Evidently diseased or eaten leaves are not marketable. Aesthetic and economic considerations intertwined send the human animal further afield, deeper into the forest, to find perfect green. Leaves that are infected are left on the growing plant, or picked off at the site of harvest, or discarded at the brush shed.

HARVEST AND SUSTAINABILITY

To date, we have relatively little research on the ecological impact of picking — or over-picking — salal. As several interviews in this book indicate, people in the field believe that, harvested responsibly, salal can be picked sustainably on a two- or three-year cycle. These same people also intimate that they know, or more likely suspect, that some pickers pick irresponsibly. The effects on other plant, bird and animal habitat are so far unexplained, but it seems inevitable that the scale of harvest will change the ecology.

An article in the *Seattle Times* discussing the huge industry of extracting non-timber forest products cites an official figure from 2002 valuing the harvest of salal and other products in Washington State at $236 million US, and quotes Washington State University's Extension Natural Resource Professor, Jim Freed, as guessing the actual take might be double that. The article says very little about ecological impact, except to note that it's difficult to assess, and that "salal ... grow[s] back quickly in the drippy Northwest." The suggestion that salal rebounds rapidly appears generally to be true: recall the struggles of many foresters to rid recently clearcut sites of the salal they believe is hampering reforestation. *Salal Complex*, a Forest Renewal BC manual, advises that "[m]anual cutting of salal stimulates re-sprouting from stem bases and rhizomes, usually resulting in an increase in salal crown closure" — in other words, more growth in the upper part of the shrub. "To be effective"—to thin salal so that newly planted trees can grow —"manual cutting is required for several consecutive years" (Boateng and Comeau 9). Even efforts to destroy the plants and to sever the rhizomes and stem fragments only tend to slow the rate of salal development, not eliminate the plant entirely (7).

Still, at the very least, over-harvesting can affect the immediate livelihoods of other pickers in the area, and animal species that rely on salal's leaves and stems may have to forage more for food.[3] Diane Doss, Professor of Botany and Horticulture at South Puget Sound Community College in Olympia, Washington, notes in an email response to the *Seattle Times* article that "[a]lthough there's little chance of salal becoming an endangered species, forest ecosystems are changed drastically when species are removed on a large scale." However, Brian Titus and Wendy Cocksedge, of the Pacific Forestry Centre and Royal Roads University respectively, observe that salal harvesters usually only take about five percent of the above-ground biomass, and do not tend to remove all leaves on a site.

If the rhizomatous riot of salal helps limit, at least to a certain extent, the impact of over-harvesting, it also serves human needs for stabilizing and protecting against erosion in disturbed areas, and especially in sand-dune environments — although Scotch broom does a better job (Brown and Hafenrichter 13). Of course, human dependency on salal might be primarily imaginative: we need the green shade of a green thought.

Although the Salal didn't house its workers like the Town Tavern did, it was also a collective, which is why it was named for the indigenous salal plant, an evergreen shrub bearing fruit in midsummer whose prolific underground root system struck the café's founders as an apt metaphor for the spirit of cooperation, grass-roots activism, friendship, and tolerance that coursed through the community as abundantly as Northwest rain.

Natalia Rachel Singer
Scraping By in the Big Eighties

Ecology understands the natural world as an infinitely extending series of reflexive dependencies. Ideally, the ecology of salal should not be the primary focus of a discrete section in a book, even one titled "Depending." The idea of ecology urges making the concept more explicit, proposing an ongoing set of intersections on almost every page. Which is to say — posing more questions. To discuss the use of salal as florist greenery together with the so-called leathery quality of the leaves might involve asking what leathery means in chemical terms, and what differentiates salal's decay rate from bigleaf maple or even kinnikinnick. What nutrients — in jelly, jam or wine — do salal berries provide in unusually large quantities? Examining harvest in a less isolated way would recognize that harvesters are habitat students — that they do not simply look for good patches of salal, but also know where to look by understanding the elevation, the slope, the canopy, and the acidity that make for best foliage. The human browser may actually function in the ecoweb to encourage growth.

Cindy Prescott's encouraging conversations about forest ecology sustain this section. She may not think of herself as a poet, but her enthusiasm for the ecology of salal seems to me moved by a poet's passion: her conversation sings an interdependency of succession, transformation, intriguing terminology, and close observation. Cindy is, of course, part of a community of scientists, themselves depending on one another. I especially enjoy her anecdote about a grad student in the field who described the moist soil at one site as "fluffy:" the term stuck in Cindy's head, echoing, until eventually it pushed her to reshape her research conclusions. I take these dependings as reason enough to include poems in this listening for ecology.

In his essay "Beyond Ecology," Neil Evernden laments that "the Arts and Humanities seem[...] to play so minor a role in the environmental movement" (92). Ecology, he claims, cannot stop at observation and recording of sets of interdependencies: the science of ecology contains its own subversiveness — the assumption of interrelatedness. So an ecological study, however much it examines physical dependencies, always requires us "to ask what it *feels* like to have a territory" (97), to ask together, interrelatedly, into which environment does this species fit? And how does that environment reciprocally define it? Evernden knows we need to incorporate in environmental studies so many elements that seem soft to the hard-headed: feeling, subjectivity, values, animism, pathetic fallacy, and metaphor.

It's just this conviction about the subversive literal intermingling at the heart of ecology (where does the human leave off and the non-human

begin?) that makes methodology, as typically required in the definition of a scholarly project, apparently unmethodological. Find out as
much as possible about salal, in as many surrounds as possible, and then
texture, intermingle, blur, and combine so that the result is somehow
"organism-plus-environment bounded by an imaginary integument"
(Evernden 97). Rather than a detached examination of the habitat of
salal, listening to understory enables "a subtle diffusion into it" (97).

I hope "subtle diffusion" describes my territory and my locale, the
movement and direction of my travels with salal. "Destination," "quest,"
and "pilgrimage" don't have much hold. Pollan's *Botany of Desire* provides
one fine model for ample ecological connection. He takes a more or
less historical approach that encourages me to ask when salal was first
picked, when first sold, however difficult such facts are to find. My travels with salal are more a spreading, happily stopped where impediment
arises, detoured, but with tribute in mind. Call it an ecology of desire.

So, I try to allow interrelatedness. Resist the straight ahead, so as
to notice what is next to you, or behind you, or at your feet. In the section titled "Arranging" that follows, for example, I try to take a story I
happened on and suggest (contrary to the obvious) that it is related, in
several ways, to poem, and corner-store bouquet, and allegiances.

Of course, my travels are also informed by the principle of doubt
that, Cindy reminds me, always operates in the sciences, and hence
in ecology:

❧ I can't think of anything we've actually nailed down in this entire field. I
recently challenged one of my students in a candidacy exam: "In this sentence,
you used the word 'undoubtedly.' Is there anything so strong, so obvious, so
well studied that we could actually use the word 'undoubtedly'?"

Sometimes we think we have a good idea, and we run with it. But it
depends on where it comes from, and what we're expecting. Sometimes
research leads to nothing and leaves us nowhere. And, of course, one
researcher depends on the work of another, and in turn another. Evernden keeps turning us to this basis of ecosystem — all parts of a system
interdepend, although the depending does not inevitably mean cause
and effect. Some things just happen. And — ecology is also a political

position — we may depend in ways we do not understand. That principle of ecology is crucial for Cindy. It depends: the colloquial throwaway, its holding alternatives in suspension, is the foundation of ecology.

ARRANGING

salal (itself a sign)
· Daphne Marlatt *Ana Historic*

All domesticated plants are in some sense artificial,
living archives of both cultural and natural information
that people have helped to "design."
· Michael Pollan *The Botany of Desire*

Cut flowers need arranging. The idea is to put the flower to best advantage, against a backdrop of green. Presumably the flower's own leaves
are insufficient. For the florist, salal provides a green more substantive,
more lasting, more black, to highlight the flower. As in so many
instances in this understory, you don't notice the salal in the bouquet.

    In flower arranging, and probably in ecological function, salal, there-
fore, is itself a sign: its role is to enhance but not to be noticed. It focuses
attention on what is near to it, or up against it. It would be noticed only
if absent. Tess Gallagher develops this attractive paradox in one of the
many poems she writes to test the dark and sustaining beneficence of
her dead husband, the short-story writer Raymond Carver. Gallagher
admires an "arrangement" apparently accidental and natural:

> … this morning
> snow lightly cupped in salal is raised against
> the hillside by fresh ardor alone. (26)

The poem's title is "He Would Have," and it speculates on how Carver's companionship would have enriched and deepened this simple experience. But, of course, Carver's presence in memory is deepening. Salal, as usual, is incidental: it is the support, the container for a spiral of snow that morphs intriguingly into the "white head" of an eagle — a "knot of infinity." Such a grand transformation might obscure the doubling of the poem's "paired attentions." Two observers pay attention to both snow and cup. Salal enhances, perhaps produces, the "pleasure" of the snow. It finds in this poem its grandest literary moment — a vessel raised by ardor becomes chalice, its contents an emblem of comfort and support: do this in remembrance of me. But still the palette of the surround makes its own "beguil[ing]," illuminating the nuance of a greenworld from "snow-lit green" to "sky-green" (26).

So beguiling is salal in flower arranging that its travels, around the neighbourhood or across the Atlantic, complement those of its admirers. If you bend to the bouquets in London's Paddington Station, at least in December 2003, you see stems of salal. You will find, that is, this sign of home while away. But one of the most unusual arrangements I have seen is a ferry ride away.

Alongside the Island Highway at Union Bay, BC, huddles a celebration of the local and crafted called Open Studio. In the studio, Corry Lunn makes slightly fantastic marine ceramics. Outside, Darrel Nygaard builds furniture and garden sculptures from driftwood. I am on the lookout for salal, and there, up against the unvisited north side of the studio, I find a bleached stump, almost a metre in diameter, and growing out of its top is a browning and spotted tangle of salal.

Many of Darrel's "recycled" sculptures — water features or planters — are made from stumps left by loggers. This stump, he has sheered off and brought home not to sell, but as a giant living bouquet for his partner. It's the largest arrangement of salal I've seen, and it comes with no flowers: Darrel has just left it to grow as he found it — a nurse log as accidental garden.[1]

This salal-sculpture is one of those fine details that folds itself into a texture of real place. The uncharismatic instance of an uncharismatic species. The unremarkable detail accumulating over the years, and in the miles of travel, does not connect to x or y, but only in the surprise of the unsurprising.

AGAINST SALAL

In a bouquet, in a cellophane bag of potpourri, or along the forest's edge, salal is background, not focus; a context, not a subject; a frame for a picture of something else. The leaf sometimes stands for a whole intact plant, a holder of blossoms, a promise or validation of an evergreen world. I have found no argument about the function of this barely noticed plant more compelling than the intriguing "turn" at the end of Richard Hugo's "Saying Goodbye to Mrs. Noraine." In the poem, Hugo, in self-critical awkwardness, discovers the humanity and acknowledges the pain of a woman who in childhood he had learned only to mock and fear. After talking to Mrs. Noraine, he notices dandelions he had been "taught … to ignore":

> … Their greens are excellent
> in salad. Their yellow flowers
> make good wine and play off like a tune
> against salal I love remembering to hum. (223)

Hugo likes weeds and often writes of them to validate the beauty of the tenaciously vital growing where it's not wanted. Here weed plays off against weed. Does salal have a tune? A rhyme with salad? Can you hum salal? Or is it just flower showing up in its yellowness? *Against* salal is as crucial a directive as it is drifting. It defines what you are looking at, and, in Hugo, what you are listening to, or waiting for. Salal is the *against* crucial to showing up what you are seeing. Take it away, and you're left with something else, something vaguely lesser. Hugo writes how the unnoticed figures to make us notice.

GARDENING

She does not know how to read this untended garden.
Her hands fondle fern, salal, driftwood,
seeking some texture reminiscent of parchment;
hoping for roses, her nose finds only ocean.

· Stephanie Bolster
   "In which Alice visits Pacific Rim National Park"

Eight inches of snow have settled on the Hoyt Arboretum overnight. On this November morning in Portland, Oregon, it is winter. But it is a green winter. Dan Moeller, Hoyt's Plant Collection Manager, has agreed to meet with me. We chat across the corner of a large conference table in the Interpretive Center. After 30 minutes or so, we go walking on the arboretum's trails, my dress shoes slipping up and sliding down the hilly paths. In our scrambling, the tape recorder misses a lot of our conversation, but it catches the passion of a dedicated educator.

❧ When you first contacted me, I was excited. I'm new to the region: I grew up on the prairies too. I lived in the Appalachian Mountains on the East Coast, then in Pittsburgh, Pennsylvania. I went to school in Boulder, Colorado, then moved to Illinois to work in the botanic gardens. My professional background is in plant biology: I studied photosynthesis and plant biochemistry. And then I got really tired of being inside. If I was going to do plants, I wanted to be out with them. So I had to move to more applied botany. That took me to public gardens, because working there is always a mix of plants, conservation, horticulture, and education ... and a little bit of research.

I was a plant guy, and I knew plants in four time zones. I thought I knew plants. And I moved to Portland, and I didn't know one. But salal was one I thought I recognized on my first day. Of course, I misidentified it, because it resembled *Gaultheria procumbens*, its sister, a plant I knew well.

I've been here three years and I come at salal from a horticultural perspective; I concentrate on its utilitarian use in the landscape. One of the things I noticed when I moved to this area is that, relative to the Midwest or East Coast, so many of the plants are evergreen — broad-leaved evergreen — not just conifers. When you have that, it affords you many things. One, it affords you four seasons of interest in a plant from an aesthetic standpoint. Another thing I like, from a maintenance standpoint, is it's not very messy. It doesn't drop a lot of leaves. People are moving toward using more evergreens in landscaping for both these reasons. Another issue here in the Northwest is that we can grow such a wide variety of plants, and as we all aspire to interesting and unusual plants from around the world, sometimes we overlook what's right in front of us. So doing that, we've inadvertently brought in plants that have become invasive. One of these is English ivy (*Hedera helix*).

As we start to educate the public about the trouble these invasives can create in reducing the diversity of our plant community, one of the things the local gardener cries out is, "What do I replace this stuff with?" There are several plants you can replace it with. But the one I really like is salal.

We have salal in the arboretum in so many different conditions. We have it on a dry, sunny south slope. We have it in a very cool, wet, moist valley. We even see areas in the arboretum that have been mowed for over 20 years, and there'll be a giant bush or shrub of salal right in the middle of a mowed lawn. It's just persisted without any encouragement. So it's been quite a strong performing plant. I'm delighted, and pleasantly surprised, at its adaptability in the landscape.

I find it quite ornamental. Even if a lot of people say it's not as showy as other plants. I'm always surprised at that commonality we have in remember-ing something, especially good times, in connection with plants. We donate pruned branches to the wreath-making program downtown. But one thing the garden volunteers do come up for every year is to cut salal. We sell some of the wreaths for the benefit of Programs and Parks. So, salal has a small economic benefit here.

From a horticultural perspective, evergreen shrubs like salal, on our small lots, provide a really interesting structural feature. And it provides a really nice background for other plantings. We put a lot of it at trail corners, where we're trying to restore a worn heavy-traffic area. By that little stone wall, in the picnic area, is probably the only spot in the whole arboretum where we have it labelled. However, we have a series of self-guiding pamphlets, and I would say on almost every one of these salal is highlighted in some sense.

When you look at plants horticulturally, you need to notice some very subtle characteristics. If you just described the plant to someone — broad-leafed evergreen, grows one to four feet tall — it might not get much notice. But it's wonderful: that red stem colour against the green leaves, and then the white flowers, and later beautiful blue berries.

Dan relies on "Wow!" to convey his admiration. Sometimes when he's listening; often when he's looking. Dan is a gardener, gardening for the public. He tends the garden, but celebrates the untended. Whether he's telling me about salal's subtle palette, or Dawn Redwood, or a plan to involve more graduate students at the arboretum, he tells me joyfully. He touches each plant for its texture. Every exclamation inclines toward an intricate elusive ecology of teaching and conservation.

PICKING

Without a complex knowledge of one's place, and without the faithfulness to one's place on which such knowledge depends, it is inevitable that the place will be used carelessly, and eventually destroyed.

· Wendell Berry "The Regional Motive"

In the salal economy, *harvesting* is the term that suits bureaucrats and policy-makers. The people who collect salal in the wild, however, don't describe themselves as harvesters, but mainly as "pickers," "picking."

The word *pick* implies care, even fastidiousness. Faithfulness to one's place. *Picking* (in contrast to, for example, *gathering*) designates a necessarily unmechanized one-by-one process. Picking often focuses on small items; the verb *peck* is an analogue. *Wildcrafting*, a term now only occasionally used, implies, like picking, a process done by hand, individually.

At the sites of other salal stories, *pick* will also mean "to attempt to find, to seek out," as in pick flaws in an argument — hence, an active and analytical and difficult *finding* moves here. On the clandestine side, think of *picking* a pocket, or a lock. All in all, picking happily combines individual, careful gathering for livelihood, and serendipity — that other dimension to which the dictionary points us, of "occasional opportunity," of "obtain[ing] casually."

WILDCRAFTING

The verb (or noun) *wildcrafting* is not listed in my desk dictionary: it evidently adheres to a specialized occupation. While *picking* is the more salal-specific term, a broader culture is evoked by *wildcrafting*. Reading *Nontimber Forest Products in the United States*, I am amazed how this technical work acknowledges the "cultural" — far more, I think, than in comparable studies of timber resources.[1] Dealing with *non*-timber seems often to honour both "wild" and "craft." You can't describe the process of harvesting the understory without thinking of the invisible economy, the income level of the people most immediately involved, and, most especially, the non-pecuniary elements that mix into, and often dominate, the wildcrafters's world. One analyst of Latino and Southeast Asian immigrants's involvement proposes that

> increased globalization of the US economy, large populations of marginalized migrants, increased inequalities in income, changing values toward resources, and government policies combine with labor conditions and erratic weather to push Latinos and others into the woods to harvest non-timber forest products. Growing use of these renewable but limited natural resources may lead to stressed ecosystems, growing conflicts among users, and increasingly tightened regulations that invite flouting. (Hansis 68)

The news media are paying increasing attention to the harvesting of non-timber forest products such as salal — especially to the clandestine, hidden, and illegal elements that adhere to the story. Robert McClure reports in the *Seattle Post-Intelligencer* that "much of the greenery sprinkled in today's bouquets is hot — illegally plucked from public and private lands by undocumented workers." The *Sun* newspaper in Bremerton, Washington, informs that a man arrested for illegal brush-picking was also wanted for "driving under the influence, theft, and hit-and-run" ("Brushpicker"). According to David Foster, reporting for the Associated Press, Alfredo Menjivar "was shot in cold blood" and died over an incident of brush theft near Aberdeen, Washington. This article closes with an account of Menjivar's fiancée, Melissa, making a scrapbook after the funeral: "In it are snapshots of Menjivar, sympathy cards and newspaper stories that got his name wrong. On one page, pressed carefully under plastic, is a single leaf of salal. Melissa put it in there in December, but the leaf is still green."

Scott Sunde, also writing for the *Seattle Post-Intelligencer*, describes efforts by the Quinault Indian tribe to halt poaching of salal, bear grass, and mushrooms. He quotes Mike Mail, who manages the Quinault harvest of special forest products: "They're like locusts in a wheat field.... They just get in there and wipe it out." Sarah Efron repeats tales of "busloads of pickers going to a mountaintop and destroying everything in sight" (59).

Widely reported in early 2004 was the story of a more lucrative leaf being shipped from Canada to the US disguised as salal. A florist greens company in Shelton, Washington, received 55 boxes of salal in excess of what they had ordered. A phone call soon explained that the boxes had been sent by mistake and that the owner's husband would come by to pick up the excess. Suspicion, a call to the police, an arrest: the boxes contained marijuana, "nearly 900 pounds with a street value estimated at $5.5 million" ("2 Arrested").

SHINY GREEN COINS

Rick Ross says we have a "window of opportunity" for picking at about 8:15 AM, just as I arrive at Western Evergreens, his floral greens business on the outskirts of Courtenay, BC. (A few months earlier Rick had taught me about processing and marketing — an encounter recorded in the section of this book titled "Containering.") Off we go promptly. "Can we take your car?" he asks. "My wife has ours." Rick puts his rain pants and rubber boots in my trunk. I wonder where our tools are. "Do we need something else?" I ask, imagining pruning shears or knives. "No, we just use our hands."

We drive maybe four or five kilometres up the highway toward Campbell River, and turn off to the right. We are to pick (with permission) on land owned by Raven Forest Products of Campbell River; north of the jouncing road is park — no picking allowed.[2] We leave the car and walk south into the bush along what Rick describes as an "old road."

I can scarcely make it out. After walking 200 metres, Rick pauses, explaining that most "pickers will flag their way in" and pointing behind us to a piece of safety ribbon; again, I can't make it out. Baffled, I try to reassure myself — perhaps somehow recalling David Wagoner's poem "Lost" — that if I can just find what this bush "does," I'll understand "wherever ... is called Here" (182). Rick begins his how-to lesson with two stems in hand, and bending over a single bush.

❧ So this was last year's single-year growth. And it would've come up to there, where the stem changes colour. This is this spring's, or this summer's growth — this one and this one. So in three years you basically have a piece that's pickable. Here, if you break this single piece off this old stem, it's gonna stimulate the plant to produce more of those. I've broken two off this one. But you can see how old this is. This is — we got one year, two years, three years, four years, five years, six years — it's about 15 or 20 years old, that one plant. And you can come back year after year and harvest it. And after we've gone through the patch, you can look back and see that it doesn't look a lot different. You really can't overpick it too badly because a lot of it's not good enough for what we're looking for, which is decorating flowers.

Once you start building up your bunches, then what I do with them is I put one under my arm, and keep picking. That way you're not constantly putting stuff down and losing it. So I'll pick about five like that, three quarters of a pound each, then I'll find a spot like this — maybe a bigger log — where I can lay them down upside down, so I can see them. I'll have them all in one spot. So I'll pick in an area, and then I'll come back, drop all my bunches there — then you're making up your bale, not floating through the woods looking for your product. A lot of times people will put a flag up. That's why when you're walking through the woods you'll sometimes see just flags, in the middle of nowhere. That's probably where a salal picker has put his tag, so he remembers where his stuff is. The other trick my dad has from years ago is, you hang one bunch up in the tree like that. You don't need any flagging, and you can see that from quite a distance, and you know all your bunches are going to be sitting right underneath it.

Over here, you see how the salal's looking for the light. It gets quite gangly at times. I've got some patches where it's all up over your head like that.

It is easy to get lost. You find the best part of a patch and, with yourself as a centre, pick in a circle. Then you see another promising patch, and another, and soon you're circling and reaching and circling — disoriented. Such a rhythm resembles the listening and the writing. I am learning the consummate craft of the salal-picker, and the rigour of the physical work required.

Rick urges me to keep my head up, to look ahead for a patch, a lighter green spray. Snap it off where green meets brown; strip the old leaves. Rick snaps and strips in one motion — snaps off the branch and, sliding his left hand down to the bottom of the stem, strips off any other bad leaves. And he's on to the next.

THE ZEN OF PICKING

Rick tells me how his father first told him to concentrate, focus, keep looking ahead to the next pick, and "you get in a zone." I think of skiing, then of soccer. Twice he repeats this reminder.

❧ You can see how great it is just being out here in the bush in the rhythm of picking. I always think of what my dad taught me when I first started picking: you're here to pick — you're not here to daydream. So if you concentrate on the picking, it's actually quite a nice freedom, you know. You're just concentrating on that. You're not thinking about too much else.

Such outdoors groovin' might be muted a little by weather: we have just come through five to six days of record-breaking rain. Courtenay recorded 176 millimetres from October 15–20, 2003. Now, on Tuesday morning, it's still grey but no rain, and warm — about 3° Celsius above the norm for this date.[3]

❧ So that's my first big bunch there. This might be $1.40, $1.35. That's a pound and a half. It depends on the patch: I might pick a variety — I might pick a few hands of long, and I might pick a few hands of short, if there's a lot of short stuff right in front of me. And a lot of pickers do that — unless they're in really, really big stuff, they won't pick all the same.

Right in front of us here is just the most beautiful patch of salal. It's sweet stuff.

Salal grows mostly by a very complicated sort of root system. It tends to pull up all the nutrients that're available. They're actually trying to eradicate it with a program on the North Island, because when they did their fertilizer test they discovered that it was going into the salal, not into the trees. Of course to a forester, that's just horrible. For us it's great — you get this beautiful, big, lush, green salal.

To make a "hand" of salal, you put the sprays in back and the single stems in front. "They like the sprays to lie flat," Jean Howarth reports in her instructions for "one of the jobs always available on Madronna Island": "This means that the best picking is on the northern side of a mountain, where there is little sun to draw the leaves out of alignment" (23).[4]

❧ Look at the green wood there — that's a beautiful, beautiful spray there. So what you're looking for is mostly sprays, because that's going to build you the most weight in the shortest period of time. So I take that one off, and that's a nice flat piece for the bottom. I'm building a big bunch, a 1½ pounder. I got lots of nice long stuff in the back, shorter stuff in the front to face it up. And it's all done with your hand.

Now, if I was going to pick for a whole day, I'd have some electrician's tape, and I'd tape my fingers. The other thing is to wear a light glove — those ones that they use on fish farms with all of those little nubblies all over them, rubber. Those are great. If you have a pair of clippers and you're trying to clip the salal, you'll constantly be losing them. A lot of people tie them with a little string to their belt, but you're constantly getting them caught up. And once you build your fingers up, you can see, you feel it on the inside of your fingers. But if you put tape on there for the whole day, or a glove, it makes a big difference.

As we pick, we wander apart —then I can't see Rick —and confusion rustles in the bush. I'm up to my elbows in salal, but I can't see a single spray to pick.

❧ What we do with a lot of new pickers is we say to them, "Go get a sample." We've shown you what to do with the plant — go get a sample, bring it in to us, and we'll go over it with you on the bench. That gives you a much better idea of what to do. Clip that one off, clip that off. Now it's a matter of putting the singles in the bunch to hold it down. And at this time of year a salal picker is also looking down, 'cause the mushrooms tend to come up in the same area you're picking salal. You'll get both the pine mushroom and the chanterelle, and so they can make a few extra dollars picking a few mushrooms at the same time. They can make a couple hundred dollars a day on the mushrooms, and then I'd only make 80 to 100 dollars a day on the salal.

All this time, I'm trying to learn to pick, occasionally twisting at a stem, mostly marvelling at Rick's speed. "Is that flat enough?" I ask, as I begin to accumulate a bunch.

❧ Yeah, that's beautiful. And that goes to the back: you get a nice big spray, you put it to the back. Small sprays and singles you put to the front. And the other trick is to learn when you've got too much in your hand, when it's time to put it down.

Then again, I ask, "Mine doesn't seem to snap off like yours. Is there a technique to that?"

❧ Well, I think there is. I put two fingers on the stem and my thumb in behind it, and just go like that. Really reef on it. It's actually even tougher in the springtime when the sap is starting to run. Then I think it's really difficult to break — every piece wants to rip, rather than break. This actually is quite crisp and breaks quite nicely. Like I say, you do wear your fingers out.

If you like being out in the forest, and you don't mind a little bit of nasty weather every now and then — 'cause the pickers tend to pick even if the weather turns a bit ugly — this is just excellent work. You're right in the middle of nature. Our main problem in the industry is that there's just so much urbanization of the whole island that we're losing huge areas that used to be picked. And when they develop this area they're going to make it into 10-acre lots — so it'll all be individual 10-acre lots that are owned by people who really don't want salal pickers coming onto their property, even if they have no use for the salal themselves.

Always put the wide stems to the back, and then you build up your hand. The whole idea is to have something that's saleable on the market, and that's what they're looking for on the market — all facing the same way. I mean, we've got the odd bug-chew mark here and there, but this stuff isn't very bad for the back. So that'll be used in a flower arrangement somewhere in Europe in about three weeks. We have a few customers in Japan too — they take a container every three weeks. But the big market is Europe. They take multiple containers from all up and down the coast.

Japan uses the salal a little bit differently, and they want different specifications on the side. So we actually take out all the small leaves — you know, sort of in this range — anything with lots of small leaves. They want that separated out. So we'll spend the time as we're checking it, and spend the time to pull out all the small leaf stuff. Also, they want their tips a little bit longer than most of the European customers do. And it all has to be hand graded and inspected by Agriculture Canada, so there's tighter sanitary concerns there.

There's 13 bunches, and we'll put your two in there and make 15. So we got a 15-hand bale, and we were probably here for, I don't know, an hour. But we'll see how many we get out of it when we get back to the plant. That'll be the test. Now, what you want to do is really cinch this up tight, and you want to overlap them so it makes a nice tight bale. I usually like to bale them upside down so I can really see how they fit. And you can really reef down on this and make a nice tight knot if you're going to be packing it out. Sometimes down the trail it's a little bit rough, you know, with logs sticking out and everything, and you don't want it to come apart. So I ran the loop through and tied it off tight. It makes a little bale that you can just sling up over your shoulders and pack out of the woods. Sometimes if it's a bigger bale, like a 30-hand bale, I'll put a stick in there as a handle. Some people use a wheelbarrow. And you want a path that's fairly open, so you're not running the bale through the branches and really damaging the leaves. It'll take a little bit of that, but it's not going to take a lot.

So that's about 20 pounds of salal that we got in this little spot here. You can see where you could spend a day and clean an area, and have your bales set up, and haul them out. Today is beautiful, it's perfect. The weather's great. And we're in a nice spot. This is pretty typical of the coast salal patch.

"I was just trying to guess how many pickers would be involved in total across the province," I muse. "It must be a hell of a lot."

❧ Oh, it is. It's hundreds and hundreds and hundreds.

When we get back to the car, Rick warns me not to set the bale on the road. We don't want to get dirt on the leaves. I'm proud to say I'd anticipated this caution, and had hesitated, waiting for instructions.

BRUSH SHED

Back at Western Evergreens, Rick's father Dick takes over and "processes" our take. Each hand he repacks — repeating the same process as in the bush — then weighs, chops lightly on a chop block with a hatchet to even up the stems, and binds with an elastic band to hold. He shows me one crucial procedure: loop one end of the elastic band around a single stem, then wrap the entire band three times around the full bundle, then hook on to another stem or three.

He counts them out, five at a time, and puts them in a large grey plastic wheeled bin. The sprays will later be washed and inspected again for insects. Our take for the morning? After re-sorting, we have 20 hands. At 70 cents a hand, this yields $14 for one veteran and one rookie, each doing probably 1 to 1¼ hours of actual picking.

All surfaces around me burst with life, with liverworts and tongues of ferns and shiny green coins of salal.

Douglas Coupland
Life After God

While I'm watching Dick sort, trim and weigh, I note that the Western Evergreens "plant," so-called, is a very happy place. A fair amount of kibbitzing, some cursing. Dick admits it's "monotonous," but he still seems, well past retirement, to be enjoying himself. And when some very new pickers come in (three young women and a man) with some mushrooms, the staffers promptly begin training them to pick salal and Christmas greens. Rick readily spends 20 minutes with them summarizing the various "crops" he is interested in.

figure 11

Bales of salal "shorts" in refrigerated storage.

WESTERN EVERGREENS, COURTENAY, BC

BLAME SALAL

Helen Heffernan's story "A Clear-cut Equation" is as much about the inevitable failure of the "narrative of retreat" as it is about a failing marriage (the overt narrative thread). Alex and Rae try to build a cabin on a small North Pacific Coast island (unnamed), but the more demanding the work, and the more self-reliant they become, the more the distance grows between man and wife, until Rae discovers Alex in a homosexual tryst with his friend Peter. Evidently, Heffernan challenges clear-cut equations. As Peter and Alex clear the forest, and build a home from scrap, they live the traditional macho narrative of "claiming" the land, as they become connected in desire.

In a story without place names, location is defined by the mix of named native plants and birds. The story opens with its ending, with Alex throwing Rae out: the first and lingering image we have of the central and sole female character is of her standing, half obscured and stunned, her feet and lower legs hidden in salal. Salal is also a "thicket" where things get lost, or want to be lost — Alex in a tantrum throws nails into the salal, as if into the sea.

For Rae, salal is also refuge. In salal, she finds, or defines, her "distance" (10); she "retreats" into salal when Alex refuses to allow her back into the cabin. I am undoubtedly inclined to overthink the significance of salal, but, along with an orange rice pot, it decidedly frames the story. Heffernan invites us, at the outset, to consider salal as cause, as instigator, maybe as rival: "Blame it [the unravelling of her marriage] on the salal" (8).

Such conviction, so compactly expressed, might warn that the story in and of itself can't provide an answer. We have to think outside to discover cause — most evidently to the sheer, multiplying, half-concealing fecundity of salal that stands in for the impossible dream of an island retreat, remote from the city. "Natural" forces are so early and often at work against their dream, blowing over walls, warping the stored plywood, or causing a tree to topple onto the cabin. And the intersecting associations of salal with the island cove location, and the sea, may also make meaning, as if the calming and tangling mystery of a sargasso of salal is somewhere behind this odd urging to "blame it on salal." Or maybe such absurd blame is index to the distressed puzzlement of the teller.

EYE-MINDEDNESS

Molly Gloss's female spirit quest *Wild Life* wanders through Charlotte Bridger Drummond's diary, published writing, notebook, and scrapbook. It's a novel haunted by Sasquatch and her variants; if ever there were a novel — filled with "otherworldly" darkness, trembling with phantoms (133) — where salal might figure, this is it. But, for all the "dense understory" (133) and the yearning it provokes, it is not until the last few pages that salal appears.

Maybe the fabular and irrational are more at home in skunk cabbage and snowberry. Yet the novel does end in some rapprochement with "skuma'qea" (253), some appreciation of the mobile interpenetration of one world and the other — here summoned in one of CBD's published stories. In the time of harvest, of gathering, of the fruiting darkness of salal, "eye-mindedness" becomes possible:

> We had been up the head of the hla'hou river, eating salal berries as they fell ripe, and then we had gone over the shoulder of the ridge to wait down there along the stucallah'wah for those sandbar willows to drop their seeds, . . . and we believed we could see his form still fluttering in the air — (252)

GREENWORLD

A depository of relics from some forest hagiography in which the saint was still named Raven. An altar freighted with amulets and fetishes. A shrine in accord and perfectly organic; a tabernacle of totems.

• David Guterson *Our Lady of the Forest*

In David Guterson's novel, Our Lady of the Forest is a "mushroom gatherer" (5); pickers of "seed cones," of "peeled yew and cascara bark," of "ornamental brush for florists," especially of mushrooms, form her society (127). The male brush-pickers wear thick beards and thick glasses and toques pulled down tight (6). The women live in shadow and might be mistaken for men. They pick where they wander — wandering is their mode, prone to interruption for sleep, or pot, or abbreviated talk. They have names such as Ann Holmes and Steven Mossberger, eco-citizens of the green world.

Immersed in this perfectly organic and saintly culture of the brush-picker, David Guterson writes a wry fable, a mock hagiography. Ann becomes Ann of Oregon, whose vision of Our Lady of the Forest becomes a magnet for desperate pilgrims who bring economic renewal along with ecological peril to the fictional North Fork (apparently in southern Washington State).

The brush-pickers's culture is trance-like, recalling the impression of automatism Rick Ross seemed to emphasize as he picked. Meditation induces visions, likely reinforced by the hallucinogenic possibilities of some of the products. So for all that *Our Lady of the Forest* emerges within the (somewhat asocial) society of the brush-picker, we get little sense of the pickers actually picking. And salal is more obstacle to, than object of, the search.

As we might expect from a locally sensitive writer, salal is one marker of the temperate rainforest through which the pilgrims traipse, quite obliviously. Although it continues to have an erotic charge, this forest is not so fecund as that in Guterson's *Snow Falling on Cedars*. This forest drips with an "oppressive pall" (212), in which tormented Romantics might write more "odes to gloom" (64). And instead of rain, the grey-green is imbued with a "mild carbonated mist" (248) ideal for a wonky West Coast Dada, more fronding and "ungovernable," to use novelist Jack Hodgins's term for the lines of the landscape (1978, 223), than linear or narrative.

Salal is impediment, most of the time. In every reference, it is joined with Oregon-grape. I'm tempted to find a Eucharistic parody here. Salal and Oregon-grape form a "thicket" (11) to be passed through, pushed through, "thrashed" through (17). Only late in the novel is a track made, worn by 5000 would-be pilgrims, in this pathlessness. Now the salal seems "trimmed artfully" (234) or "sheared" (265). Carolyn's picking bucket becomes an alms plate, stuffed with money by degenerate gull-ibles (215). A path is made, but the way is lost. Moss, fern, and green are landscape for a new church, and the tabernacle of totems is no more.

COLLECTING

**marked by a
leaf**
· **William Carlos Williams** *Paterson*

Sometimes, in my courtship of salal, I just wanted to give up. Wanted
to return to the comfortably familiar — to count, say, the references
to dust in Sinclair Ross's novel *As For Me and My House,* to follow the
intricate variations of words puzzled in mind. One such moment was
the mid-December midday I spent in the herbarium at Kew Gardens. I
had not until recently thought of an archive as anything else but folders
filled with papers, a few photos, and the occasional keepsake. Now I was
learning how to read the many dried and pressed leaves and stems, flowers, and berries, usually carefully dated and located, that were crucial to
botanical knowledge. Ushered from the Botanical Library downstairs
and around corners and through several keypad-guarded doors, I felt
lost. And seated in a window seat that served less as a desk than a radia-
tor cover, I felt as chilled as the wan December sunlight that warmed
neither me nor the two bulging folders set in front of me.

Dr. Rogier P. J. de Kok is a friendly and smiling man with the
impressive title of Systematic Botanist, Head of South East Asia and
Pacific Regional Team, Royal Botanic Gardens. He tries to assure me

figure 12

Sample of Gaultheria shallon collected by early botanizer David Douglas.

FIELDING-DRUCE HERBARIUM, OXFORD UNIVERSITY, OXFORD, ENGLAND

Printed with the permission of Oxford University Herbaria, Department of Plant Sciences

The New York Botanical Garden

Gaultheria shallon Pursh

det. James L. Luteyn

1989

that it will be easy to find my way back to the library — the building is on a square that it will and you want to go back over there, he says, pointing — and leaves me with two precious bundles of *Gaultheria shallon*. Now I try to read not guidebooks or memoirs or research journals, but a collection of actual plant samples — crumbling.

My only previous experience with a herbarium had been in the Lewis and Clark Herbarium at the Academy of Natural Sciences, Philadelphia, two months earlier. And, although the access there seemed similarly labyrinthine to a visitor, the care for the samples was much more overt. In the collections vault, I felt the temperature difference from the surrounding rooms instantly; the samples were mounted so as not to be in contact with any other surface. A curator stayed with me the whole time.

Maybe the relative ancientness or abundance (over seven million specimens) of the Kew collection breeds casualness. I was left alone with 40 folders, and best wishes. In many of the folders, two separate samples are preserved: over 50 examples in total. What to make of this? The exactness of the visual evidence only bewilders and here I yearn for the understanding of a good poem. Odd how we would cut a single stem, detach it from soil, sun, thrush and sea-air, press it flat and brown, and then rely on it as a realistic representation of a living thing. Here I wonder about the wisdom of fieldwork.

The samples represent 150 years of collecting.[1] Some collectors simply list place names (Ketchikan or Crescent City) as a source, while others attempt to describe the immediate habitat: "slightly shady places in muskeg." Many have an official and institutional imprimatur: "Oregon Boundary Commission 1858" or "California Academy of Sciences."[2] At least as many seem to have been collected and volunteered by amateur collectors and herbarists.

I want to make something of such range and enthusiasm. I want to find the stories in this collection that say something other than "plants very plentiful."[3] I do not have time to compare the number of samples of, say, salmonberry and Oregon-grape, to determine if salal has any special "profusion" at this herbarium.[4] I welcome the apparent indiscriminate recklessness of this collection — as the Kew website explains, because the plant comes from many places in many times, any particular specimen is, or could be, a resource for DNA/genetic research on differences in habitat, climate, even botanic evolution.[5] Reading in these files of salal is to appreciate what it means to be "marked by a/ leaf." I register the contrast between the places where these leaves were collected — in suburban London they can only be imagined — and the regimented coolness of the rooms in which they are now housed. All these many hands that have touched and transported and treasured — and found some measure and meaning in — a stem of salal. Appreciation shifts to awe — the strict simplicity of the venture, the enormous historicity of it. Salal is a story happening many times. And one of the story lines may be buried in my herbarium poem.

Working at Kew, I yield to a certain reverence, a sense maybe of the regality and mission that goes with being the *Royal* Kew. This sense is reinforced by the security — electronic passes, multiple locked doors, signatures required, registers to be filled in. Then there are the actual documents I'm reading, which are everywhere filled with His Majesty this and Sir that and the whole sense of your obedient humble and respectful servant on a mission to make the King's garden the best — home to the most species, boasting of the most rarities. Yet richness and regulation mix with a bit of higgledy-piggledyness. I'm not quite sure why the office is smack in the middle of the stacks. New books, old books, books under glass, stunning extra-folio size drawings, diaries, paintings of plants crowd the small table provided for the visiting researcher. Kew's herbarium collection, in particular, with no separate sleeves for dozens of samples and bits of leaf shredding as I turn from one sample to the next, is quite a contrast to the austere but solicitous system at Philadelphia. I get the impression of a vast and disparate operation — and wonder how it is all managed, if it is all managed, and if in any sense it coheres. The tourist aspect dominates: the park is big, and in it are many buildings, such as the Palm House, that must need discrete directors. Kew also is labs, the slightly freakish Economic Botany Collection with its electronically controlled compact shelving, and numerous other remote sites.[6] The influence and the relative wealth of this imperial centre have waned, but the empire of botany still extends. Paradoxically, this institution of imperial exploration, with an implicitly monocultural mission, labours mightily to remember and preserve biodiversity. And where does *Gaultheria shallon* fit in all this? Obviously, within the Kew complex, salal plays a minor role, but — as this condensation of herbarial annotation hints — still a richly connected one:

Write on Kew
              (a found poem)
bluish
reddish
color waxy white
black berry
corolla white to pink
mature fruit purple-black

common on cliffs
along rocky shoreline
in dense shade
very common in woods
soil dry and rocky
altitude sea level
on exposed rock outcrop
in muskeg
seashore
common over a vast extent of country

coll
recd
ab
ex
herb
hab
HMS
NW America

Tlell
Clallam
Tacoma
Semiahmoo
Ketchikan
Chilakwe yuk
Taken in old Indian Cemetery

This attempt at a poem is my way of collecting the notion of collecting. On a late June morning, I am trying to make myself spend a couple of hours with this manuscript while most of the passengers on the *Nautilus Explorer* are on watch for humpback whales in the foggy and still sun-sparkling waters of Frederick Sound. This particular context makes the poem's reliance on list, for all its prosiness, seem appropriate.

I have been nine days on this boat, one of a scattering of topsiders among 15 dedicated divers. Living with these divers for the past week and more, I've often been puzzled — why would people do this? The thought of being underwater, in a clinging suit and mask, is suffocating. But I have been impressed, day by day, at such uniform devotion to collecting. To a person, the divers, within a half hour of returning to the ship, are at their logbooks. Several have laptops; all the rest have paper logs — books or sets of interchangeable cards.

Donna Gibbs, the irrepressibly joyful naturalist from the Vancouver Aquarium, brings five or six species to the surface each day. We stare, and after 20 minutes she returns the animals to the sea. "That's an orange peel nudibranch," she exults. (I remember David Douglas, early botanizer, delighted by his first encounter with salal.) So pleased was she that I could scarcely see anything but it. Donna shows me a page of her species log, a program running in MS-DOS called MAKELOG. For each dive, she records Dive Number, Date, Time, Bottom, Location, Area/Region, Latitude, Longitude, Access (in this case, the name of the dive boat), Purpose (naturalist), Weather, Tide, Buddies, Equipment, Depth, Visibility, Air Temperature, Water Temperature, PSI Start/ End. Then follows a list of species; to compile their lists, these divers pore over 40 guidebooks after each dive.

Maybe humans are the collecting species. Twenty categories to record each encounter: a trace of our living, of our knowing. Home is our collections.

"Write on Kew" is my collection of phrases from the herbarium. It's a tribute to the species logs of 160 years of often anonymous salal-collectors. It speaks, I like to think, to the persistence of salal as honoured by Briony Penn: "If you have seen a heather species in action, you know that once they take root, they cling tenaciously to their spot and love a challenge" (161). They try to collect the colour of berry and flower.

They collect location. They collect abbreviations: divers, herbarists, academics all have their own codes and shorthand. They collect collections (coll.). They collect the connections to first peoples that give the plant both its aboriginal and Latin names.[7]

The herbarium collects (fragments of) the memory of my plant: a history of multiple human encounters, a record of its range, a record of slight variations in shape and veining, and even to a degree the texture of leaf and flower and berry. The colours transform into sepia but the colour of language remains. In an old Indian Cemetery.

GETTING NATIVE

Even the best intentioned of us techno-industrial humans are mired in cash-driven, car-propelled lives. These lives render us so non-indigenous that the word *native* is an honor we must earn afresh, every day.

· David James Duncan *My Story as Told by Water*

Earning the honour of the word "native" would not concern birthplace. Travelling reveals the multiple origins that grow a sense of place. My journey has at various times, as in "Naming," included honouring the languages of those who talked about salal before salal was a word in English. Before Pursh Latinized a Salish word. And, of course, learning words requires cherishing some sort of understanding of stem and leaf and berry that precedes the techno-industrial mire.

Then Jim Freed freshened the word for me. "You get so involved, you get so native," he said earnestly, "you start missing stuff." Well, I hadn't thought of it that way before.

Jim Freed may be the best-informed authority on non-timber forest products in the Pacific Northwest.[1] As Extension Natural Resource Professor at Washington State University, his classroom is all of Mason County. And despite his publications and his credentials in the fields of forestry stewardship and special forest products, it is talk that is his scholarship. I leaned into his openness and willingness; Jim's surname seems superbly apt.

In Jim's talking, *getting native* carries both meanings that keep dancing through place — an illusion of lifelong connection and an obligation to listen to the ancestors. Both aspirations are felt behind the phrase. We were sitting on stools, at a high bar table in Applebee's, just north of Olympia, over a lunch of greens and club sandwiches. A non-indigenous life, to be sure. But immediately Jim began to urge on me, and on himself, a caution about habit, about getting so accustomed to a culture, so inbred in an academic world, so undistanced from our dailiness, that we forget "what is real on the ground" and we "miss asking what a researcher should ask."

Freed came to the Northwest from Ohio. His degree work, he explains briefly, is in forestry, agriculture, natural resources. "I was studying to work for Weyerhaeuser," he jokes, "and to determine the feasibility of selling 2 x 4s in the Chinese market." Self-awareness keeps smiling through favourite phrases: "That's cool" and "I kind of like that," gestures of his tolerance and openness.

JUST WONDERFUL STUFF

As we wandered along the shoreline, we ducked under Douglas-fir trees laden with cones, Arbutus trees heavy with scarlet berries, thickets full of white Snowberries, blood-red Nootka Rose hips, dark green Salal and holly-like Oregon-grape. We were living in the midst of one giant Christmas decoration.

Briony Penn

A Year on the Wild Side

Freed moved to Washington State in the late 1970s: "They needed someone to work with the Christmas tree industry. I had some experience, and Mason County had the five largest Christmas tree companies in the world." And Christmas trees led inevitably to other festive season foliage. Jim keeps detouring — or is language his primary topic? — to tell me about terminology. *Brush*, as in brush-picking and brush sheds, according to Jim, is only for the pioneers, the old-time pickers. "The big guys use a grander term: 'Wholesale Greenery Industry.'"

Steal is another word Jim teaches me. "So many people are disparaging about the pickers," he says. "The pickers are 'stealing.' But some Vietnamese asked me, 'How can you steal something that nobody wants?' It was very hard for Laotians, Cambodians, Vietnamese, to understand that in America, if you own it, you can let it rot, you can burn it, . . . whatever you want. They have a whole different understanding of what the forest is."

Jim's interest in economics allows him to appreciate the historical shifts. Around 1982, he suggests, the occasional pickers (the men who had low-paying forest jobs, and picked Saturday and Sunday) started being able to earn higher wages operating computer-driven harvesters rather than chainsaws. But the market for greens was still there, and large numbers of Southeast Asian refugees were looking for work.

❧ At a conference in 1979, I listened to repeated estimates that "minor forest products" represented about 3 million a year. But I knew *one company* that did three times that. So they [the Bureau of Land Management] commissioned me to do a survey. Very unscientific, but I came up with a figure of $183 million in 1979. And that didn't include things like firewood and Christmas trees.

Salal was the backbone. Seagrass, sword fern, evergreen huckleberry, Oregon-grape, holly. Oh, and we also do mushrooms. They were opportunists . . . they didn't move too far.

But the pickers are outside society. You drive up the driveway . . . big road shrinks down to the little road, finally gets down to the gravel road with the trees hanging down both sides. And there's a house sitting up here with Forest Service land or big company land all around it. And they can see down their driveway clearly. And this house could be a trailer, or something quite nice, but most of the time they've built it themselves. . . . The old-time pickers were really wonderful people. Vietnam vets, or veterans of the forest industry: choker setters, whistle punks . . . the people on the ground stomping around.

Jim talks of a shift in "mapping." The worker population and regulations change configurations of space. Where the former forest workers knew their way around logging roads and had some tacit agreement about who picked where, these protocols all had to become public and institutional knowledge once permits were introduced, and picking shifted to Southeast Asians.

❧ We had no permit structure up to 1982. Everyone carried a gun. Wildlife agents would talk about how they would find "salal juice" running out of the back of a truck, and it would be *red*. And they'd lift up the salal and there'd be a deer underneath.

NO LONGER JUST PICKERS

❧ This association we put together [of workers in the greens industry]: one of the requirements is the members have to help with research. It was done on purpose so that they felt they weren't just pickers now. What they had in their head was valuable.

Heidi [Ballard, a non-timber forest product researcher,] asked these two guys to help her. Well, they kind of hmmed and they hawed around. Finally, just by accident, I said, "Do you have any money you could pay them?" "I could pay them a basic wage." So, people came out. There were not many days they didn't work — Sundays they only worked half a day. So, she started working with the harvesters and they helped her redesign her research plots, so they met what was real on the ground versus what a researcher is taught to ask.

What she taught me was that these people are very interested in what is happening out here and they want to be managers, to be stewards of the land, farmers of the land, gardeners — whatever term you want to use. But typically they can't. The land managers still basically consider them "scum" at worst — at best they consider them a pain.

Right in the middle of the Christmas tree season, all the local people who were hired to load the trucks, work in the yards — there were three or four hundred hired — said no, we're not going to do it any more. They wanted, you know, a guaranteed wage, and a whole bunch of stuff.

So next summer I got this phone call. Is there any way you can find us some migrant workers? Yeah. I have some contacts. We made arrangements in '83 to bring in three Hispanic crews, the smallest was a hundred people. In '84, the Christmas greens industry was starting to grow. This is an industry where ladies made extra dollars making Christmas wreaths, couple of thousand, 10,000 wreaths a year. They started seeing the demand increase, but they didn't have a work force. We helped set up housing and everything for the Hispanic workers. From the east side of Washington, Oregon, they came over. Well, pretty soon they're like, "Why go home?" You know, they looked around and they saw there's some pretty good opportunity here.

Some of them stayed around. Three or four the first year. Fifteen-twenty the next year. They were out there on other people's permits picking salal and evergreen huckleberries. At the same time, the Vietnamese, Cambodians, started moving up. And they began to realize there was money to be made getting the leases and getting someone else to pick for you.

People in the industry — it sounds like a negative word, but I mean it very positively — they're opportunists, they're survivors. They kind of sit on the edge. You know, you and I look at it and say whoa: a lot of hard work to make $50 a day.

Okay, make 50 bucks a day. If ten of us work together, pool our pay cheques, we can send $40 a day back to our families. I mean, that's the kind of thing that happens now with the Hispanic people. And the Vietnamese did it too. They weren't poor, these people who came over; they were the shopkeepers and doctors and lawyers who picked the wrong side. Cambodians were more bush people. Laotians, the same way. These were country people who lived in the forest. Hell, you dropped them off in the forest out here, and they could live three or four days without even thinking twice about it.

The Hispanic harvesters — the Spanish-speaking harvesters — began coming from *southern* Mexico, and Guatemala, and they were Native people. They spoke about as much Spanish as I do. And they looked at the forest. And they said "Wow! Look at all this stuff that nobody wants. And somebody wants to buy it."

Our association [the Northwest Researchers and Harvesters Association] has 48 members: most of them are families now. From being temporary migrant workers, in the late 1980s and early 1990s they started bringing their families in. In Mason County now, the Catholic church has 700 Hispanic families. Of the 48 members of the association, there are eight white, and of those, two of them are brush-pickers; the rest are mushroom pickers, wild edibles. So, conservatively, the high 80s percentile.

The other big change occurred about the time the land managers thought they had a gold mine out here. (They do. But it's not for the reason they think they do.) The Hispanic people weren't looking for a permanent career. The white guys we talked about were doing it as a supplemental — it wasn't something they were going to do forever.

Used to be able to talk to pickers like Don Collins — people with 40 years of experience. But the Hispanics might have only two years experience. Most of them are gleaners: you know, whatever is there is what they're taking out. Most of them come from a forestry or agriculture background. And here I'm on my soapbox. So, given an opportunity, they'd just love to have their own 200 acres or 2000 acres — whatever it would take to have their families sustained. If they were just doing salal, they'd need 2000 acres for a family.

Within the forestry industry, there's a lot of emotion. A lot of fear. Until forest health became an issue, at most 10 years ago, salal — anything that wasn't trees — was considered competition. There's still no real good research. Royal Roads [University near Victoria, BC] is talking about doing it.

Is there any genetic difference? Between north [Vancouver] island and south [Vancouver] island? I mean you and I don't have to be geniuses to know that the salal in Crescent City, California, that grows 12 feet tall might have a little different genetics after thousands of years from what grows on the north end of the Island. And what's growing over in eastern Washington, northern Idaho — the salal there doesn't get very big. They just call it "wild wintergreen."

During our conversation, Jim several times mentioned Heidi Ballard, whose PhD research on harvesting salal (undertaken at the University of California, Berkeley) included extensive field work near Olympia, and on the Olympic Peninsula. Jim particularly praised her involving of harvesters and managers in her research — work which extended his own efforts as a field professor. Ballard's projects included designing and implementing a participatory inventory of non-timber forest products on the Makah Indian Reservation.[2]

❧ The work that Heidi is doing is the first real work to get at best management practices. Her three years of work kind of supports my hypothesis. If you have a good site that's really ideal for salal, and you pick only quality greens on site, not leaving it to the brush sheds to sort out, you can't overpick. The amount of stuff you're going to get the first year, if it hasn't been picked, is the least amount you get, because it responds to pruning.

The wildlife group has been most helpful to me. They've done browsing studies. The elk and deer mow it down to the ground, but if it's a really good site, you come back in three years and you can barely walk through it.

Now we have a lot of people looking at the total range of salal — southern Alaska, all the way down to California. Salal has this absolutely wonderful range. But the problem is where it does really well — close to salt water, temperate conditions, frost-free — in those areas, *people* are living there now. People want to live where salal wants to live. The woodlots have been cut up into 20-acre parcels. People are building homes on them. So, prime salal habitat went from public land ownership to private small parcels.

Most of the good salal sites have homes on them. But the harvesters are realizing most of these people go off to work during the day, and they have no idea whether the salal's gone from their property or not. We've pushed the high-intensity commercial salal to the margins.

When we use the word sustainability, we have to be cautious with understanding plants. It's not the sustainable "growing a tree on there for 500 years." From the first light shade of trees to the really dense shade — of course, there's things you can do — but if you're talking about natural sustainability of salal there's only a window of 15 to 20 years.

In a natural setting, if you don't harvest it and don't do anything to enhance it, it's going to go away anyway. A number of environmental communities will say, oh, look over here, there's no salal and it's been heavily picked. Yeah. But no one has the intestinal fortitude to stand up and say *it wasn't going to be there anyway*.

People in our BLM [Bureau of Land Management] say you have to prove it's sustainable before we allow you to harvest it any more. But nobody knows what sustainable *is*, okay? I mean *nobody*. The closest to knowing are people like Don [Collins] and some of these old-timers who've been picking the same general area back to the 1940s. They'll pick it hard and take off half and come back.

Researchers and scientists and environmentalists and land managers, we don't look at the harvesters's knowledge as valuable data. The pickers are people we've been trying to get involved. They are the ones who really know. You don't have to write a "Best Management Practices" for them, because when it doesn't produce they stop picking.

Traditional harvesters will tell you the same thing. They don't use the words "synergy" or "symbiotic relationship." They think you know that these roots join: if you dig them up and look at them they're all covered with little white

It really irks me to go hiking ... and find once-beautiful valleys stripped of their salal.... This is nothing but forest rape, and it makes me sick.... [T]ell your florist "I don't want any salal in my bouquet, thanks."
Tom Eberhardt, letter to the editor.
Victoria Times–Colonist 14 December 2003

Maybe the letter writer should learn more of this forest product before he carries on further with his dictatorial floral industry boycott of some people's livelihood.... Salal is a multi-million dollar regulated business that was audited approximately 10 years ago by the federal government tax auditors, leaving the business well observed and taxed.
Bruce Smith, letter to the editor.
Victoria Times–Colonist 18 December 2003

fuzzy stuff [mycorrhizae]. That's got to be doing something good.

Photosynthesis. Their leaves are locking up food, which they're dropping every three years or so, so they're increasing the forest litter. The other thing the pickers keep bringing up: "They [salal plants] cool the site, Jim. They keep the trees's roots cool, so in the summertime, when it's real dry, the trees aren't under as much stress as they would be without it."

If they're looking for chanterelles, they're looking for 20-year-old Douglas-firs; they're looking for salal; they're looking for "spring" in the soil. They know what environmental conditions are ideal for finding the best yellow or white chanterelles. They're wonderful store-banks of knowledge.

Don and I can take you out and show you sites where the salal has been overpicked and they're dry anyway, and the trees are small and not doing well. So, I totally agree [with what Cindy Prescott's saying about salal-tree symbiosis]. If you have this smorgasbord of trees, then the seedlings (not of Douglas-fir but of cedar) planted right in the salal will be protected from browsing, and the moist shade will nurture it. The knowledge is there. Is it in the university? No.

It's not in the Native Americans's hands. I have a project I'm doing with the Makahs. They're not much on salal. My experience has shown that all around the world special forest products is pretty much a woman's domain. And it would be here. What I'm finding is that if the Hispanic family sets up house, one woman will continue picking, even if the husband goes into landscaping. The men move on soon as they can — picking's not very sexy: you don't need a chainsaw, you don't need a four-wheel drive, or a backhoe. I mean, some rubber bands, sometimes you don't even use a box knife — just snap it off. Throw it in the back of the station wagon.

So the women in the community valued the berries, knew the medicinal value as a kind of antiseptic when crushed and put on wounds. Salal may be even more valuable in the future for its medicinal qualities. The Oregon State Health Center out of Portland, Oregon, is doing research on the salal flower, for its natural antibiotics. Especially for skin diseases. If you start saying instead of $1.10 for greens, you'll give them $25 a pound for dry-weight flowers, the value of an organic natural fresh poultice is going to be way higher. Though there's a real question of sustainability when you're harvesting the reproductive component.

You guys up there. If I was in Canada, I'd be going down to the international district, to Chinatown, and saying, "Excuse me guys, what would you pay for this stuff? It's a wintergreen." And let them figure it out. The salal may not be any good for greens. But if it grows on harsh sites, the tannins will be high. That's the kind of stuff where the future's going to be.

You work with people, but you go native. I went native — according to one of the bosses I had. And I was worried about what these people wanted more than what the university wanted. So instead of doing the program the university had, I was doing what the people wanted.

I was really out here on the edge. Working with the Latinos, and the Cambodians, and the Vietnamese. You know, I had guys that were really good. My information came from some of these people who grew up, basically, just inside the law. One summer I had three guys on community service. One of the sheriff's deputies said to me one day, "We have three guys now who say they make a substantial part of their income working with special forest products, with brush. Do you have anything that you could do?"

So even though I've worked a lot with regular people, and I thought I knew a lot about the industry, the opportunist picker knows best.

"Native," at least as it applies to plants, is historically contingent. Jim Freed and seedsman Forest Shomer, the men in this book who overtly associate themselves with concepts of "native," are generous, tolerant — advocates indeed for the mixing and diversity of human communities. But they and I need always to advocate for native plants with a parenthesis, with continuing consciousness of Stephen Jay Gould's admonition: "How slippery the slope between *genius loci* ... and 'my locus is best'" (13). With the support of specific examples, including truly frightening ones from Nazi Germany, Gould continues: "How easy the fallacious transition between a biological argument and a political campaign" (13). Although he allows some case for natives as a "protection ... against our [i.e., humans'] overweening arrogance" (17), his crucial reminder is that "organisms (and their areas of habitation) are products of a history laced with chaos, contingency and genuine randomness" (16).

So listening to Jim's listening is getting inside words: gleaner, brush, opportunist, picker, poor, steal. It's getting inside getting native.

GATHERING

**No wonder that the earth expresses itself outwardly
in leaves, it so labors with the idea inwardly.**

· Henry David Thoreau *Walden*

To listen to Jim Freed was to learn about living both inside and outside
the story at the same time. His definition of getting native implied
no superficial identification with Native American understanding. His
notion had more to do with gathering: the more information you gathered, especially from varied perspectives, the more comfortable and
inside you were likely to feel. Yet, paradoxically, in such comfort you
were prone "to miss stuff."

Not long after I moved to British Columbia, when I was gathering
works to include in a course on West Coast writing, I read Bill Holm's
Northwest Coast Indian Art: An Analysis of Form. That book, both probing
and yet helpfully elementary, goes a long way to helping an outsider feel
some insider perspective on the design conventions and representational
elements of a profoundly local and powerful art. Recently, returning
hopefully to Holm's book with salal in mind, I was not surprised to
find no leaf in sight.

The apparent absence of plants in Northwest aboriginal art, as in
most literature and clan names, seems to offer yet another example

of salal's anonymity. Plants, especially cedar, provide the foundational material for art and artifact, but are seldom represented. Even in a book promisingly titled *The Magic Leaves,* Peter Macnair and Alan Hoover's commentary on how the Haida rework the suppleness of argillite, we can detect very few leaves of any sort — eight or nine instances among 230 carvings. That inward and mysterious process through which leaves make the earth's food and maintain its critical atmospheric balance is essential to wolf or frog or orca or raven, but unlike those more mobile and vocal species, unrecognized in art. While salal is aesthetically desirable and a commodity in a post-contact bouquet-for-all-occasions floriculture, its beauty is either assumed or, more likely, undifferentiated in Haida or Tsimshian culture.

When we came back to Masset from the cannery I used to pick berries with my mother. We went up to New Masset for salal. There weren't any white people there then, just all kinds of berries. My mother also used to go to Watun River for red huckleberries and I went with her. She'd bring the berries home and cook them with salmon eggs for thickening. She boiled them till they were dry. She put the berries in a bentwood box with a cloth covering over them, then thimbleberry leaves and skunk cabbage leaves on top before she put the lid on. She cooked her berries in the shed behind the house where my dad carved and she stored them there, too.... My mother put up huckleberries, salal, and cranberries in boxes, five or six of them, for the winter.

Florence Edenshaw Davidson
During My Time: Florence Edenshaw Davidson, A Haida Woman[1]

Yet salal is hardly unregarded among Northwest aboriginal peoples, as ethnobotanist Nancy Turner's work amply shows. Among many aboriginal peoples, berry patches, like hunting grounds and fishing sites, were the property of a particular clan or lineage group, and passed down from one generation to the next. It was the responsibility of clan members to serve as guardians of the patch, tending to the plants when necessary (Turner 2005, 164–65). Perhaps key to understanding the absence of salal in aboriginal art is a gender element: gathering berries as staple food, making berry-cakes for ceremonial occasions, weaving plants and roots into baskets, and using leaves for cooking may all have been primarily female responsibilities, at least traditionally, whereas the making of totem poles, jade carvings, and masks may have mostly been designated male. However, as Philip Kevin Paul's poem, discussed earlier in the section "Naming," implies, the pronounced division is changing: in the poem, a mother teaches her son the precious importance of gathering.

I did find one extended, explicit use of leaf in *The Magic Leaves*: "Many ship panel pipes feature floral motifs in the form of lanceolate leaves and berries.... [T]here may be an explanation for these designs that is closer to the Haida world than the alien source might suggest.... [W]e suggest that the native tobacco plant is intended in many of these renderings" (Macnair and Hoover 40). Macnair and Hoover's title comes from a story by Skaay of the Qquuna Qiighawaay, recorded by the linguist John Swanton, and recently translated by poet Robert Bringhurst. It concludes a series of adventures with birds and fire and "spirit beings you haven't so much as imagined," when the hero Born through Her Wound brings down from a "big tree" seeds and leaves of native tobacco to be planted restoratively throughout Haida Gwaii (Bringhurst 2001, 267). Hence, we may say that the only leaves in Northwest Coast visual art are narcotic and sacred — that leaves figure in art where they enable humans to approach the supernatural and transcendent. (Intriguingly, the wound from which Born through Her Wound is given birth is treated by unspecified "healing leaves" [Bringhurst 2001, 247].)

Few leaves, it seems, appear in the art of the Northwest aboriginal peoples. Yet always and everywhere that ovoid form integrates, and manifests interior structures — "eyes, joints, and various space fillers," as Holm puts it (37). James Swan, Holm reminds us, links this ovoid form to the "elliptical spots ... on a young skate" (37). But to me, as an untutored observer of such motifs, I can't help thinking, in ignorance, that the shadow of that ovate salal leaf is continually emerging in masks and prints and feast bowls.

WORKING

The Northwest is for people more interested
in being than achieving.
· Thomas Griffith "The Pacific Northwest"

On a half-warm, mostly cloudy day, late in August, the atrium of the
Pacific Forestry Centre, as Brian Titus points out, is filled with silver
light. On one side of the foyer is a yellow-cedar relief map of the North
Pacific Slope carved by D. M. Murdoch and dated 1970. The map,
I learn from Brian, is shaped to the exact curvature of the Earth, its
vertical scale increased tenfold to accentuate the relief of the region. I
can't help thinking: a giant map of the range of salal. Brian, a research
scientist at the centre, moves with quick enthusiasm, wound tight with
stories. He shows me several possible meeting rooms, and then we
head back to the ground floor cafeteria for coffee. Wendy Cocksedge
soon joins us. Wendy, coordinator of Research and Extension at Royal
Roads University's Centre for Non-Timber Resources, initiated the
arrangements for this meeting. So, I know already that she has nurtured
a mutual trust and respect among salal pickers, has enabled a person-to-
person contact that eluded me for two years. Wendy is reverent about
plants, but also passionately tolerant: a few minutes conversation and I
am beginning to think of her as Canada's custodian of salal.

We are to meet with Chuong Chau (Mr. Chuong) at 10:30.[1] Meanwhile, we trade place stories, habitat stories, salal moments.

Mr. Chuong brings with him Mean A. L. Khim and Sok Kosal. We assemble in the Sage Room, a spartan and light-filled space with a 12-foot glass-top conference table. I regret that I must begin with bureaucratic niceties; the permissions sheets and protocols introduce a formality out of rhythm with the open invitation I want to encourage. Nonetheless, each man (where are the women?) tests determinedly his English, not hesitating to try a way into answering my questions.

Mr. Chuong is the buddha, the overseer, the "money-man" according to Brian. He speaks deliberately and with a magisterial placidness, but nonetheless leans forward from his chair, as if intent that the tape recorder hear his story and his opinion. Mr. Sok is only an occasional contributor, but, for all his quiet observation, he too conveys an intensity — my school was destroyed in the civil war and I could not finish my education, he says sadly — and what might be called, in recognition of the paradox, a deferential confidence.

Mr. Khim is the most entertaining, and despite groping for an English term here and there, is clearly the storyteller in this group. He creates a vivid word-picture of walking out of the forest with a 130-pound bale over his shoulder. And when he tells us of the urgency of taking his son picking, Brian, Wendy, and I are rapt and moved. He wants his son to realize that he must work very hard to get a degree and qualifications so that he will have a career and success in Canada. But he also wants his son to know what his father does, where he does it, how hard it is, and how — somehow — his work expresses his love, his masculinity (his responsibility to provide for his family, his key to being a "man"). This advocacy, this claim — no, this apologia — for respect, or just appreciation of the integrity of his work, is surely the active principle of the whole morning's talking — and of every day's working for these three.

Mr. Chuong begins by explaining that the picking season begins in earnest in September:

❧ But some buyers here sell in the local area, like in Vancouver, and for them we can start early in August. In August, salal still soft — not hard enough — so it cannot ship far away. We pick from August through to April or May. From

April or May until July, salal gets really black on leaves. It's called pepper mould. If we ship far away, if only on one leaf in the whole pile, overnight it can spread over salal.

Mr. Khim elaborates:

❧ It will leak, salal leak, because we have something like a dark, dark dot.

Brian adds that "it looks like you took pepper and sprayed it over the leaves. But it can spread overnight through a box, from one leaf. It's bizarre how it can ruin a whole load."

Mr. Chuong tells us he has been picking for about 10 years. Mr. Khim and Mr. Sok have been on the job for five years. "Why did you start picking salal?" I ask. Mr. Khim explains:

❧ The first time, I need to find job. And I know some people who pick salal. You don't have to talk. Because you do it without people. So I asked to go with them. And the first time I got sometime $10 a day. It takes me about three months like this, and then I can pick a bit better.

"And now?" we ask.

❧ Right now around $100 a day. Some people pick really fast, and you can make more money. And some people like me are slower. I have no muscle!

Mr. Chuong adds:

❧ Yeah, you need muscle when in bush. And climb high in mountain. And sometimes, according to the price too. Right now, from August to November, the price goes low. So even if you pick more salal, still get less money. And then if the temperature's under minus four you have to stay home, because the leaf is frozen — you cannot use it.

I should mention that last year we can get more money, but this year, it's turned down. Because the economy, I think, is low. [Salal] has two prices: I think one is called "tips," and one is called "longs." Some will buy 70 cents, and some other buy 75 [for tips]. But longs are one [dollar] thirty for a hand.

Mr. Khim explains further:

❧ Right now, in the summertime, every house, every day, you can find
flowers, so you don't need salal in the house. It just makes sense. And right
now, salal, it's not hard enough, it's still soft, so we use the local only — that's
why the price is low. When salal is hard enough, we can ship it overseas.
That's the best time — the prices are higher.

Brian notes that "we don't know much about what you get paid, how
much salal is taken when, and what they do in Europe — we don't know
much about that structure. We don't know if maybe the Europeans are
selling cheaply."

And Wendy remembers, "When we were down talking with Hiawatha
[a greenery wholesaler in Nanaimo], they said that they'll buy it cheaply
now. Or actually, more in September when they can store it, and then
they'll just store it in their warehouse, because it will last so long. And
then when the price is higher in the spring, they don't need to buy as
much because they have a big store. They have millions of dollars worth
of salal sitting there in boxes."

"When you go out picking," I ask, "do you go early in the day? Does it
take the whole day? Do you pick by hand or do you use an instrument?"

Mr. Chuong says:

❧ [To get to] my place of working, it takes about two and a half hours —
five hours back and forth. So we have to wake up early. My wife wake up at
five o'clock in morning, and the time I'm back is eight o'clock at night."

Mr. Khim volunteers to show us the procedure for picking. He has
come with several props to help with the demonstration — gloves,
elastics, twine — and proceeds to go through the picking sequence
all in mime, accompanied by rapid, enthusiastic patter. He shows us
how to gather enough stems for a "hand." (A "hand" of tips weighs
¾s of a pound; a "hand" of longs weighs 1¼ pounds.) When he's holding enough for a hand, he wraps an elastic band onto one stem, then
quickly stretches it to hold the whole hand. He is proud — many
pickers can only hold two or three at a time — that he is able to hold

six hands of salal, three in the left, three in the right, and still pick effectively.

Once he has six hands, "you put it somewhere where you can remember where to find it." The lengths of twine are already prepared with a loop in one end. Mr. Khim ties a noose of twine around an imaginary twenty hands of cut salal to make a "belt."

❧ When you have six belts, then you have to put on your shoulder and carry out of the bush wherever you want to take it to — to go to the parking. Sometimes I carry 140 pounds. If I go up on the hill high, I have to cut down — maybe 130, 120. You have to work hard to get muscle up, increase muscle. But if you cannot stand to go up too many times, you might run away, you might quit. But for me, first when I start, oh. Really tough life. I say well, I must do this, because I'm here, and that kind of job don't need degree. But my heart still is unhappy, so I have to do this — I must do it! And then I go up to the hill until I go on top of the hill. And then go down that hill and start another hill. Keep going. Sometimes we might walk about three kilometre away from the parking. Sometime, there a lot of old cutting log in the forest — you have to walk there and it gets hard to carry. Very difficult.

"The slash in some of these sites," Brian adds, "is incredible. The logs, and the physical difficulty. Sometimes, a picker I know spends a week working, and then has to take a day off work just to recover. The bruising — she showed me once just her shins, just the physical difficulty. It's a lot. Another interesting thing," he continues. "We weighed what Mr. Chuong and his people picked, because we wanted some data for science, and it was exactly what they said. And I decided then, there was no point in me weighing, because if they say, 'There's a belt, it's 130 pounds, 120 pounds,' I know it is. And I think what amazed me was the accuracy. It's not worth my time to check, because it's very accurate."

Mr. Khim explains how he learned the weights:

❧ Oh, you get used to it. First, you have to pick it up, and you have to bring a little scale along, and you weigh it up, and it's "Oh!" Then you start, you say, "Oh, I've got enough weight for this hand. Ha!" And you start the next one.

And then you come back and weigh it again. But now I don't weigh it, because you know how, like, between your thumb and your finger here, you say, "Well, it's this much. That means it's enough weight." It take you about three week to a month to get used to it, and then easier for you. But people first time, they cannot make very much because they're concerned about the weight. And the most important way to know the weight is when you can feel just small like this, this enough pound. Short stems, you need more; long stems, you need less. And it also depend on the land. Some land feed up really good juice inside the stem, and some land it sucks the juice out of the plant — it's lighter. Even if thicker and longer, but it's still lighter. So we have to watch about that too.

We return to talking about the work day, and Mr. Chuong explains:

❧ Usually, my wife get up at five, one hour before me. She cook — prepare and cook everything. And then by the time that she done — probably 30 minute, 40 minute — we all get up and ready to go, and say, "Well, we're ready to go." And take everything out, put it in the truck, start it up, and go. The latest, probably six o'clock. Sometime five-thirty. And then we go there. Sometime the area is a bumpy road — got to go slow in there, otherwise get into the ditch — and then if the highway is too wet you cannot go faster because it's too slippery, so to prevent accident. But if it dry — like the summertime it is — from here to there [Jordan River] probably two-hour drive from Victoria, but in the wintertime probably more than that. And we come home around nine o'clock, nine-thirty at night.

Mr. Chuong keeps repeating his concerns for safety:

❧ Bring to the warehouse is not very much important, but important is the highway and also the mountain road. Because the mountain road is sometimes bumpy, like go like that, like that, and then sometimes go on the side of the cliff. You have to be careful — otherwise, you're going to steer and then go in there. And when it happens, he can contact Forest Services. But if he not, nobody can know where we are. Must be careful.

And you have to sleep really good. You have to make sure you have enough sleep. Because of preventing accidents on the road, to keep something between us and the other driver, to be safe together. And the second thing, to prevent wasting a day or two and then we lost the income. You might put the brakes on, but the tire won't stay — it still moving, it goes down like this. It's really steep in some places.

I have to mention that I think it was about a year ago, one woman from Nanaimo die. She died because the accident. Probably something wrong with the brake or something wrong with the driver — he fell asleep or something like that. And the truck flies from one side to this side, and the one or probably two in the back. Gone. I read in the paper — I didn't see it.

And then we have to watch the trees, too, if it's windy. Some days, too heavy rainy and windy — must move out from the forest quickly because the big tree fall down, or if go in the road there the tree fall, block up the road, and you have nothing to move the tree, and you have to stay there for a day or two.

"So if you're going out at six o'clock in the morning," I wonder, "and you come back at nine-thirty at night, how many days would you do that in a week?" Mr. Khim answers:

❧ Sometimes five days, six days. As soon as we get tired, stop take a rest for one or two days. If you feel better, start working again.

And Mr. Chuong adds:

❧ As long as you have enough energy and not feel like sleeping. Like I said, if we start at 6 in the morning until 9:30 at night, and we come home, you have no time to talk or run around or call anyone — just go to bed right away.

Sometimes we just go there, we got there, and we go home with nothing. Not even one hand. Because we go there, we just start something, we've just finished breakfast, and snow start coming, and we have to go home, we have to leave. We cannot go up the hill because it's too slippery. If the truck cannot go up, we come back. Here we close to the ocean, and plus we have flat land here. But over there [that is, toward Jordan river], some deep and some high, but have the big big tree, so it's really difficult to tell from the weather forecast. For example, today, here, there's a little cloud but it bright and it dry, but over there, no. Raining and cloudy — you cannot see very good. A lot of cloud.

Mr. Chuong, in all this conversation about safety and difficulty, mentions the "next generation," and Mr. Khim explains how he introduced his son to picking. He said to his son:

❧ If you stay home, and just come back to see me at home, you don't know what I'm doing. So you have to come with me and see how hard I work, and how long a way is the drive from home to there, and how difficult for walking in the forest. So I'd like you to come along and learn how to pick like me. If you don't want to do the professional picking, but you want to learn something about what happen in life, and why I recommend for you to study harder, to get some degree, to make yourself a better job. I came from Cambodia to Canada: I need my kids to have a good lifestyle. So I don't have enough degree to have any kind of office work or any kind of different work. So this is the job that I choose for my life from now, because if I'm just waiting to study or something else, probably my life will be gone. So I must do it now, while I'm alive. Do whatever I can to help you and help my life, because I'm too late to get a degree. And you must work hard at school to get a degree, to do something else while I'm supporting you. I told him that, and took him along to show him some things.

"What about competition," I ask. "Do you go and find other people in your spot, in the place you want to pick? Is there any conflict with other pickers?"

Mr. Chuong says:

❧ If we're talking about the Crown land, you must go there earlier. If not go early, somebody found first, they pick first. You're not allowed to start picking — you have to leave. But if in the property, like what we doing now — no, we not happy to see someone going in there.

"Yeah, yeah. Mr. Chuong has a very unusual situation," adds Brian. He explains that the reference to "property" comes from Mr. Chuong's having arranged consecutive leases with a company that has given him continuous access to one piece of land for over 10 years.

Wendy notes, "It's very rare. Western Forest Products is the only company that does the area-based tenures for salal. All the other forest companies, if it's on private land, they'll issue permits. But they'll issue any number of permits. Then you'll be competing with everybody else, even though it's private land. Western I think is really good, because then you guys can pick sustainably, and you can make sure that it's not over-harvested. So it's a really good arrangement."

Mr. Chuong describes the problem of sustainability:

❧ Sometimes, when it's a good place, you can pick the same place the next year, and next year again. But right now salal is getting less and less every year. The trees grow bigger, and steal salal. Before, we can pick around 100 hands a day; right now, about 70 or 80 hands. But I have to work harder and harder.

"You talked about the danger and safety, but are there other things," I wonder, "that you don't like about this job? What's the worst part of picking?"

Mr. Chuong is quick to propose:

❧ The worst part of picking is the price and also the quality of the land that salal grow in. That's two concerns. So everybody who do this work must depend on salal. And the price must be stable, must not go down, and the buyer must not cut out, must be open all the time. This is very important for us.

Finally, we turn to the story of immigration to Canada. "What did you do in Cambodia before you came to Canada?" I ask, and Mr. Sok, who has been mostly listening, wants to respond:

❧ Oh, because my country is a long time ago in a civil war. So civil war start in 1970. At that time I'm in the high school. And when the civil war start, it destroy the school, and because of the war, I stopped school. So I didn't go again. And we stayed long time in a refugee camp in Thailand, and apply to go to Canada or Europe or Australia, like that.

Mr. Khim picks up the story.

❧ For me, my home is a small town — I don't know how many people, because at that time I was young. But most of the time I was helping my parents do around-the-house stuff, plus farming. In the morning time, I would get up at four o'clock, sometime three-thirty, if I had a lot of work — 250 to 300 cattle in the big barn there. And also poultry we have a lot, like I'd say about 150 ducks and five hundred chickens, and have one house for them. And we clean up underneath, have to open gate to see if they have egg, and put in the basket. Then start cleaning up from the cow, uh, shit. And the chicken too. After everything done and put in one place, and done next thing, then I go check and make sure all my work done, and when my mum get up in the morning she move around and check if I've done a good job. And then after I done the job — seven o'clock, seven-thirty — I have to go to school. Yeah, I start school at eight-thirty, up until two o'clock, come back home again. And right away I come back to the barn, go inside the barn, check make sure my cattle have enough to eat, clean place, and go back to the duck, make sure the duck have good water to swim in.

And the war broke out in my town there. And probably — I'm not sure — Khmer Rouge or whoever came over to our town in the early morning. They asked us to leave the town — we cannot stay, nobody allowed to stay, have to leave. And then we don't know where to go. And then from that time, my parents have no job, no nothing. I have nothing to work. And then no school. And we moved up to the really deep countryside somewhere, and then we had to find a big leaf, like this size, and then as soon as we had to start there we had no — what do you call the plastic thing? [Brian suggests "tarp."] We had no tarp or nothing to make a shelter, must use a leaf. And we had to cut a tree, and we stick together to make a shelter. I have no school from that time on. Work, work, work, until the adult they took away from the children, that time too. And then they move us to work in one part, and the parent they have to stay in one part. And that time they start to say whoever good or bad, they will send to different way — I don't know what they do.

Photographs often fascinate for what's not there. What's just out-side the frame? What happened just before? How did the expressions change after the shutter clicked? Something of the same puzzle occurs with tape recordings. Sometimes, a new intrigue surfaces after the tape recorder is turned off, or two sides of tape have run out — most memorably, in this project, when Wendy Cocksedge, Brian Titus, and I were listening to the stories of Mr. Chuong, Mr. Khim, and Mr. Sok. When the tape ended, Mr. Chuong was still keen to tell us his history. I had another tape, but I was too absorbed to want to interrupt.

Mr. Chuong lived in a refugee camp in Thailand beginning in 1979. Trying to give us some idea of the conditions they had escaped, Mr. Khim told us he had lived in a camp with 70 other families, where they were forced to work from 6:00 AM to midnight for "zero pay." Mr. Chuong came first to Canada, to Calgary, in 1986. Through connections in the Cambodian community, he began to work cleaning dishes on a shift that began at 5:00 in the afternoon and ended at 10:00 the following morning. Depleted by three months of this schedule, he collapsed one morning while waiting for a bus home.

He was hospitalized for exhaustion. Years after, Mr. Chuong still marvels in grateful disbelief that a young doctor completed paperwork for him affirming that he was medically unfit for work, and allowing him to collect welfare during eight months of rest and regaining his strength.

Since then, he has tried to repay his new country with hard work and independence. He is proud of getting a job cleaning at the Southern Alberta Institute of Technology. He is also proud to have earned a certificate as a bakery worker.

Eventually, he moved to Victoria, partly because of ties to the Cambodian community there, but especially because his wife had been unable to find much work in Calgary, and harvesting salal provided an opportunity where "my wife can pick with me." "I feel safer in the forest," he says. "I grew up in the forest. But here is better: there's no danger — no big snakes, no wild boars."

The story of Mr. Chuong's life in North America, here recounted imperfectly and no doubt inaccurately, stilled Wendy and Brian and me — and I think his fellow workers — into reflection. Here was a reminder that the understanding of place (and of native plant) will differ greatly from one subgroup (based, say, in gender, or ethnic background, or class) to another. Mr. Chuong's story again complicated a place and a region I treasured as home, with a world I knew but by a single name. I realized, listening to Mr. Chuong, that however happy I am to have their voices in this book, their reading of salal habitat may have little of the sublimity and transcendence of the nature writing I have been taught by. Their story, the story outside the mainstream and yet at the centre of the thicket of salal culture, must be acknowledged here to be an untold story, a still-to-be-told story. Mr. Chuong washing dishes and being hospitalized in Calgary is a "supplement" to this book. Call his story of migration and work and gratitude another version of the understory.

This is just the point Wendy emphasizes in her parting comment to me. "People don't know about these pickers — or if they do, they look down on them," she observes, "but they deserve honouring." She is the catalyst in this group of five men and one woman; her smile, her quiet animation, her empathy, make her by far the best interviewer.

INHABITING

Corollaries, capillaries, tributaries: any lesser form
of "ownership" than full self-forgetful entry into
a thing seems, in comparison, like a fleeting legal
fiction.... I believe what we seek, ultimately, is not
to possess but to be possessed by what we love.

· David James Duncan *My Story as Told by Water*

THATCH

If salal has a characteristic season, we might find it in H. L. Davis's
Honey in the Horn: salal occurs in that odd coastal northwest season
where "though all the leaves were dead and drying up, there was not
enough strength in the sun, and not enough difference between summer
and autumn to make them shed or color" (258).

This unresolved and indistinct season is also space, the edge of
the continent (245). In this dizzying boom of a novel, when Clay and
Luce drift and yarn their way out onto the hard Oregon beaches, salal
makes its singular appearance. Given that he is writing in the 1930s,
in the genre of the community chronicle, Davis might be said to be
ecologically prescient. Seldom does a plant appear in solitude, but
in association with the species that share its habitat: "all the slopes

were one solid thatch of stiff salal and deer-brush and balm-bush and mountain-laurel" (259). Impenetrability layers itself into roofing and shelter and associations of yeoman stolidity and enduring quaintness. Given the resoluteness of thatch, it's not surprising that the salal is nearly rigid, or at least strong enough, along with these other bushes, to bear the weight of any man fallen from a horse, as if he had tumbled onto a "stiff set of bedsprings" (259).

Maybe it's the season, maybe it's a place to land, maybe it's part of the long ubiquitous invisibilty of the plant, but the cranky narrator makes the salal-season not a month of wild berries picking, but "worthless" (260).

figure 13

Salal rooted on tree trunk.
CHESTERMAN BEACH,
TOFINO, BC
Photo credit: Treva Ricou

SHELTER

Timothy Taylor's *Stanley Park* is a novel to delight West Coasters. The novel's central character is Jeremy, a chef and restaurant owner who sets out to recreate a French relais in Vancouver, BC, using entirely locally sourced ingredients. For various reasons, the restaurant's financial difficulties require selling out to a food financier (whose chain of coffee shops bear a hardly accidental similarity to the shops all decorated in forest green and founded in Seattle). The new owner demands a shift to cuisine known as "global fusion." The novel's morphing restaurants extend to the nearby large urban park (styled as wilderness) where the homeless make their home and survive on yet other forms of urban cuisine.

Such a novel is a fine companion to this book's wondering about the narratives of globalization and local knowledge rooted in salal. Aptly, Taylor pays a fair bit of attention to the plant. Salal, in *Stanley Park*, marks the local. In the first reference to salal, Jeremy's father, "the Professor," stands "in the shelter of a salal bush" (11–12). The salal supplies a hiding place, but Taylor chooses his vocabulary carefully. He does not write, as might certainly be justified for the context, "he stood concealed in (or behind) a salal bush." Rather, the word "shelter" proclaims protection: a single bush provides a habitat, a home.

The reader comes to this initial mention of salal by way of a passage, just a few paragraphs prior, that makes a great deal of the singularity of "leaf." The quite unsheltered Caruzo, the spirit of this wilderness islanded in the city, declaims how he came to be at home in the park: "From a leaf to a lifer.... That's me. A lifer to a leaf" (10). Jeremy's father has always studied the transient — first gypsies, later stowaways and squatters. Now, in the late stages of his career, he is living among the homeless in the park, and lets his son do his library research for him. His study is now participatory not only in the sense that the observer is also the observed, but also in recognizing that a community's customs and behaviour alter as they are lived. In some way, he has come to understand research as "lean[ing] back" and "only listen[ing]" (9). The Professor tries to puzzle out, not too successfully, the meaning of Caruzo's equation: his uncertainty encourages the reader to speculate. Salal is mainly valued as *leaf*, to be sure, although Caruzo makes no immediate reference to *salal* leaf. Caruzo might be slightly mad, and his connections are more aural and oral than intellectual or semantic.

Stanley Park is especially relevant and disconcerting for plant-thinking, because the Professor's project is both passionate and, on many levels, absurd. One reading of Taylor's story makes a compelling case for alternative ownership, the ownership that rests in full, self-forgetful entry into a thing. Another reading would detect not an honouring of the local and bioregional connection, but a send-up of the fetishization of food, and of "nature"— of a much revered "park" whose creation displaced aboriginal people and will not now house the homeless. Taylor's burlesque of "participatory anthropology" inevitably implies criticism of an academic trend, the social and well-meaning desire both to identify with those of another class and lifestyle, and to understand one's self and one's place, or culture or region, through telling someone else's stories, indeed by almost living "their" stories. Yet *Stanley Park* is someone else's story — one it's worth trying to inhabit.

We intuit a connection, somehow, that a leaf is alive, that it is vital essence, that you can live your life through a leaf. That salal would be a habitat. The sustained reference to salal throughout the novel (20 times or more — it's the most salal-littered novel I know) makes *Stanley Park* another sort of salal habitat: an imagined habitat, a thicket of words, within which you read yourself into place.

SOURCING

**I'll say, "Have you ever eaten salal?" They'll say,
"No." That surprises me. Because to me it just
seems that people would find out which berries
are which and eat them because they're so prevalent.**

· Forest Shomer

I drafted much of this book in the home of friend Bob McDonald, on
Saturna Island, BC, where salal is up close and everywhere. Yet I spent
much of the time just staring from Old Point Farm southwest across
Plumber Sound. Salal grows behind the small house, but in front of me,
distracting, are the sculptures of a dozen arbutus in full bloom and the
craggy barkscapes of seven Douglas-firs. And, on this last morning of
my stay, four browsing deer.

Writing usually involves more staring than pen moving on paper.
But when desperate, I hoped I could always get going by writing about
writing. And then I read the introduction to Robert Bringhurst's *Carving
the Elements*, in which he groans inwardly at the thought of one more
"piece of *writing about writing*" (13). Profession, job title, credential, institution have shaped a habit that is hard to break. So writing about
writing about salal gave me a tenuous narrative line and, I fancied, a
signature. But, I'd say to Robert, I *am* telling the story of salal. And,

in several parts of this book, I couldn't bring myself to write about writing, to intrude on the story. I tried to slip outside and listen, listen deeply, to story, to tellers telling.

So I listened when food columnist Anne Gardiner told me her dog eats salal berries and salal leaves. Why not? If they're nourishing for bears and deer, if they're undiscovered herbals, then why not for Anne's dog?

Salal as dog food is, still and all, food. And maybe the fact should be mentioned in conjunction with eating or Bowen Island ecology. But, in writing on sourcing, I want to get at the edge of this sea-edge subject. And Spot's feeding preferences seem pretty unusual.

"Sourcing" as a verb isn't even listed in many dictionaries. As noun, it relates to origin, beginning, or the parenthetical citations in this book that point you to the authors and talkers that provided information. But sourcing as verb, as in the frequent use of outsource, means "to obtain the raw materials, the components of manufacture." Better, and more relevant here, might be to recall that source comes from the Latin verb *surgere*. To spring forth. Unexpected salal connections feel as if they are springing forth: I think of the exhibits staff at the Royal British Columbia Museum first thing in the morning, before the museum opens, carefully replacing the salal in the forest dioramas

figure 14

Sourcing Northwest.
BELLINGHAM, WA

(Davey). Wreath makers also source salal. According to its website, the family-owned and operated Silk Bouquets make wedding hairpieces of roses and salal; so, too, is the bored guy in Captain Cook's Pub in Tahsis, BC, sourcing salal when he reports from the woods on the *blue* bear scat he's seen (Smith 26). And when you're a long way from a pub or crockery, you can serve your supper on salal, as did the early botanist David Douglas and members of the 1825 British expedition to the Pacific Northwest: "Mackay made us some fine steaks.... The meal [was] laid on the clean mossy foliage of *Gaultheria shallon* in lieu of a plate" (Douglas 221).

Sourcing Northwest, despite the name and its location on the Mount Baker Highway, "sources" from all over the world. The hibiscus comes from Thailand. Most of the pungency arrives from India. And salal, a ton a year, comes from the immediately surrounding forest. Sourcing Northwest makes potent potpourri. It's a business devoted to mixture, to the miscellaneous, to the unrelated. Sourcing Northwest, paradoxically, does little of its sourcing in the Northwest — except for salal, the rare local item that makes the pot green.[1]

SOURCING NORTHWEST

My wife Treva and I visited Sourcing Northwest about 1:30 PM on a bright Friday afternoon in July. Along the Mount Baker highway, about seven miles out of Bellingham, marked by a rustic ranch-style sign, huddles a slightly random collection of buildings and add-ons with a clutch of small almost-huts and older cars under the trees near the entrance — presumably accommodation for some of the workers. It didn't seem like a tape recorder kind of place.

Although we'd arranged the visit the day before by phone, owner and founder Ann Stewart seems slightly startled to see us and a little impatient at first. But she starts to show us around immediately, and seems, on a very hot day, to grow enthusiasm as the tour proceeds.

First, she grabs a small, well-used plastic bag of dried salal and invites us to smell it. I can't make out much of an odour, other than a faint earthy smell, but Ann suggests that the bouquet is not especially attractive, and that she advises the workers to put the salal well down in the bags of potpourri.

Then, she scrabbles through 30 or 40 bags of potpourri looking, unsuccessfully, for one with salal. Finding a lonely bag about 10 feet away, she identifies the salal. When I ask if I can buy it, she cheerfully gives it to me.

Sourcing Northwest is a rather astonishing business — more or less entirely devoted to the "manufacture" and wholesaling of potpourri. We can only guess at the scale, but Ann reports (very vaguely) on a core of about 12 employees — and on this day "around 35," it being the peak season: that is, the period of preparation for the Christmas market. When I ask about salal, she reports buying most of it direct from the pickers at a price of $9 per pound. I am both intimidated enough, and distracted enough by this unusual place, that I don't think to question such a high price. Ann notes that salal was one of the smallest ingredients in volume or weight of materials purchased — "less than one ton a year" she says. Other materials, we presume, would be in container-size loads.

She notes, in contrast to the cost of salal, that she can bring material in from India at $2 a pound or less, including shipping. What these products might be, we do not enumerate, given our focus on salal.

We walk through the narrow, cluttered office, and turn right into a bigger room: on one side, several men work with unidentified bulk materials and, on the other side, a plywood box sits on the floor, about seven-by-seven feet and 30 inches deep. The bin is surrounded by perhaps eight women, who might all be Mexican. They are packing the mix from the box into individual cellophane bags.

Ann makes no reference to this process, nor to the people, but she shows us the "recipe" for the fragrant mix, done by weight on a computer program, or profile, developed by her partner, Charles Walsh. She points across the room to the mixer, the size of an oil barrel, painted orange-red, but offers no details.

We hasten on to the dryer, passing through a two-storey-high warehouse, a mini-barn, stacked with, among other things, sacks and sacks of aspen curls dyed orange, green, blue, purple, and red. These curls provide the bulk in most of the potpourri.

We pass through a covered outdoor area that appears to serve as the heart of the shipping and receiving zone — the only place where we see anyone wearing a face mask. Then we pass into a large receiving room where a big dryer whooshes. It is the size of a large dumpster and when in operation gives off a lot of heat. Spread over the concrete floor in front of the dryer lie perhaps 100 square feet of cedar tips either waiting to be dried or just out of the dryer. I'm not surprised to see the cedar, given the business's emphasis on Christmas packages.

In the same room is a dock into which trucks can be backed, and where salal and other products are accepted. The product is immediately weighed as it is unloaded, and a cheque is issued on the spot.

Ann remarks that salal is tricky to dry, since it "will turn" brown or black if it gets too much heat. It is best to air-dry it, but that would be impractical. I ask how they contact their pickers. Mostly she mails out postcards saying something like "now buying salal," but she is not keen, or even perhaps able, to put me in contact with individual pickers.

Ann wears a fatigued denim dress that speaks of a lot of hard work. In appearance, she is an unlikely entrepreneur, but I have no doubt she knows what she is about, and good at it. Ann is a once-upon-a-time English major who's been in this business 15 years. But we don't talk about books, or local ecology. I don't detect any sense of a "mission," as I'm probably hoping for. Still, I wander around delighting to have found another unexpected and surprising use for salal. In this specialized market, global sourcing (especially from Asia and other low labour-cost environments) meets the more expensive local native plant. Whatever the possibilities of a "Northwest fragrance," salal is used here not for its bouquet, which Ann thinks dubious at best, but for its aesthetic elements: in the cellophane bags it is placed

When I'm travelling, I suppose I'm still sourcing Northwest. Although I do not have time to search out the "living specimens" at Kew Gardens, I have no trouble finding salal in London. It's there, in a plastic pail, on the steps of St. Pancras Parish Church, just across the street from Euston Station – the shop of a casual flower-seller who sets up in the morning and disappears at night. So too at a florist's kiosk in King's Cross Station, and in bouquets set out in front of a florist shop in Kew Village I see salal amid other, less durable, greenery.

on the outside and lower down to give a "leafy" appearance — that is, the salal leaf in dimension, colour, and ovate contour, staying intact (not crumbling) even after drying, speaks to the buyer of freshness and renewal, at least in the mauvy five-quart "Spring" potpourri we were given as an example.

CONTAINERING

Wilderness is a great reminder of the
limits of human perception. Where there
are no clocks or roads, time and distance
behave differently, and without signs or labels,
everything appears able to shift its shape.

· Molly Gloss *Wild Life*

"Turn right at the little church. It's the second left." Three hundred
metres up and Courtenay's Western Road runs out at the site of Western Evergreens. On one side, 100 metres of loading ramp, a big white
refrigerator truck, a pickup; some of the buildings are faded green,
others look unpainted, stained possibly with preservative, something
oily, almost like tar.

Owner Rick Ross is the guide who will, on a later visit, give me
a hands-on lesson in picking. Although on this day he's busy with a
small shipment (figure 15), he is immediately welcoming, and Bill, the
guy who is doing the shipping (from Campbell River), is also kind.
Bill doesn't scoff at the idea of a salal book (though he warns that one
has already been written),[1] and he announces proudly that he still goes
picking himself sometimes.

figure 15

Western's salal boxes are a deep blue — a navy blue almost, with a hint of royal. They are stacked up, some on skids, in a covered lean-to shed, at the northwest corner of the complex. So, with boxes in his arms and more behind him, Rick begins to tell me about his life with evergreens:

❧ You've picked an interesting subject, as far as I'm concerned, but I've been immersed in it my whole life. Most people, if you ask them what salal is, they don't really know.

It's used a lot along the roadways, because it stays short, and it fills in beautifully, and it's used to the environment, so you don't have water requirements. It must be very difficult to process the seed. It's a very sticky capsule the seeds are in.

This business, Western Evergreens, was started by my father back in 1970. He had been working for a company in Vancouver doing similar things. The way he got involved is he'd had polio. They told him he'd always be weak and that he could never handle a heavy job. So he started selling from store to store in Vancouver. From there — he never really had any physical problems — he decided he'd start his own company. And he moved here to Courtenay — I was 16 at the time. My sister stayed in Vancouver. I worked for him on and off while I was in school. Then I went to university in Victoria. Got a Bachelor's degree in Botany and Environmental Studies: I was one of the first people through the Environmental Studies program. It wasn't a degree or anything — just a certificate with your degree saying "Environmental Studies Program." I worked for the Canadian Forest Service in Victoria doing research at the federal research station as a lab technician. When I got married, I decided it was time to move back, because it's such a beautiful place — I couldn't imagine living anywhere else.

So I came and worked with my dad, and eventually became a partner. And he's just recently, in the last seven or eight years, retired. But he still comes in to work every day because he loves it. We've been doing this for a lot of years — about 33 years we've been doing the same business.

There's been tough years, and there's been good years. It's never a huge moneymaker for the exporter. We take a lot of the risk — because if the product goes bad somewhere along the line, we can't go back to the picker and say we're going to take your money back. And there can be problems, especially at this time of year, when it's very hot, especially with air shipments.

Basically, we buy product from the people who go out and harvest it in the forest. They bring it in to us. We pay them on a weekly basis. Today is payday, Friday, and we give them a cheque for what they've picked for the whole week, up to last night. Some of the pickers we've had for 33 years; some of them still pick who started with us.

But in the old days, when we first started, there were two large American companies, who have since gone out of business. They were huge, and they were buying all their product to send down to the States, and we were buying our product to send across Canada. We were mainly just a Canadian business. Probably about 20 years ago, we started doing a little exporting to Europe. It became *the* business. Now, most of the companies on the Island, that's what they're doing. It's a huge market. The only problem with that is that in the last few years, there's so many companies doing it that the margins have come way down.

I've had people say to me before, "Oh, wow, you're getting that for free — you should be making bundles of money." But it doesn't work that way. We have to process it, we have to package it, we have to do the transport. And then we have to wait for the person we're sending it to to pay us. And I can tell you about lots of accounts that haven't been paid over the years. There's a lot of risk involved.

There's probably only about 20 large wholesalers in Europe. So you get to know who's who, and you set yourself up with one or two companies. We're exporting to two companies in Germany, two in Holland. We export to Japan. And we do a lot of Canadian business, and some US business as well.

That's one reason we're still around — because we've really diversified in where we ship it. And we've tried to have a product that's a little big higher quality. It's very difficult to do these days, because of the volumes that are being picked. We talk to the pickers, check the product, make sure they understand all the different rules — in the hot weather we've had for the last week we only have an early shift, from six o'clock in the morning till noon. Then they bring it in and put it right in the cooler. It cools down; the heat of the forest goes out of it. And then we start packaging it in the evening: I have a crew that comes in at night.

We export a product to Japan that is probably higher quality than anyone else is doing. And it's our secret sort of process. We can get it to Japan, which requires very stringent phyto-sanitary rules: you can have no insects, no live insects, in your load, so we have to have a process to get rid of them. It's quite lengthy and time-consuming, but we get a better product. Most of the product that goes from the States gets fumigated. Of course, that lowers the quality of the product. We're lucky that we have a Japanese market for this product — we get a better price for it.[2]

Salal is by far 95 percent of our market. We do have other products that we ship. There's evergreen huckleberry, which mostly comes from Texada Island. And there's cedar boughs, sword ferns. Some other companies ship a smaller fern called the deer fern. Oregon-grape. An escapee from gardens here locally is *Daphne,* a species of *Daphne* [*Daphne laureola*] — it's escaped to the forest and some people harvest it. Some companies were calling it madrona, but you're not allowed to ship madrona, so we've changed the name to medrona (with an "e" in it). It's a growing market. We also have some products that we produce later in the season: bare branches with no foliage on them. One of them is the red-berry huckleberry. We market just the sticks, when the foliage falls off, as a product called pearl fern.

A lot of these stick items are really increasing, too. I know some companies in Vancouver that are doing red-osier dogwood. We do the blueberry, the *Vaccinium* that grows up the mountains with the blueberries on it. When the leaves have fallen off, it turns bright red. And they use it a lot in Christmas decorations. Another one is bog myrtle — a beautiful plant. When its leaves drop off, it has this bud at the top that just looks gorgeous: it's a sort of mahogany colour. A lot of florists really like that, especially in spring arrangements. There's a lot of other items, but they are miniscule in comparison to salal.

The container season, which is the big volume season, usually begins about the middle of August, early September, and we normally ship two to three containers — 40-foot ocean-going containers — per week, during that season, which is about 30 weeks, maybe 32 weeks. And the rest of the time, the product can only go by air. There's a season when you can't harvest, and that's the end of May to the beginning of July. So there's six weeks when you can't harvest at all. And most companies would have storage product to cover that period. But it doesn't always hold up that great. So you usually run out before the season's over.

When the new crop is hard enough, you can ship it by air. That usually lasts till the first containers arrive, usually about the middle of September. And there's usually no air shipments after that. So that's about 50 containers to Europe.

What most of Europe is doing is bouquets. And there's a step-level of sales. We're a wholesaler who sells to wholesalers in Europe. Those wholesalers will bring in product from around the world, and divide it all up, and sell it to wholesalers in each country. And these wholesalers will sell to the individual florists. So there is a chain there.

For more specifics, Rick directs me a few steps from the very hot parking lot into the refrigerated warehouse.

❧ Have a look here. That's a bale of 25 salal tips that a picker would've picked yesterday. It has to be done properly — that's the main thing. What we're looking for is the quality of the product. The main thing is you have to clean all the old leaves off. When he picked this piece, there would have been old leaves that ran all the way down the stems. So they strip all those old leaves off, just leaving the last seven to eight leaves. That's what we're looking for: just this year's growth. Everything else has to be stripped off. Those old leaves turn black very quickly.

Approximately the right height for salal tips is between 20 and 24 inches. And three quarters of a pound, or just slightly more (it can't be slightly less). A lot of the pickers will have a small fish scale they hang in a tree and they'll weigh it.

In the old days, everything used to come in in bales. And there would be a whole crew of women who cleaned it and bunched it and made it up to weight. But about 15 years ago — maybe a bit more — bush-bunching became the big thing. The picker bunched out in the field and they got slightly more for their product. Some pickers really caught on to it and do a really good job, and some don't.

This is what they're looking for in Europe — the salal tip. In the Canadian and US market, there's a lot more "long salal," which are 1½ pounds and 28–30 inches. And if it's a really good growth year, that's not a problem. But we've had drought years when the growth has been very minimal. Or early in the spring, we've had too much wet weather. It's a bit weather-dependent.

The other thing that can happen: when the new leaves are just out, and still a little bit soft, and you get a hail storm — that can ruin huge areas, because it just puts holes through the leaves. In flower arrangements, you want leaves without holes, bug-chew marks. It has to look very nice. It's only two pieces of greenery in the back of a bouquet, but we take a lot of time and effort to make sure it's what the customer wants.

Another problem we have here is a lot of it gets picked out in the forest. And you get road dirt if it travels maybe even half a kilometre into the bush. And if it's on the leaves it's very difficult to get off. You can try washing the leaves, but it never quite comes off. It has a scummy look to it.

The bunch should have a front and a back. A lot of new pickers tend to hold it too tightly, and they get it kind of twisting and rotating. This is what the customer wants — a spray, a nice flat bunch that's really dark green on one side, and you can see all the backs on the other side.

If it's going to Europe, it would be slightly wet down, and packaged in cardboard containers with a plastic liner. When we first started we used boxes similar to a cabbage box, waxed inside and out. With the environmental standards now in Europe, we couldn't ship these. Now we use the recyclable box, which keeps it in good shape, keeps it moist. We keep it at this temperature, which is about 4–6° Celsius.

The other thing you don't want is brown on the stem — a woody look to the stem. That means they're picking the salal too far down the stem. When you get into this dark wood, it's probably five, six, seven years old, and it just doesn't regenerate well. The pickers look for the green stem, and where the green stem ends, that's where they try to pick it.

It regenerates every year, so you can go back year after year to the same patches. That's sort of the basis of our industry. You can harvest year after year, and there's really no depletion of the resource. Our biggest problem is the de-activation of logging roads, and the shrinking land base because of the development on Vancouver Island. When we first moved here in 1970, it was bush from our back door all the way to Black Creek. I could have gone out and picked, when I was a kid, right out my back door. Now pickers travel a long way, sometimes, to get the product.

We pay pickers by the bunch. For the ¾-pound bunch, today, it would be 70 cents. Some pickers prefer tips and some prefer longs. A good picker will bring in 150 tips in a day, so that's about 90 dollars. A picker of longs brings in around 70, even up to 100 hands. We have all levels of pickers. We have people who do it part-time — a lot of fishermen will go pick when it's off-season for extra money. We have seniors who are bored, and decide they want to pick — they might go out just for two hours in the afternoon. We have people who pick it for a living, and people who just pick it for extra money.

This [Rick points] is the only item we import. It's called bear-grass. Grows on the Olympic Peninsula and the Cascade Mountains. That's the only item that doesn't grow on Vancouver Island that we have to bring in. It's probably second biggest in volume, after salal — they ship container-loads of it out of Seattle.

The American companies are magnitudes larger than any in Canada. They ship huge volumes. And most of them have buying stations here on the Island. Hiawatha is one in Nanaimo, But there are quite a few others that buy here — they may not have the same name, but they just ship to one US company — because the salal on Vancouver Island is the best salal in the world.

Alberni Valley and the surrounding area is [sic] rapidly becoming reknowned [sic] on the Pacific Coast and eastern Canada as a shipping centre for floral greenery – Salal and Huckleberry.

Although in its infancy – just about three months old – Kirks Limited of Port Alberni are shipping about 3,000 pounds of these twigs per week, and it is expected this will increase to about 8,000 per week within the next couple of months.

Kirks Limited, an American firm with headquarters in Tacoma, Washington, are one of the largest suppliers of this type of greenery on the North American continent.... The [branch] here in Port is the only one in Canada....

One feature that makes the enterprise unique is the fact the company do not have to plant in order to secure the crop – Nature takes care of these plants, in the Barkley Sound area.

All production of the local plant is being shipped to Ontario and Montreal at the present time.

"Salal and Huckleberry Creates [sic] New Industry"
West Coast Advocate 2 February 1956

It's such a big market — it's huge. There's probably 40 or 50 containers a week, I would think, leaving the Puget Sound area, the Seattle area.

There's lots more competition now. A couple of Canadian companies have opened. There's BC Floral Greens and Canada Floral. They've been really intensively hitting the European market. It is a commodity — a worldwide item that's traded. The price fluctuates: lowest in summer, rising in December. We usually see another rise in spring. The reason is demand — there's a huge demand, just after the Christmas stuff is done, for Valentine's. Mother's Day and Valentine's are the two biggest flower days of the year. The volumes that have to go out at those times are phenomenal.

I've seen the prices as high as $1.15, $1.20 for tips at the end of the season. We get a lot of haggling. There's at least five companies in the Comox Valley that buy salal. And there's eight in Nanaimo. We have two plants — another Western Evergreens in Campbell River. I buy a little bit from other companies; they provide me with huckleberry, evergreen huckleberry, so I don't have to send my own crew over to Texada.

We also do a lot of Christmas greens. That's a whole other business that all of a sudden gets added to our main business. Cedar boughs, silver fir boughs, white pine, hemlock, jack pine. To compound things even further, we also do wild mushrooms. You get all three of these together, and we're pretty busy in October — maybe triple what we do the rest of the year.

In many ways, my visit to Western Evergreens has been an encounter with numbers — whole container loads a week from this one wholesaler. And this volume is multiplied many times over.

"How would you describe the typical picker?" I ask, just as I'm about to leave.

❧ They're a very independent person. They're someone who likes to work for themselves and be their own boss. If they decide they want to take time off, they take it off. If they want to work 14 hours a day, they do. I think for the most part they really enjoy it.

A person who likes to be in the forest, to be outdoors — a lot of them go out in weather I wouldn't even try to go out in. They'll go out in monsoon rain, not because they're desperate — it's just part of the culture of harvesting these products.

I was asked by a North Island group trying to organize pickers up there. One of my suggestions to people who wanted to set up plants was to go and pick it first. You don't have any idea of what's involved till you've actually gone out and picked it. You've got to go out and be in the bush, and find out what it takes, and how it has to be done properly, before you become a buyer.

When I sit down, four days later, to try to write about this visit, I have on the oak table where I often work copies of Kim Stafford's books *Having Everything Right* and *Lochsa Road*. Kim — at the time I hadn't seen him for 10 years, but he's the sort of person, and writer, that you feel you must refer to by his first name — writes a lot about place. By reflecting on being *out* of place, he writes his way back or through to a sense of home.

Because I felt out of place at Western Evergreens, I re-read Kim's line "For I am an idiot with a PhD" with assent and relief (1991, 23). Yes, to the sense of discomfort. But I also like that Kim doesn't pretend, even to himself, that he isn't bound, in some measure, to credential, and to institution, and hence to an urban home in an urban environment with a personal webpage. Maybe the idiot part is not so much a contrast as integral — a dimension and measure of the ties, economic and avocational, to having a PhD.

Kim needs to teach. Teaching for him is not only mission but personal necessity. He can't go too long without it. He teaches me, and allows me, to admit ignorance. But his choice of noun goes beyond signalling book-ignorance, goes beyond even the foolishness of the Fool at play. The term *idiot* implies an aspiring learner so remote, so unattached, so without a mental framework or capacity, that remembering or analyzing — say, how to snap a stem efficiently, or how rhizomes behave — seems impossible. *Idiot* also suggests that beyond rationalizing and beyond talk, some sensory, pre-linguistic understanding might open up.

Idiot comes from the Greek *idios*, "own" and "personal" — think of idiom and idiosyncrasy — implying a special and individual way of understanding. You're an idiot when you push yourself, when you try to make sense of something that doesn't make any sense to anyone else. "Why is an *English professor* writing a book about a shrub?"

So, thinking back to my visit to Courtenay, it makes idiotic sense that this warehouse on the shore of the westernmost inland sea on the continent should be called Western Evergreens and found at the end of Western Road. A slightly ramshackle and piecemeal architecture evokes a backlot set for Dodge City or Salal Gulch. And, for all that the name and the surround are green, the dusty tints of the buildings and the baked expanse of gravel out front speak of desert. Rick chooses to hold most of our conversation in the parking lot, in the full noon-hour August sun, at 30° Celsius.

Inside, whatever the astonishing coolness, I sense mainly spaces and volumes and emptiness. And when the pickers drift in from the range, backseat of the '84 Toyota stuffed with salal tips, they carry their harvest into rooms that remind me of a small barn. There's a table built of unfinished rough lumber, a rusted spring-loaded scale, and a gathering of cut twine hanging from above (figure 16). Here the trading is done, with sometimes some jawing thrown in. Although I hear only a little of their conversation, the shed seems a congenial space for the typical pickers Rick has described: independent, out-in-all-weathers, hard-working, but unpredictable — maybe a little of the "cowboy" in them.

RAMBLING

**What will be called home one century from now
— a thicket, a nation, the Earth itself?**
· **Kim Stafford** *Having Everything Right*

BREAD AND WATER

During my first visit with Rick Ross, owner of Western Evergreens, a
slightly rumpled light-blue Toyota pulled up beside us, and a slightly
rumpled 20-something couple got out and began to unload salal from
the back seat. Rick didn't introduce me to them — maybe he didn't
know their names. Ten minutes later, we met them again in the sorting room. Although we pretended not to notice one another, I watched
them obliquely for three or four minutes, and suddenly I pictured them
up to their armpits in a nearby salal patch, snipping quickly, not talking
much. They had tied maybe 15 hands, I would guess, and I imagined
them taking their $10.50 earnings, buying a jar of peanut butter, some
seven-grain bread, a bottle of water, and retiring to eat a simple supper
on the shell midden in front of their small tent, just overlooking the
sunbright black waters of Georgia Strait. And behind them, a swelling
of salal so intact no picker could possibly have been there. "A green,"
in Daphne Marlatt's phrase, "so green it outgreened itself" (1988, 15).

If you were kayaking in the Broken Group Islands, in Barkley Sound, on the west coast of Vancouver Island, you could stop in Turtle Bay, a natural harbour formed by Willis, Dodd, and Turtle Islands, and detect the presence — "dilapidated fencing" and a "few fruit trees" — of a presiding spirit named Salal Joe (Snowden 176).

From about 1960 to 1980, Joe Wilkowski, Iranian immigrant, lived a hermit's life at Turtle Bay. His name came from his sometime occupation of "collecting salal branches and shipping them to distant florists via the *Lady Rose*" (176). In 1980, Salal Joe disappeared; his outboard *Hello Nature* was found on the rocks of nearby Chalk Island, "throttle wide open" (176). But he continues to appear to visiting kayakers, through the night mists and cedar branches, to ensure that the garden he created still blossoms (Steel 1996, 73–75).[1]

The legend of Salal Joe grows into a hello-nature story. It is possible to live and die, remote and alone, harvesting salal, selling "nature." When the Broken Group Islands became the Pacific Rim National Park, Joe was permitted to stay (Snowden 176). His story is still told — I heard it first from Erin Peters, a friend of my son. Joe is an ordinary name; salal is an ordinary bush; joined inside/out. Salal Joe makes sure the islands get the space, air and food they need.

Rambling from occasional pickers near Courtenay, BC, to the durable legend of Salal Joe shows something of the range of the pickers' story. Another favourite salal trip took me just a few kilometres from home, if decidedly sideways from my habitual routes. On a Tuesday afternoon in July, I go to Adanac Street in Vancouver's Strathcona district to talk to Ernie Myer, wholesale florist. Myer is a middle man, buying greens from the brush sheds and marketing them to retailers.

Ernie might be *the* salal cowboy, although he is uneasy about American business, and admires Native Americans. Maybe cowboy here becomes boss and manager. Ernie's story incorporates cross-border tension, ethnic stereotyping, and nationalism — he only sells in Canada (or almost only). But he has little or no use for government.

In our conversation, he's very good at keeping the focus on salal — it really is quite prominent in his business. But he's hard as hell to pin down for details. He gets up to give me addresses of jobbers from his files, and maybe names of pickers, but another strong opinion intrudes and the specifics never emerge. Although, right at the end, he does give me three telephone numbers of "white guys" who have been or are pickers and might be able to help me.

Ernie's office in a warehouse, this whole warehouse as an office, makes me feel privy to an amorphous and unregulated economy, or sub-economy. In Ernie's mind, it seems, the only company being regulated and taxed (and yet operating ethically) is Myer Floral. Most of the rest is rumour and instinct and guesswork, with no names attached. He praises the Indo-Canadian community. Maybe there's more bluster here than bite?

Salal, this apparently simple plant I'm after, this apparently grounded topic, is located in speculation and ramble. I teeter on the edge of specifics, but they dissipate in rapture and sometimes anger. And, in looking for an ordinary plant, I become a visitor to my own home place.

Ernie has a booming voice and booming opinions. His office — glassed-in but hardly soundproof — is in the corner of the two-storey grey-dark space that houses Myer Floral. There's a feel here of a trans-shipment zone, with boxes stacked and scattered, a solitary half-full box of salal on the floor near the centre of the room.

Business seems to be the last thing on Ernie's mind. As Bob Kroetsch might say in enthusiastic admiration, he's an A-1 Pacific Northwestern bullshitter. He leans back in his chair, often rests his heels on the desk, and blasts at everyone in sight. It was both easy to talk to Ernie — I hardly had to say a thing — and difficult. I wanted to let him have his fury, but I didn't question enough.

When I walk in, he is smoking — there is no query, commonplace now, "Is it okay if I smoke?" I suspect if I object, I'll be on my way in two minutes. Much deep coughing and scrambling for some kind of gum to allow his vocal chords to keep working. But 20 minutes in he is busy with another cigarette — his use of roll-your-owns a signal of a generation and culture I link to some black-and-white film I might have seen on *Horse Opera*. They declare his self-reliance, financial shrewdness, and fierce "independence." His first comment when I turn the tape recorder on is to describe the form I have come to think defines salal culture.

❧ If you don't mind me rambling, because I will ramble on.... I got mixed up in this industry about 20 years ago. What salal was primarily used for then was funeral work. If someone makes a casket spray, the flowers go into an oasis holder, and that has to be covered because it's very unsightly.[2] The public doesn't want to see that. So the sprays would drape over the oasis holder and make it look very natural. Some people used cedar for it; some used dagger fern, or sword fern, for it. But it doesn't last. Dries up in hot funeral homes or whatever.

Since then, salal has got into everything from arrangements to supermarket bouquets. Now you've got, out of the port of Seattle alone, 25 containers a week going to Europe. It's come a long way that way. Twenty years ago, I was selling it for $22 a case; now we sell it for $70 a case. I started out with an Indian fellow. For 25 years he's raised his kids, bought houses, cars, whatever have you — all on salal. He's done very, very, remarkably well. He's worked very hard. He's not always reliable ... but you take what you can get in this business.

Our heaviest competition is from the Americans. And the Americans have a funny way of competing. Salal to them, in Washington State, is a hobby. A lucrative hobby, but a hobby nonetheless. They make all their money on Christmas greens. What they did when they saw the Canadian guys up here, chipping away at their marketplace, they dropped their price below their cost. Knowing full well we couldn't compete. I got back at them by getting some of their best customers, faxing them a price list, which I knew they would have to match to keep the customer — which I could never afford. I did this for about three months at a ridiculously low price. Two can play that game, right? I can price anything I want — doesn't mean I've got it.

The Americans don't like me much. That's neither here nor there.

Subsequent to that, the Americans opened up plants on Vancouver Island. They will raise the price to the picker on Vancouver Island. When they do that, we have to match. And our price has to go up. Meanwhile, their price in Washington State hasn't been raised. I'm not sure if that's illegal or not — but I have a feeling it is. Nobody can prove anything.

It's not quite the salal wars, but cross-border tensions in the Northwest focus on resources — salmon and softwood especially — and environmental concerns: the City of Victoria's untreated sewage, the Sumas power project. The nursery trade in salal, Washington State nursery owners Tom Wilkins and Ingrid Wachtler told me hesitantly, sees free trade as a problem in the US.

❧ They can buy it here, especially with the dollar the way it's been, ship it right down to the States. There's no tariff on it. And sell it there. They still make a good dollar. Meanwhile, we can't.

Dealing with the Americans, it's tricky. They're a funny people. One of the biggest companies opposing them is Canadian Evergreens. And they're making maybe a dollar profit a case. Six hundred sixty cases in a can. So they're making 650 bucks every time they send a can to Europe — it's not a lot of money.

For the picker it's great — he still gets his money. But for the guy who's actually doing the paperwork, supplying the warehouse ... you've gotta sell a lot of product.

Which brings me to a modern-day event, where you've got people now selling to Europe at a price they can't be selling at and still making money. Which makes me wonder what's going on there! Nobody does things like that for nothing. So it makes you wonder who's running that operation. I heard the RCMP is investigating some of that operation at this particular time. So, we'll see what comes of that.

Throughout this inverview I keep offering an encouraging, assenting "Right" and "Uh huh" to Ernie's stories and speculations. I want to stop to ask who? which? what? It's hard to interrupt. But I do stop here to say, "How do we *know* there's 10 containers going a week?" Ernie shuffles paper, turns to his files, looks for the documents, but finally provides little detail:

❦ — The rumours just fly, absolutely fly …
  — There's all kinds of statistics and …
  — The Americans collect better information than we do …
  — None of it I consider to be particularly up to date, even when they put it out …
  — "Forest Practices" hang on there …
  — I think there was an overview done in '97 …
  — This one here from Washington State. I think it was '97, but what they've got written in the book, and what it actually was: you could double what is in the book and maybe still not come up with a proper figure …
  — I know a picker who knows a picker. So this picker tells that picker that he was down delivering a load to … and they're loading up three containers to go to Montreal. Another guy comes in and says that some guy is doing two containers to go to Italy. So you add it all together. But that's all word of mouth …

As with Jim Freed, the special forest products researcher who insisted on the value of pickers's talk, the rambling oral culture is the backbone of a secretive industry. Hyperbole is the dynamic.

❦ So when I'm saying 25 containers going out of Seattle a week, it could be 50. But 25 is what I've heard about. Another guy over here is doing 10 containers. Another guy over here is doing two containers.

If I'm getting two bucks profit a case, then I'm working too hard. It's not worth my time. I'd rather do Christmas greens, where the percentage is way higher. So, in salal, in the Canadian market, if you're doing 200 cases a week, you're doing well.

Canadians will pay a fair price. So will Americans, if you could get the market. Europeans? Not a chance. Not a hope. They're so cheap, they squeak.

How we do it is this. We have jobbers. The jobbers hire the pickers. The pickers deliver to the jobber. The jobbers grade and pack bunches for us. And then the jobber sends it to us. We have four separate jobbers who ship product to us. Then we, as distributors, either sell to other wholesalers, or as wholesalers sell to the retail market. The jobbers have plants, which means they have coolers. We pay any jobber $6 a case to handle.

My sources are Powell River, Sechelt, Vancouver Island, Campbell River. The early stuff we're getting is from the Gulf Islands, which is kind of nice. It started 10 days ago. It hardens off quicker on the Gulf Islands — you need to watch that. Other wholesalers, they go dry. We were first off the mark this year. For the first two or three weeks we have the advantage. First, we can get any price we want. But "B," people know that we're reliable. "They must know what they're doing ..."

Some guys are still closed. They don't care.... Of course, he's the same guy who gets a government grant for hiring handicapped people. So the government subsidizes his labour costs, so he can sell salal cheaper than anyone else — in competition with proper businessmen. Which I consider to be bullshit. Right? The government is helping that guy compete against me. That's bullshit!

Meeting Ernie Myer was one of the genuine privileges and pleasures of my salal roadshow. True, in some ways I felt most out of my element during and after this interview. And part of me wanted to call "Whoa!": "Isn't there a bigger social advantage," I might have asked, "to providing wage work for disabled persons?" But I knew this complex I was trying to get at wouldn't have much value to me, or to a reader, if it sidestepped, or censored, or euphemized the unsettling stuff.

Much of the story of salal I could never get at. We might catch a corner of it in an advisory in *National Geographic*. And we might expand on that rumour reported in the *Seattle Times* concerning a shipper from Vancouver Island accused by Seattle police of using shipments of salal to conceal more potent medicinal greens. And because salal pickers seek out remote locations, sometimes relying on secrecy to safeguard choice patches of salal, hints of intrigue and bits of innuendo tend to cling to their accounts. The "under" in this story gestures toward the hidden and incomplete.

> At Olympic [National Park], they're ... concerned about plant thieves....
> The top illegal crop is salal.... If you see signs of poachers, such as rubber bands (used to secure bunches of stalks) littering the side of the road, notify a ranger.
> **"Get Involved: Brush Plant Poachers"**
> ***National Geographic* July 2004**

I've affectionately called Ernie a cowboy because I like his maverick side. And in a book wanting to disrupt some border-crossing myths, I think it's worth imagining the cowboy *north* of the 49th parallel. But also in the revisionist history of work in the West, we have realized how overdone is the image of the gunslinger on Main Street or in Myer's Saloon. Cowboy means strength, an ability to defy the elements, long hours of demanding physical work. Those attributes were felt in the listening, what I heard in the intonation and emphasis that might not translate onto the page. I recognized tenderness in Ernie's wish to do well by his own son, and his son's generation. I heard integrity in his desire that his son should be brought up in a society where indentured labour and environmental recklessness, of whatever sort, would be eliminated. Ernie speaks for the intensities of a free and frantic picker's and salal-seller's world — but his greatest intensity is to make things right.

❧ What gives them the right to do that? If you're going to give every Tom, Dick, and Harry a hundred grand a year to operate, give *me* a hundred grand. Right? So where is that fair? There's your money for hiring the mentally handicapped. So what does he do? He knocks the price of his salal down so he can sell it cheaper than anybody else! Excuse me! That wasn't the deal.

It's just like CIDA. Canadian Economic Development Association [*sic*]. They set up with a single distributor — gave them a whole stack of money. Whatever. To help undercut the market for everyone else. So this guy's got a place in Vancouver, buys salal with government money, ships it to Montreal to cut the market down.

Economic development. These poor bastards, they're some religious outfit. They're saying they don't make any money — it's all for whatever religion they've got going. But what about me? I'm supposed to sit here and like it? What kind of bullshit is that? They've got my share of the business, and the government helped them get it.

Now you go and figure the logistics of that one out … That's your federal government and provincial government! Never mind what else goes on in this industry! Alright? I won't even go there.

Now how did it all start? Little Greek fellow in Washington. He was a florist out of New York City and moved to Washington. Something like that. Maybe it was his brother moved to Washington. That was in the '40s or something. Early '40s. Guy spotted salal, which they called lemon leaf. Said, Hey: this would be a great cheap filler. I'll send it to my people in New York — see what they think. That's how it all started. Now I heard tell it's also used in the perfume industry. I'm not sure what part it plays there.

"How," I ask, "could I get to talk to some of the pickers? Would any-one dare?"

❧ How do I say this? There are a lot of people out there who consider that to be part-time income (and don't pay taxes whatsoever). And because they work on a part-time basis, there's no record of who they are.

There are some people who would shoot you. There are some who would tell you it's nobody's damn business but their own.

But I'll tell you there are some people that are indentured into it. I don't deal with any of these people, myself. But, uh, there's several stories I heard that people from certain parts of the Orient come over and they are basically chained to someone for years, because a guy signed papers to get them over here. Guy takes a chance with wife and kids and he's indentured to the guy for signing the paper. And he'll work five or ten years under this guy's thumb. Salal's now $2 a bunch for the picker — he'll be lucky to see 50 cents. Which I consider criminal. I don't like that. That to me is more criminal than anything else. Money laundering? I don't really give a shit.

But captive labour affects not only the generation it's happening to, but the following generation. That's what I'm so bitter about — so I warn my kids about that horrific stuff. It affects everybody down the line. It's not right. That's slavery. Or very close to it. I thought we got rid of that shit, but apparently it still goes on. Modern-day slavery.

I won't tell you what nationalities are the worst for that ... but we had a war with them. And we were all for keeping peace in the '60s and not having a war with them. These people have absolutely no idea how North Americans live and how to live in North America. They have some very feudal systems. Kids go to the same schools as their kids — and they're walking around in rags and the other kids aren't. Well, what's wrong with your dad? Doesn't he work? Yeah, he works every day, 12 hours a day.

Other things go on. Like salal. Sometimes it's very hard to go right into the depth of the brush to get salal. So what a lot of guys do when they're lazy is they'll take their crew out. And they'll see a stretch of road, all covered in salal. And the men will go first and rip up the salal, the whole plant. Five feet in from the road, rip 'em up, throw them onto the road. And the women and children come along behind them, break off all the twigs and bunch it up right then and there. Load it up in the truck, take it off to the jobber.

Well, what have they just done? They've ruined six years of crop. And this happens a lot. Not just a little thing. They cut down cedars for the boughs. They rake up pine mushroom spots and destroy all the peat.

"Isn't there a case here for some sort of permit system?" I ask. "Isn't that something that would help?"

❧ Well, I was invited to go to one of their stupid meetings. These fly-by-night jackasses that are in the Liberal government. First of all, they set up a competition to me. Now they try to ding me for stuff I'm not buying. Right? Now how the hell does that work? I know they're not going to ding the guy they set up. They can't. They're giving him money.

They're going to take an average. And then nail every distributor. For stumpage, right? Two cents a bunch — it's going to affect me. Not my pickers or anybody else. It's going to affect *me*. I'm the only guy with written records.

I can't see the US system working here. My pickers would just say "Go away." Who is going to monitor the permits? Who's going to police it? Who's going to care? So of course the thing they're going to do is they're going to attack me as the seller.

Same group of people responsible for a lot of problems in this province. Used to be another group of people. But they've cleaned up their act. Canadian East Indians. And they're Canadians. They started out being a little rough on the environment. Now they're doing things the right way — it's taken them 25 years. But these people are very conscientious. It's nice to see, you know. They've been 'round long enough.

What am I going to see in the future? Next 10 years? You'll see an explosion of Mexican labour up here. They already have the problem in Washington State. NAFTA agreement, all that other stuff. They'll come up here in mushroom season, salal season, Christmas-bough season. And that'll be the next problem. In Washington State, they kick 'em out every six months, and two months later they're back again. New truckload comes in. Land of opportunity.

Fresh air. No cares. Go out four hours a day. Pick a little here, pick a little there. Every three days go to the jobber. Here's your money. Goodbye. Great. I'm 55. I figure in 15 years, tired of living in the city. Move up to Sechelt and away you go. Bit of fun. Gotta watch out for cougars and bears.

BOTANIZING

What it thinks it is. What's taken in at root
is complete at leaf. It flowers
into a dream of seeds that we wake
to what they were before.

· Brian Swann "Plant Mind"

I have not written much about walking, the body movement and pace
so often invoked in nature writing. Yet, in these various encounters
with the odd notion of "plant mind," I suppose my turning and paus-
ing amidst sentences and sections might touch what Gretel Erlich calls
"an ambulation of mind" (qtd. in Anderson 2003, 114). Ambulation, I
hope, promotes local knowledge, close-up looking, and a lot of dream-
ing. But, perhaps, not much history.

Ambling tends to give way to ecstasy — for instance, to experiencing
seeds as "a dream." Inclining to ecstasy puts me in that long post-
Romantic history of spontaneity and overflowing feelings. Botanizing
in that field sidesteps collecting plants for botanical investigation in
favour of collecting impressions that might lead to connections. This
book botanizes in print. Or, given its focus on one plant, quite the
contrary of the usual eclectic and voracious side of the sport, maybe it's
an exercise in mono-botanizing.

"Botanizing" takes that verb that a short time ago seemed to me a surprising and original coinage, historicizes it (according to the *Oxford English Dictionary* its first recorded use was in 1767), and situates the botanizing of salal in a history of voyage and empire. In the eighteenth century, as better sailing technology, navigational skills, and gunpowder enabled Europeans to visit, and claim, and begin to occupy waters and lands beyond what showed on the maps they carried, botanizing became imperializing. Raised on the political and military versions of history (when raised on history at all), we seldom ponder how extensively European exploration concerned collecting, describing, transporting, and testing plants.

While James Cook (1728–1779) roamed the Pacific, microscopes and telescopes (invented in the seventeenth century) increasingly gave humans a sense of the infinitudes within and beyond what unaided eyes can see. Carl Linnaeus (1707–1778) developed a classification scheme with the promise (however illusory) that all animals and plants could be understood within a single system. A growing leisure class, and the proliferation and portability of print materials, seemed to collapse distinctions between curiosity (always a powerful motivator) and scientific calibration — even while specialization and disciplinary differentiations grew in scientific circles.

So, while Captain Vancouver sailed around the Pacific Northwest, leaving behind place names that assert British military possession (Puget, Baker, Howe) and his own crabbed emotional spectrum (Cape Disappointment), the expedition's surgeon did the walking and the botanizing. The prominent naturalist, Joseph Banks, honorary director of the Royal Botanic Gardens, taking little account of the limitations, gave Archibald Menzies the responsibility to catalogue plants, to bring home samples, and to test soil and climate conditions. Menzies looked for what might be useful and profitable — but he also needed to report on how British colonists (and their crops) might thrive in a different land.

Botanizing, we might say, was both centripetal and centrifugal: plant knowledge was to be brought back to the imperial centre, where study, organization, and preservation would reinforce the control of information; habitat knowledge would also enable the establishment of colonies to reinforce networks of control.[1]

Menzies, maybe overworked and under-equipped, took little notice of Banks's instructions to enquire into the "present state and comparative degree of civilization of the Inhabitants you meet with" (qtd. in Mackay 48). So the flora of the North Pacific Coast settle into a European mindset with no daring to imagine how what we call Douglas-fir or salmonberry might think. Menzies's account of his encounter with salal, if under a different name, is the first printed record of European "contact" with the plant.[2] There is no sense of a local context, but a glow of enthusiasm to harmonize with the public's enthusiasm for the adventure of discovery. On December 21, 1792, he records finding on a ridge west of the Presidio (at the western edge of San Francisco) "several of the more Northern plants, such as are commonly met with about Nootka and in New Georgia. Of these the following three beautiful Evergreens were here in abundance: *Gualtheria* [*sic*] *fruticosa* [*Gaultheria shallon* Pursh], *Arbutus glauca*, *Vaccinium lucidum* [*Vaccinium ovatum* Pursh], which are all new and peculiar as far as I know to this side of America" (qtd. in McKelvey 47). This first Latin naming by an English speaker configures salal both as plentiful and as aesthetically pleasing — not, that is, as food or herbal or tool. Indeed, in a later footnote, McKelvey reminds us of Menzies's prescience by remarking how "great quantities" are now sold by florists (285 *n.* 6).

Thirty-three years later, with Menzies's sense of abundant beauty preparing the encounter, and having certainly consulted Menzies's dried sample in the London Royal Horticultural Society's herbarium, the amazing David Douglas — mono-botanizing for a moment — writes salal into his journal on April 8, 1825:

> On stepping on the shore *Gaultheria Shallon* was the first plant I took in my hands. So pleased was I that I could scarcely see anything but it. Mr. Menzies correctly observes that it grows under thick pine-forests in great luxuriance and would make a valuable addition to our gardens. It grows most luxuriantly on the margins of woods, particularly near the ocean. Pursh's figure of it is very correct. *Rubus spectabilis* was also abundant; both these delightful plants in blossom. (102)

Seduced by salal, Douglas writes his encounter as a dizzying, almost hypnotic experience. Salal is both close up and wide angle: it fills the screen of his brain. And it fills the brains of his successors, almost all of whom quote his description. Walking here is crucial: after eight months and 14 days on board ship, Douglas dreams the walk, "ranging through the long wished-for spot" (102). But the walk, in this case, has no range or amble: it halts immediately — maybe while he gains his land legs — and bends to luxuriance and delight.[3]

Salal is Douglas's first Northwest native plant, and to it he devotes his first ecstatic description. Not, if we can trust the account, picking leaf or blossom, not touching for texture, but apparently cupping the whole plant, as if reverently, respectfully, in near meditation. Salal flowers into a dream.

Douglas's biographer, Athelstan George Harvey, describes him as exceptionally diligent and dedicated, excessively modest and shy (39). Maybe the modest Douglas empathizes with the unpretentious salal. The "shady stillness" of the rainforest, discouraging to many, is congenial to Douglas — according to his biographer, the shade-loving Douglas makes the shade-loving *Gaultheria* his favourite. He leaves the first encounter "amply gratified" (Douglas 102).

Known to the aboriginal peoples as both *Olla-piska* (Chinook for "fire") after lighting his pipe with a magnifying glass, and as the "Grass Man" for his devotion to collecting plants (Harvey 54–5), Douglas, during his first year in the Northwest, collected over 500 plants, seeds, and cuttings, and sent them to England.[4] Authors of a biography intended for young readers imagine him appropriately with "hands . . . streaked with green juice" after his first visit ashore (Stoutenberg & Baker 53).

Between Menzies's spare account and Douglas's "green feast" (Stoutenberg & Baker 53) comes the "descriptive gatherer," Meriwether Lewis (Moulton 1). Lewis may not have been the first Westerner to identify salal, but he certainly is the first to describe it in detail. When his expedition's transcontinental trek pauses at the Pacific, sustained purposeful travel slows to attentive ramble. In the relative leisure of the expedition's wintering at Fort Clatsop, near the mouth of the Columbia, Lewis's fullest description of salal extends to some 400 words, incorporating measurements and a good deal of specialized vocabulary.

Meriwether Lewis's mother "was a recognized herbalist." Prior to the famous expedition, he was private secretary to Thomas Jefferson, the naturalist president. Preparing for the expedition, and to meet Jefferson's instructions to examine and collect plants, Lewis studied with Benjamin Smith Barton, professor of botany at the University of Pennsylvania (Moulton 1–2). So the surprising detail, and what we might now label ecological awareness, should perhaps not be surprising.

Lewis distinguishes salal from loval (laurel). He notes that elk feed on its leaves. He distinguishes the "redish [sic] brown colour" of the older stems from the "younger branches ... red where most exposed to the sun." He measures the leaf at "4 & ¾ inches in length," and tempers his own green feast: "the upper disk of a glossey [sic] deep green, the under disk of a pale green." "The fruit" he continues, "is a deep perple [sic] berry about the size of a buck short [shot] or common black cherry, of an ovate form tho reather [sic] more bluntly pointed than at the insertion of the pedunde" (Journals 6:287–88).

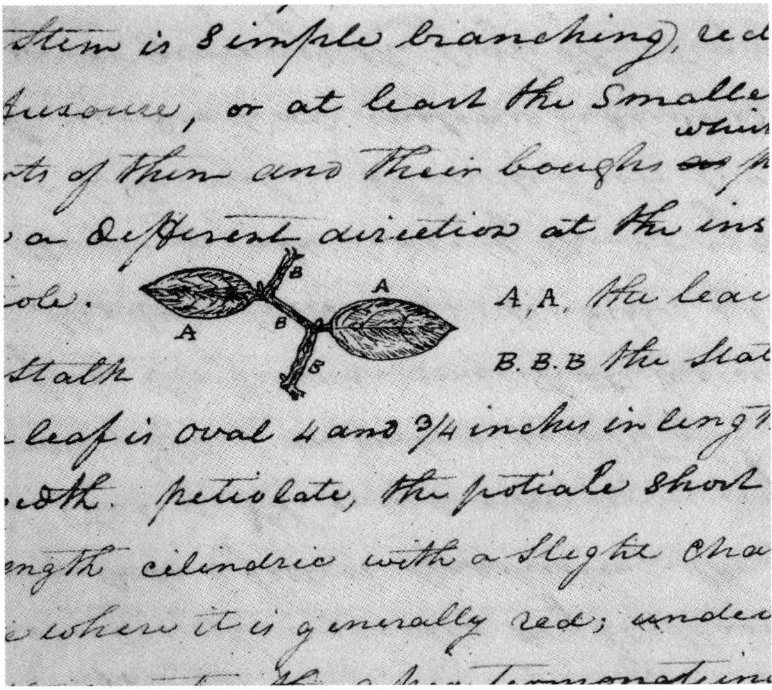

figure 17

Stalk and Leaves of the Shallon, by William Clark at Fort Clatsop (Oregon)

8 February 1806, Voorhis No. 2 Journal.

Printed with the permission of the Missouri Historical Society, St. Louis

Though it was Meriwether Lewis who produced the rich textual account of salal, the editors of *The Journals of the Lewis and Clark Expedition* speculate that William Clark was the artist for the plant sketches made at Fort Clatsop

(Journals 6: 290)

This account of salal is by any measure quite staggering. In my own study of Western literature, I have been slow to warm to Lewis and Clark. US American hero-worship, I thought. All those thousands of places and institutions named after these two. A mythology of unrelenting movement westward: Lewis and Clark endlessly retold to validate Manifest Destiny. An ignoring of Alexander MacKenzie and Simon Fraser, a privileging of the native-born.[5] But, narrowing my encounter down to *Gaultheria shallon*, I've developed my own enthusiastic admiration for the pair: the meticulousness of the botanical description, the amazing preservation of the samples of salal on the cross-continental return trip, the scrupulous recording of determined botanizers whose travel involved extremes of hunger, weather, and illness. This book appears just after the Lewis and Clark bicentennial, and I would be pleased if it were considered in some small way part of that celebration.

Salal appears several times in Lewis and Clark's journals. It first appears as food. Patient attention to the shape of the berries reflects both the length and season of the encounter. But, unlike the accounts of Menzies and Douglas, here (whatever the insensitivities and ethnocentric assumptions of the expedition) the attention to foodstuffs and language is crucial. Lewis and Clark are the vanguard of a massive displacement of native peoples — a process that will have genocidal dimensions on both sides of the national border. But just at that moment of cultural blindness, we can also recognize in the journals the first signs of the way into, or beyond that sad history. However tenuous and limited their contact, the immediacy and detail of observation enable and urge a twenty-first-century reader to write back.

Menzies collects a sample but guesses wrong at the name. Lewis listens to the local and Chinookan variants of the name, and eats the berries. And as the homebound taxonomist, Pursh names the plant based on a Lewis sample. Douglas, a few years later, carries that Latin name firmly in mind when he first alights from the ship.

To think now of the subsequent history of salal, it is surely Douglas's caressing thralldom that has figured centrally in the marketplace: "great luxuriance" sells salal as garden plant and florist greenery. In the market economy, salal is only incidentally food and medicine, although special forest products researcher Jim Freed speculates that the situation may be changing.

From 1792 to 1826, the central period of European discovery, the hobby of botanizing goes from amateur to professional, from individual to institutional. However, as it does so, polite recreational botanizing apparently hardly wanes: it becomes an essential part of female society (Cook 258).[6] Donna Landry traces a cultural shift from game hunting to alert wandering, locating the beginnings of the change in the early nineteenth century, where Menzies, Douglas, and Romanticism also thrive. Landry, as it were, provides a social and economic explanation of the understory (70–71). Walking promotes continuous attention to "what can be seen from a ground-level point of view" (209).[7]

The practical or scientific garden (for herbs, for example) gives way in the mid-nineteenth century, at least in sheer numbers, to the garden as delight, with emphasis on design and ornamental value. Plant collecting equipment improves,

When I watch our son explore the forest,
I see him crouch low wherever there is a secret.
Kim Stafford
An Intricacy of Simple Means

making it possible to transport live plants on long sea voyages. Commercial nurseries grow and expand. In England, about 80 introduced species are recorded in the mid-sixteenth century; by 1900, some 10,000 imported species are estimated to be cultivated. Douglas's work in 1825 gives particular impetus to promoting woody species (Jarvis 151–55).

According to Alfred Rehder, salal is introduced into cultivation in 1826 (738). Hence, it must have been planted from seed the moment the Douglas shipment arrived in England. William Curtis's *Botanical Magazine* reports that salal blossomed in the Glasgow Botanical Gardens in 1828 (Justice np) (figure 18). In the later nineteenth century, the emerging fashion for woodland or "wild" gardens — a reaction to geometrical and symmetrical principles of gardening — proves particularly congenial to the use of salal.[8] Remarking on the "useful and handsome shrub [that] is one of the best we have for forming a dense evergreen thicket in moist, shady spots," W. J. Bean, writing in 1914, proposes that salal might "be recommended as cover for game" (261). A few decades later, another gardener advises that "it thrives under

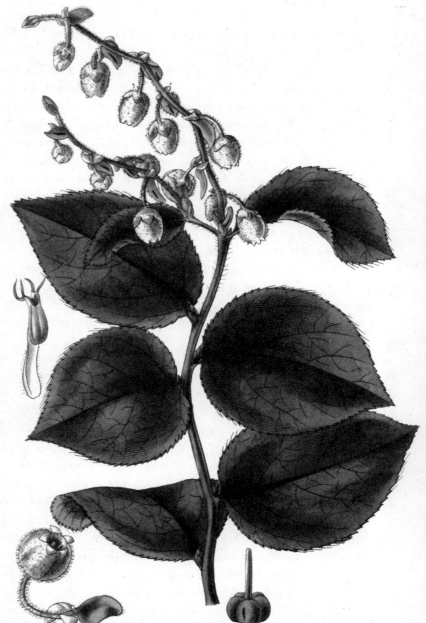

figure 18

Botanical painting of Gaultheria shallon, based on the first salal plant grown from seed in England.

By William Hooker

Curtis's Botanical Magazine, 1828

Printed with the permission of Glasgow University Library, Department of Special Collections

1.

2.

W. J. H. del.ᵗ   Pub. by S. Curtis Walworth Augᵗ 1.1828.

trees and is useful for forming game thickets" (Osborn 354).[9] However, salal may not be so confined: today *Gaultheria shallon* can be found, for instance, in Irish public gardens in counties Donegal, Wexford and Down (Forrest), and in the Royal Botanic Garden in Madrid.

Maybe the hunting is disappearing, and walking is making another comeback. If so, you might amble in places far from the Pacific Coast of North America to find salal growing overseas. Going on foot, and often slightly dreamily, teaches the significance of sustaining healthy growth beneath the trees, including shade-resistant underplanting for bird habitat. It inhibits shooting or hounding whatever might be sheltering there.

DREAMLAND

Anna Zeigler, in the course of studying Pacific Northwest writing, nicely expressed the unending curiosity of the low-crouching botanizer when she wrote to me: "I had a dream last night about salal. I was walking when I came upon a lake, and there in the lake, written in silver, was the meaning of salal. But I woke up before I could write it down, record it, read it."

Plant pursued — secret — dream. It is a familiar concatenation in the falling light of the understory. I like the version in Carol Windley's "Dreamland."

I dream salal and salmonberry.
Salal forming the understory, thick
and leathery leaves sleek to the
tip of the tooth
that shields the urn-shaped flowers
bearing blood dark sepals.

…

I dream the polyphony
of the constant rain that delivers us
into a primordial past, into a history
where life emerges from water.
Lee Gulyás
"North Coast Meditation"

Like many of the best short stories, "Dreamland" compels us in its foreshortening: it *stops* after eleven pages, but it has no "ending" — and, for that matter, not much of a "middle." Lillian's unnamed husband, a long-time career civil servant in British India, announces, bizarrely but definitely, that as his career nears an end they will retire not to olde England but to the west coast of Canada, to somewhere he imagines as quintessentially temperate and benign — and also silent and distant (250).

And mostly mysterious. He buys a house in a remote fishing village accessible only by water, presumably on the west coast of Vancouver Island, and then returns to India to do three more years of tax collecting, bizarrely leaving Lillian and four sons in the house on their own. Maybe he's more concerned to retire from family than from imperial bureaucracy?

Windley's story draws the reader into deciphering a marriage, its permutations woven in the shifting associations attached to a tiger rug, the result of Lillian's husband's rare and maybe uncharacteristic hunting expedition. But Lillian might be Emily Carr's reincarnation, or, given the date of the story, 1918–1921, her visionary predecessor. On this edge of land belonging to nothing, feeling an "incomprehensible absence" in several senses, Lillian dares again, and then again, to follow a trail, apparently purposeless — a "diversion," no more. Not cedars or rocks or fog command attention, but the undergrowth:

> Underneath the trees she sees a surprising number of plants: sword fern, salal, thimbleberry, water hemlock and a species of frail wild lily, the name unknown to her. She begins to make a project of naming as many of these plants as she can, and to make sketches of those she cannot yet name. (253)

In order to grow into an alien space, without an adult partner, Lillian sets herself to botanizing. But, as she tries the trail again, and again, she gives up on the names she has just begun to learn. Lillian is an artist, a dreamer in dreamland, and as she draws and dreams she enters into some intuitive, synaesthetic empathy reminiscent of the sensuous awareness celebrated by David Abram. A fearful ecological symmetry balances salal and sword fern and thimbleberry. Human contact is replaced, or superseded, by a metonymy of ferns and branches and snuffling animal and the smell of damp earth (254); "shapes and forms" (383) hiding in the "dank vegetation" (382), at once salalean and feline (another echo of Carr), provide companionship.

MOSTLY SHINING

"Oh, everything in nature has something to tell
me," said the little botanist, fingers still busy as if
making messages in the soil around the greenery.

· George Bowering *Burning Water*

Much of my salal travelling feels like unravelling. It's more about displacement — intellectual displacement — than about visiting places of
allure and promise. Take the standard reference work on regional native
plants. Here is how C. Leo Hitchcock and Arthur Cronquist's *Flora of
the Pacific Northwest* describes salal:

> Fls white or pinkish, solitary in the axils or in axillary or terminal racemes,
> 4–5-merous, gamopet; calyx mostly deeply lobed, becoming thickened
> and fleshy in fr; corolla camp to urnshaped; stamens 8 or 10, filaments
> basally expanded; anthers awned or unawned, opening by terminal pores;
> caps ∝-seeded, surrounded by persistent but scarcely adnate calyx, the
> whole berrylike; lvs persistent, leathery, mostly shining....
>
> Lvs mostly much > 10 mm; fls mostly 5-merous, often racemose,
> subtending bracts, if any, much < calyx; anthers sometimes awned; fr
> red or bluish-black....

Fls 5–15 in terminal and subterminal bracteate racemes, pinkish, 7–10
mm; anthers with 4 slender apical awns; creeping to erect shrub 1–20
dm; lvs ovate-elliptic, 5–9 x 3–5 cm, sharply serrulate; fr purplish, 6–10
mm thick.... (343–44)

Being in the middle of this taxonomic exposition feels like being dropped
into some city you've never asked to visit, surrounded by voices and signs
in a language you can't read, unsure which way is north and which west.

Despite 35 years of teaching English, 20 words in two paragraphs
seem completely new to me. Several more I can guess at, unconfidently.
The shorthand is baffling, especially when no periods identify abbre-
viation. When I consult a glossary and dictionary, I stumble over more
alien terminology. Friendly words, such as "persistent" or "scarcely,"
seem unfamiliar in this landscape.

My impulse, of course, is to approach this as I might an at-first-baffling
poem, say by bpNichol or Robinson Jeffers. Find out what might be
denoted and connoted and make connections. I know there's an egg,
some sort of beginning, lying in the leaf shape. And I see that botanists
have at least 36 terms to differentiate leaf shapes, and that none quite
fits salal. Not to mention another 10 to describe the leaf bases, and 18
to describe the end of the leaf.

A *cap* stands for capsule, a dry dehiscent fruit. *Dehiscent* means opening at maturity, or when ripe, to release the contents. I have not seen
evidence of salal fruit opening and releasing. The word derives from
the Latin *de-hiscere:* to gape or yawn. I like that, maybe because I'm both
gaping and yawning.

Gamopet stands for the wonderful mouthful *gamopetalous,* meaning
that the petals are truly attached or grow together, especially at the
base. The understory here is the Greek word *gãmos,* meaning marriage.

The more familiar word *corolla* has a nice forgotten dimension: I
read back from a little garland to *corona,* through crown and wreath to
find that *koronis* comes from *korax,* the Greek for crow or raven. It somehow makes sense that there is a black crow strutting and a black raven
speaking in the crowning colour of every corolla.

And along the finely toothed edge of the leaf is the diminutive of the
Latin word *serra,* or saw.

No single feature defines a species or a subspecies. But whether it be the colour of berries, or the grape-like cluster of bell-shaped flowers (*raceme* derives from the Latin *racemus,* meaning a cluster, especially of grapes), or the four apical awns, the overtly distinguishing feature in this account is the size, the measurement of the leaves: 5–9 cm long is 2.5 times the size of the other *Gaultheria* listed. And I guess the limits may be conservative. The leaves are persistent, mostly shining.

BROWSING

If the background and foreground are reversed....
We could say a food brings a form into existence.
Huckleberries and salmon call for bears, the clouds
of plankton of the North Pacific call for salmon,
and salmon call for seals and thus orcas.

· Gary Snyder *The Practice of the Wild*

On January 9, 2002, I gave a luncheon talk for 25 colleagues at the
Peter Wall Institute at the University of British Columbia. I talked
about long rhizomes, David Douglas's desire, and the legend of Salal
Joe. Chris McGill, the institute's administrative assistant, had arranged
for salal table centres. During coffee and dessert, I opened a jar of salal
jelly from Moss Cottage Kitchen and we had a salal tasting. Please
record your observations on colour, bouquet, taste, and aftertaste, I
asked. "Sweet," "pleasant," "mild," "nice": the tasters's comments clus-
tered around the amiably unremarkable. As with the shrub along the
roadside, even those who noticed didn't take much notice. The evalua-
tor who tried the hardest used the word "natural" twice, once for bouquet and again for taste. Perhaps tutored by the advertising industry's
relentless promoting of the all-natural, taster Tom Hutton reached for
some way to distinguish the salal jelly from the jelly more familiar in

his own kitchen, maybe crabapple or mint. I gathered the forms and haven't returned to them until this writing. So I didn't press for more. But in a sketch by Vancouver writer Guy Babineau I found a line that refines the odour of North Pacific Coast natural. The second-person narrator writes of the dark early morning in Seattle. He starts, like our tasters, with the most readily available modifiers: "the air smells fine and pure." But immediately a shining synaesthesia —"The smell the colour of an amethyst"— embraces a complicated bouquet: "Wood smoke, camphor, soil, salal, the sea. Ozone." "Wow!" the speaker draws in his breath: "Green in January." Yes, *green* on January 9. And purple, wine-dark jelly might be the taste of amethyst.

However green it might be year round, salal is the colour of amethyst only in August and September. Northwest aboriginal peoples gathered the berries of salal — along with blackberry, blackcaps, serviceberry, cranberry, thimbleberry, and huckleberry. However primeval the tangled understory may have appeared to early European invaders, environmental historian Richard White has shown that the forest was often extensively "farmed" (18). The Salish repeatedly set fires to eliminate the most impenetrable undergrowth. The burnt-over land then renewed itself into "good hunting grounds and abundant berries" (78–9).

Salal berries are hardly a prominent ingredient in what is widely known and promoted as Northwest cuisine. But they are not unheard of either. The Wickaninnish Inn near Tofino, BC, packs a hiking picnic for its guests featuring "Fig-stuffed Breast of Chicken with Salal Berry and Apple Relish." The recipe begins with onion in olive oil, then diced apple and salal berries, cooked with champagne vinegar and

Day after day ... my sisters and I would repair to our Ravine for play. This was our special preserve, our forest retreat, our playground, and my own personal conception of a fairyland on earth!... In summer time, we sampled fully of the crops which the Ravine so generously provided for our delectation. We hunted out the buried liquorice root and chewed it assiduously. We coloured our lips with the juice of salal berries. We ate the yellow and red salmon berries, the thimble berries and the wild raspberries. Also we picked bucketsful of blue berries, red huckleberries, black caps and blackberries to take home to Mother for pies or winter preserves.

Dr. Gladys C. Schwesinger
"Where Brewery Creek Emptied
into False Creek"
Reflections of Early Vancouver
in My Childhood, 1893-1912

apple juice (Hamilton 48). And a few minutes searching on the Web will find you recipes for salal berry wine, jellied salal, Oregon-grape and salal jam, salal jelly, salal tea, and pies in various combinations. A former student, Christie Collis, told me that in leading summer kayaking tours for mainly US visitors, she would pack salal berries into an old sock and wring out the juice over the guests' morning pancakes: a syrup the taste of amethyst. Convincingly "authentic," she enthused. Maybe she was having me on, rather than those she was guiding.

Among the many berries growing wild, Briony Penn recommends salal "for bulk" (100–101). She tells of the Berry People on Saltspring Island, a group in the 1960s "who attempted to live entirely off berries" (101). At a Vancouver reading in March 2001, Gail Anderson-Dargatz said her favourite recipe in her novel *The Cure for Death by Lightning* is a "recipe for picking berries" which advises that "you approach each fruit, like each lover, differently" (158). Angela Newitt recalls the "ever-popular salal" at Clo'oose, on the west coast of Vancouver Island: "We were shown how to pinch the stem end of the berry to make the petal-like end open up, so we could be sure there were no worms or insects in it" (19).

For all the careful measurements and botanical exactness in the Lewis and Clark journals, Meriwether Lewis's first mention of salal focuses on berries and their use as food. In this account, infused with equal parts gratitude and confusion, Lewis and Clark indulge a new gourmet sensation:

> in the eveng an old woman presented a bowl made of a light Coloured
> horn a kind of Surup made of Dried berries which is common to this
> Countrey which the natives Call *Shele wele* this Surup I though was
> pleasent, they Gave me Cockle Shells to eate a kind of Seuip made of
> bread of the *Shele well* berries mixed with roots in which they presented
> in neet trenchers made of wood. (*Journals* 6: 119)

Here, I thought, is a small study in human ecology. Here was what Tom Hutton was trying to get at with the word *natural*. A native berry preserved, later cooked, seasoned with roots, served in vessels of horn or wood, and spooned up with shells. In a few appetizing phrases, the elk, the cedar, the intertidal plenty, the salal berry, and the rainwater combine on the table. Picked by women, and stewed by women.

I have since enjoyed my own comfortable tourist version of the legendary Lewis and Clark expeditions, watching out always for salal food. Then, reduced to approximate "kind ofs" to celebrate the salal-flavoured honey and jelly and vinaigrette I have been surprised to find. Character and community reside in those who would go out of their daily urbanized way to concoct salal recipes or market salal wine. Jeremy, the chef who obsesses on local ingredients in Timothy Taylor's novel *Stanley Park,* is their fictional patron saint. He will honour the berry:

> Let not your life be wholly without an object, though it only be to
> ascertain the flavor of a cranberry; for it will not only be the quality of
> an insignificant berry that you will have tasted, but the flavor of your
> life to that extent, and it will be such a sauce as no wealth can buy.
> (Thoreau 1962, 37)

For poet George McWhirter, as for my eager-to-please but perplexed tasters, browsing is a decidedly mixed experience. In slightly strained diction and stumbling syntax, the poet tries to explain himself to the salal berry. Maybe he overdoes it. But in the process, he finds his own way to celebrate the berry's ineffable flavour:

> to you, the edibles of the bush, who hang in slack bags or tight pods
>> of black porridge
>>> (dark podge, star
>>>> /stodge
>>>>> /gleam)
> in the umber of the forest,
> under the gloss of the leaf, the verdiglaze.
>>> What a dull jam your berries
> bubble into — an overly dun poi Hawaiians would appreciate, be made
> peaceable and at home by, if they ever came paddling by these beachheads
> with the beaks of thunderbirds and maw of every bear on every totem
> aimed their way. Or would you be confitured,
>> poor berry,

fed as syrup and dried cake?
　　　　　I am afraid
I don't eat you happily and can't quite like those few handfuls
I pick close to home. To be honest, most favour the verdiglaze,
the precious gloss of the leaf for a crèche or Christmas wreath,
or bold natural bouquet and floral display. Like so many, many things,
your talented plant can survive obscurity
but not a surplus
of appreciation

...

I confess I haven't told you all. I did disdain — until I nibbled on a number
beside the blueberries on a mountain top, after you had been winter-cured,
prepped under metres of snow and clean rain, I misprized and I misappraised
until I spied the blue taste of you that sizzled under pot holes in the snow
and savoured your small drizzle of the celestial on my tongue.

January 2002 was my second attempt at convening a salal tasting. Two years earlier, my students in a Northwest writing class sampled salal jam made by Margaret Mayhew of Victoria — at the time it was purchased, in June 2000, she had just turned 80.[1] "It tastes like honey but with little seeds," wrote one student, who thought it smelled "like seaweed." Gillian, less enthusiastic, spoke of a "woolly sweater consistency," echoing Tobias who suggested it was similar to eating fur. "Now I know," summed up Gillian, "why black bear poop looks the way it does." Most of the tasters also reached for that taste of horn and roots that Tom was trying for. Alexis thought it tasted "like something you'd eat when you're stuck in the woods." Gillian thought the jam should only be eaten out of doors. Theresa found the taste "prehistoric, dusty": "I wish it would go away," she concluded. Tobias noted that the jam was "in berry clumps." You could still eat it berry by berry: "I eat a salal berry. Sweet, a texture of paper and then earth: roots, mulch, decomposition."

　　Salal is earth and roots. Christie (she of the berries squeezed in socks) tries familiar comparisons — "texture ... somewhat like blueberries ... flavour ... somewhat like black currants" — and then pauses, looking for the difference, "but with a 'wild' undertone, as cheezy as that may sound — like with wild game, people comment that it tastes 'rangey'.— this is rangey jam. It is not something grandmother would serve on buttered scones at an English tea."

So often our experience of eating is an experience of words. Words stimulate our desire: chicken breast stuffed with figs napped in salal relish. Reading gives us a way to write the tastes and smells we have no words for: soil-salal-sea. I set out to write about salal as foodstuff. I ended up learning that my students could out-write their professors.

STORYING

You know, I think if people stay somewhere
long enough — even white people —
the spirits will begin to speak to them.
It's the power of the spirits coming up
from the land.

· a Crow Elder, Bozeman, Montana,
  as quoted by Gary Snyder
  The Practice of the Wild

Audrey Thomas's story "Kill Day on the Government Wharf" shapes a
glimpse — a study, maybe, if a study can be so short — of husband and
wife, of the tension between island-country and city, between living
a dream of "primitive" retreat and actually committing to the grimy,
bloody reality of living off the land, between the dreamer (wife, the
centre of intelligence) and the doer (husband, returner).

In this account of watchful intimacy, I am especially tantalized by
the graphically distinct list that sits at the story's disappearing centre.
In the unnamed narrator's dream of something "more primitive" (a
sustainability, perhaps), she writes a list:

cod	thistles	pick salal
salmon	stinging nettles	? maybe sell some of our apples
oysters	blackberries	? my bread
mussels	apples	
	mushrooms	
	dandelions	

plant a garden, make beer? a goat and chickens for Robert and the baby. (130)

This odd interruption to the typographical regularity of the story might be read as three lists: seafood, landfood, and commerce. Maybe it is three poems, swelling and then getting shorter. Maybe we are to understand the increasingly extravagant aspiration for family at the end as underlining all three lists. Maybe the list is merely bookish, the confirmation of her "forever yearning after the names of things" (130).

In the narrative, this list is no sooner made than its maker laughs, crumples it, and throws it in the fire. Just this tease of invisibility makes the passage the more intriguing for the reader. In print, as I read it, the list remains, unburned and defining. Indeed, when you browse the book, its separateness stands out, and you stop to read it even if you're just flipping pages.

Among the verbs, the imperatives, the directions to self, only the advice or reminder or proposal to "pick salal" is direct, without interrogative. Thomas doesn't write *catch* salmon or *gather* oysters or *pick* blackberries. And, as the reader is left to ponder the gaps and futures of this marriage, so is she left puzzled by the motive (why salal and not sword fern?), the intention (to sell? to decorate? to relate to other pickers?), the promise (of income? of independence? of connection?). The lure of the local seems to rest in the bland and enigmatic reminder to "pick salal." It's a lure I have heard often in my travels.

SHALLON WINERY

I drove to Astoria, on the northwest Oregon coast, with friends Bob Thacker and Mike Peterman. On a late November morning, we left Portland about 11:00 AM via Highway 26 and came down out of the snow and rain of the Coast Range summit to sun and mist on the headlands, and enough warmth for boys to be playing basketball bare-chested on the outdoor courts.

On a hilly street, we find the winery named for *Gaultheria shallon*. It is larger than I'd expected, and painted light robin's egg blue. At the entrance are two wooden planters containing four or five stunted salal plants. Inside, up several steps, is a small tasting room that also serves as a mini-museum, and a large fermenting room and storage. We notice several stainless vats, and designs painted on the wall — but they are obscured in the dark and no one invites us to go in.

Turns out Paul van der Veldt, the owner, is away. But the man in charge, Rod Stagner, is delightful, four or five days of white stubble on his face, slightly tremulous, but with a strong Texan accent. When asked about salal wine, he launches into an almost breathless ramble about Native Americans's use of salal. They would pick the berries, he tells us, put them in long cedar-plank troughs, then pound the salal berries and let the mixture dry. They would roll it up, he advises, slowly, bit by bit as it cured — and then use it for winter food.

Once Mother made a batch of salal wine, put it under the house to ferment, and promptly forgot all about it. One day an oldtimer came to call and Mother needed something to offer him. She remembered the brew down below and came back up with a glassful, but our guest claimed that the first sip practically blew his head off!

Angela Newitt

"Some Childhood Memories of Clo'oose"

With that essential historical lineage in place, he turns to the question of how you make salal wine. Paul's original plan, he claims, was to make salal wine, harvest lots of salal, and thus give employment to local people. But the resulting wine was essentially undrinkable. Very strong. Oh, you could dilute it with some other fruit but then — let's say you used blueberry — you couldn't call it *salal* wine. The same thing, he speculates, whatever fungus or property it is that allowed those salal cakes to last for months without decaying, is the same thing that made the wine undrinkable. And so, in this flourish of conclusion, the story finds shape.[1]

As our conversation proceeds, the stories get slightly more incoherent and strident. The wild blackberry-raspberry wine sold at the Shallon Winery costs $85 a bottle. When we ask about the high cost, Rod says that they can't get wild blackberries any more. The guy who harvests them — he shows us a photo of a man in his late 20s — got murdered:

❧ Out in the woods, bullet in the head. Dumped him down a latrine on the Washington side. Washington police wouldn't investigate! Said there was no proof. I go out in the woods all the time and I hear shots, in hunting season or not, and you know that noise when the bullet hits something? Could be animal, might be a human. But you can definitely hear them hit something.

The room has a midriff-high wooden bar along one side, about seven or eight feet long. At one end, in a 10-inch terracotta pot, a salal plant, with the nursery's plastic label (*Gaultheria shallon*) still on it. Oddly, no seating is available. Framed clippings about the winery decorate the room. A letter from Gary Snyder says how much he likes the blackberry wine. A wine bottle label, "Under the Bridge," is also framed — the label rejected by the Oregon Liquor Control Commission because the drawing depicts real *named* businesses, even if they were only actual at the turn of the century and have not existed for many decades. The Shallon Winery champions salal, even though it no longer sells salal wine. Appropriately, it seems also to function as an institution for quietly protesting any neglect of the powerfully local.

GLEANING

Employed myself gleaning a few seeds of choice
plants collected last year: *Ribes sanguineum,
Gaultheria shallon, Acer macrophyllum...*
· David Douglas *Journal*, September 2–15, 1826

INSIDE PASSAGE SEEDS

We meet at the Tyler Street Coffee House in Port Townsend, Washington. We sit and talk at one of two black tin tables outside. It's a balmy morning, probably around 26° Celsius.

Forest Shomer is a slim man, at once almost relaxed and yet passionate about the environment — about changing, in however small a way, the habits of foresters and road pavers. He wears a pink T-shirt with a crowded mandala emblem, maybe Mexican, and cotton shorts in another lighter pink shade. His hair curls with wooly knots of blonde-grey, balding on top.

As he talks I keep noticing his eyes, which seem to have something in them of the cloudless sky and the waters of the Inside Passage (Puget Sound), both of which I can see behind him. I feel that watery blue not perhaps as intense or haunting so much as pleading, pleading a love of the place, pleading for one more convert to maintaining biodiversity.

Can you be both rueful and polemical at the same time? Forest keeps opening up his strong convictions but leavening them with pragmatics. What can *I* do, as a business person, as a citizen, he wonders, given *my* expertise?

Forest Shomer has dedicated his life to gathering a few seeds of choice plants. It might seem an unlikely way to make a living, but a short conversation (interrupted by chats with passersby and hugs from friends) points the way into a big world with the tiny seeds of native plants at its bursting centre. Inside Passage Seeds seems a name chosen with a poet's care to suggest the traffic in *only natives.* "Passage" speaks of transfer and transmittal, or permission, of moving from one condition to another — but always *inside* — maybe hidden, quiet, within. "Inside" implies not grand gestures and visible profile, but mind and feelings. And passage also tells of gait — *pace* being an analogue — the speed of walking, step by step, almost suspended. Forest begins:

❧ I've been a seedsman for almost 30 years. Since July 1973 — full time. My initial project was called Abundant Life Seed Foundation, a non-profit foundation that handled, in addition to native species, cultivated plants that are not hybrid — vegetables, herbs, and flowers — plants best adapted to our region, rather than really exotic things that I will say are inappropriate to our climate and conditions.

Native seeds were a building interest, but not really an important part of the business; most of the interest was the vegetables. When I left the foundation in 1992, I decided to start a new business focused only on natives. I felt like the time had come. So that's called Inside Passage. I handle tree, shrub, flower, and grass seeds of our coastal region. Basically, Inside Passage would be defined as from Olympia, Washington, to southeast Alaska. I have collected all along that area, but of course mostly at the south end.

"Do you do most of the collecting yourself?" I ask.

❧ I do most of the diverse species — I collect some 100 species a year. Then I have associates who collect large amounts, generally of a few species — one of those would be salal. By now I know where and how to collect the wide range of things — which is most important to me philosophically. But because the demand for some species is disproportionate to others, I have these people who concentrate on a few species.

I encourage people to pick a full bucket of salal before I'm ready to do business with them. That would be about 25 pounds. I have a tool I recommend they use (though they don't always): it's a berry rake that's like a toothed metal implement. The ones that I have are made and fashioned in Sweden.[1] It's a version of the traditional, let's say, coffee can, serrated. A frontier product. People would take a coffee can, make vertical cuts in it so it had teeth, then rake the berries in. Basically the twigs slip through the teeth and it pulls the berries off.

I found that the rake makes a very practical tool for gathering salal berries. People can do 10–15 pounds an hour in a good location, which is quite a lot. If one were doing it ethnobotanically, culturally, for food, it would certainly be very practical, because it's an effortless piece of work, and you can get enormous amounts of fruit in a very short time. I'd like to see people doing it a lot more.

They could buy this instrument from me. Or typically we would make a trade for the first few pounds of berries, barter for the value of the scoop in berries. Some people have produced hundreds of pounds of fruit for me. Most would use that scoop. Some people prefer not to, because of the way they like to relate to the forest. With the tool you can get several branches at once if you do it right. The berries come popping right off. Very fast. Also, it leaves all the leaves behind, which is key.

I buy the rake from a company in Anchorage, Alaska, that imports them direct from Sweden. There's such an abundance of berries in Alaska — they have a bigger market. There's a dozen fruits you can use it on.

For salal berries, by the pound, I usually pay in the neighbourhood of $2.85 US; the price varies a bit depending on the quality (lower if there's a lot of leaves mixed in or twigs). So a bucket would be worth in the order of $70–80. Remarkably, in the last number of years, I have not gotten as much fruit as I actually needed for the potential sales that I have.

That's partly a reflection these days of getting people to work for themselves, I guess. It just requires a certain amount of initiative. It's a second job for them: they're moonlighting on their main job. They come home, they're tired, they think, well I wanted to pick that salal today but I'll wait till tomorrow. And tomorrow. And it rains a few times.... People who are more professional at it often have to choose between products. Salal is a fairly late fruit, and it partially overlaps with the mushroom season. Some professional wildcrafters would go for the mushroom for higher value.

For my own picking, if I have to choose between something as common as salal and some of the rarer things, I tend to go for the rarer ones. [In this preference, Forest becomes linked to the culture of collectors and botanizers.] Partly I enjoy my work as an adventure, and if it takes me, say, into a high mountain meadow instead of just along the roadside somewhere, I'll go for that.

The demand for salal seed has been building steadily. It's not overwhelming. It's certainly not the biggest item I deal with. I'd say there's a floor for many of these species, and the demand might rest there for a long time. The reason salal is taking off out of proportion to some of the others is because it makes such a great landscape plant. I get calls from either gardening contractors or others who are doing landscapes with salal and Oregon-grape. Around schools notably. It's a low maintenance mix.

"Something like that wouldn't be grown from seed?" I wonder aloud.

❧ Well, the landscaper might be hydroseeding. Typically, the first autumn they might sow something that would be stabilizing a slope. Something like annual rye. The second year they would probably plant a sterile rye so it wouldn't reproduce. Meanwhile they'd be hydroseeding in the salal, Oregon-grape, or whatever else. So next summer, when the rye was starting to die off there'd be this carpet of seedlings of the start species. Then they'd have to weed for a year because some of these things will outgrow the salal. But once they've got those two off and running there's not much more maintenance.

I mention my "delight" at discovering that salal is extensively used as landscaping at the Microsoft "campus." It seems a signal of Forest's allegiance to a world before electronics that he responds not at all but turns to a more fundamental roadside attraction.

❧ Typically, salal is already there and it can be managed into almost a non-maintenance condition. In this area, we have a struggle going on between different agencies of government and citizens who don't want herbicides used. One assumption to justify this is that the "edge plants are eating into the asphalt." I kind of see it the opposite, but . . .

I spent four years on the Noxious Weed Board, so I have a fairly good idea. Killing one plant — such as Scotch broom — with a spray simply opens up the habitat for all the seeds that are already stored in the soil from however many years that plant had already seeded. The important thing is to prevent the weed from seeding. It doesn't spread by root, it only spreads by seed. So even a mowing regime is better. It prevents seeds from growing and the situation is stabilized as long as you keep the mowing up.

I do see salal, wherever it's already present, as the ideal way to maintain that roadside because it suppresses most of the noxious weeds. It's deep enough: not enough light gets to the seeds and they don't germinate. No doubt seeds are already there — for broom, and poison hemlock, and any number of others.

They won't emerge until someone comes and mows the salal; mowing the salal, to me, is totally foolish. We can still get further with this regime, and it will cut costs for the highway people in the end — to have these salal-managed roadsides. Plus, they have a beauty. You know, it's an elegant plant.

I process the seeds. Right now I'm using what is called a cocktail blender; it's much larger than your standard counter-top machine. I can run through a bucket of salal in half an hour maybe. Then I float off the pulp; the seed is heavier and it sinks. Then a series of rinses till I've got just salal seed left, juice and pulp removed. Then I spread that seed out on a very fine screen — it has to be because the seed is minute — and dry it. That's the whole process. I'll do a final screening if I'm not satisfied with the quality completely. The quality of what I'm producing I think excels anybody else's right now. Sometimes there's little stems, the ones that attach the fruit to the spur. Once they dry, they're quite small. They're not really interfering with the product, but I'm trying to be impeccable so I'll screen those out. It looks like a very good product: I package it in transparent plastic

Humble Salal Bush
Praised As Saviour
Of Timber in BC

British Columbia owes its fine commercial timber to the humble salal bush, the pioneer plant which prevents the soil from washing away during heavy precipitation in the winter, Prof. John Davidson told the Gyro Club Monday in a talk on "Economic Aspects of Botany." If salal bushes had been planted on Marine drive [sic]*, where the bank washed away last winter, there would have been no washout and no expensive fill to make, he said. He explained the function of the salal bush on unprotected dykes and in burned-over areas.*
The Daily Province 14 May 1935

figure 19

Seed package.
VANCOUVER, BC

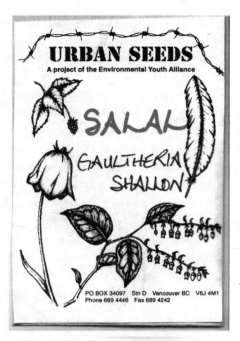

URBAN SEEDS

A project of the Environmental Youth Alliance

SALAL
GAULTHERIA
SHALLON

PO BOX 34097   Stn D   Vancouver BC   V6J 4M1
Phone 689 4446   Fax 689 4242

URBAN SEEDS

Our urban environment is destroying
the native plant population. You can help
out by planting some of these native plant
seeds on your school ground, at your local
park, in your own back yard, or anywhere
you want. They're easy to take care of and
you can watch them grow! Help restore
some of the native plants and create
more green-spaces in your community!

Our vision is to build
community and environmental health
through an understanding of our
interconnectedness to each other and
the earth. We promote this vision through
skill building youth centred projects, that create
long term legacies for the community.

Native Plant Project Sponsors:
The City of Vancouver, Human Resources,
Development Canada, Ministry of Environment,
Lands and Parks.

so people can see just how good it is. Also, it has a tendency to leak out of paper envelopes, they're so small.

"Where do you market it?" I ask.

❧ Rarely outside of North America. There's some interest in the Orient. Having been a noxious weed person for some years, I'm reluctant to spread plants to environments where they may become weeds. I'm told some of our Northwest shrubs have become weeds in Europe. The one I wouldn't call a weed, but a "spreading exotic," is the red-flowering currant. I'm very fond of that plant.

It's the first shrub to bloom in the spring — it really lights up the woods. But, in the British Isles, it's on the move. It doesn't seem to detract from the landscape there. But it's a point of view. Is this good or not?

I have sent some salal to either Japan or Korea, maybe both. Basically, to similar maritime climates, maybe a little bit warmer than ours.

Whenever you prevent one species, you enable another. If the forest industry looked at the big picture, they'd realize that salal would be preferred to most of the other things that might spread on that [clearcut] land —tansy ragwort being a good example of a weed liberated when there's no salal. For many of us, the timber industry is the invader in this picture. A plantation is not a healthy environment. It may be successful in the goal of creating a quantifiable timber harvest, but at what cost? To me, when the industry is doing its job properly, it's not disturbing the understory at all. There's great examples. That gentleman up on Vancouver Island, for instance. His name is Merv Wilkinson. Set up a managed forest not using clearcut techniques, and it's been studied by people all over the world.[2]

Typically, salal is second to mushrooms in the animosities it's raised. Those people who don't speak English very well make less of an effort to communicate with the landowners who might be involved. And picking on public lands makes everyone resentful. It's a sensitive thing.

I ask Forest if he feels that salal is under threat. He responds at once:

❧ Red spots on the salal. I think they are pollution myself. But looking more widely at the health of the salal species region-wide, and all the implications for the ecology, it's not good news that salal is deteriorating. It's hard to imagine what would replace it.

On the one hand, I don't support the possibility of salal plantations philosophically. But I feel that the part I'm doing makes things better than they were otherwise. I was persuaded by friends of mine that are native plant people to go out and look at a quarry restoration that has been controversial here and caused lots of lawsuits. I finally proposed a seed mix that they could use as an understory to the planting they're required to do — basically fir trees over the quarried land. It's marginal, no soil left, they have to do a lot of irrigation — and then there's no diversity. I thought we had something going, but as of last Monday, they told me it's not in their budget this year. Their hesitation shows the ideology of plantations of any kind (that is, timber, salal, or restoration). Their actual intent is to do the least they have to do by law.

When you're travelling you move in fear of the snafus. The expensive whale-watching trip when not a single dorsal fin or blowhole can be detected. The reservation made five months ago, and carefully confirmed, that draws nothing but blank stares from the desk clerk. The lost luggage. The missed connections.

But when you're writing a travel book, even such a sideways-on version as this one, you're comforted by the snafus. You're grateful that things don't always work out. Lose your luggage — good. Miss a connection — comforting. What you go in search of doesn't show up, is not there, eludes you: thank you. In Port Townsend, I don't get to see salal seed, or processing, or packaging. But I photograph the Salal Café (closed at the time) (figure 1).[3] And I learn that Forest Shomer's dedication to native seeds is a commitment to 200 different seeds. He feels for a watchful diversity over monoplanting — everywhere, all the time.

Forest tells me that he'd thought before our meeting about one thing he'd like to leave me with (and to give to readers). He'd decided it would be to urge his program and vision for salal restoration of road cuts. Salal-ing the ditches would be the Forest Shomer story. A man named Forest, whose childhood included no knowledge of plants, becomes a gardener, then a seedman, and now a designer and promoter of restoration projects.

❧ I'm trying to keep them accountable, and I'm trying to get them to do the right thing, through things that are within my reach. If they don't respond, then I'm on the other side. Because what they're doing is literally creating hundreds of acres of uninhabitable land. Replanting fir trees at great cost of irrigation water is not a solution. I'm willing to be an accessory, rather than just be a mute witness to something much worse. And I usually recommend salal as one of the constituents in such mixes. Basically to help close canopy at the ground level — that's to prevent weeds. Once you prevent weeds, nature will sort out the species that will grow after that. So I see salal as being very useful that way.

When I started Inside Passage Seeds, I chose not to do retail. I'd been in retail for 20 years. I used to get a lot of what I call "slug questions." People would assume, because I was selling seed, I'd have an antidote for slugs. The professionals I'm dealing with now don't have to phone and say "I've got this salal seed. So how do you grow it?" I'd reached the point where I was spending 90 percent of my time in the office answering slug questions. What I wanted to do was spend 90 percent of my time in the field.

Forest's motivation resonates with the mythology of an environmentally aware region. Working in the field, and its possibility for keeping long-rooted local species alive and flourishing, is more important than customer service for profit.

Forest Shomer has lived in the Northwest for 33 of his 50-something years. He's no insider, but I get a feeling for how much he's inside his place: in his learning plant names, in his pressing for planting that will grow a mix of homes. He admires ethnobotanist Nancy Turner for setting "such high standards," and looks forward to a time when native plants will be held in higher esteem again. "There's much more need," he says, "than my ability to tell. There's more need than my ability to fill it."

SALAL-SEEING

She feels the watchfulness
of ferns, salal, alders, birds, sky
     does not mind them seeing.
...
She steps up to baby salal
presses the cool, soothing leaf
to her mouth.
Closes her eyes on green.

  · Christine Lowther "New Power"

It has been a long time since there's been a major exhibition of the paintings of BC artist E. J. Hughes, so the Hughes retrospective at the Vancouver Art Gallery in 2003 is special.[1] On a misty day of floating greys, and with good friends Bill and Sharon Baker to share, I look forward to the faux-naïve images and exuberant colour of Hughes's coastal marinescapes. Inside the gallery, I feel very guilty that I keep taking off my glasses and squinting up close, not to appreciate the flourish of a brush stroke, but to see if I can recognize any salal.

There's so much to look at in Hughes's paintings. Defiant patches of red-orange, of glossy yellow, of royal blue, astonish where most North Pacific Coast painters would choose muted grey-blues or the black side of green. And all those crazy boats — a carnival of defiance, with the water lines too high and the angles askew. Hughes's preliminary "studies" are meticulously annotated, I discover: the colour and form of the final paintings are mostly written in words before they are realized in paint.

SALAL AS A WAY OF SEEING

Hughes relies on pencil-grey words to remember and imagine. Colour words and the colour of words: I take these as one more reason for teaching poetry. But still, for all the pattern and celebration, I'm looking for salal. Like Maggie Kyle in Jack Hodgins's novel *The Invention of the World*, I'm prepared to believe there are "bushes which [choose] to bloom light instead of flowers" (53). Reading Hughes for the bloom of his bushes urges the virtue of obsession. A problem lurks, as poet Jan Zwicky once reminded me, if a singular species singularly nurtured breeds monoculture. But, in the idea of obsession — whether the focus is salal or soccer — you have a way of enquiring and you have, if you need it, an entry point, a fund of questions to start with. To detect the web of connections that forms an ecology, and a diverse culture, the understanding has to start somewhere, and it has to start with a specific.

figure 20
E. J. Hughes
Hopkins Landing,
Howe Sound, 1935
drypoint etching on paper

Collection of the
Vancouver Art Gallery,
Gift of the Allumnae of
the Vancouver Art Gallery
Association
Photo: Trevor Mills,
Vancouver Art Gallery
VAG 86.91

Among the interpretive materials mounted at the Hughes retrospective, a quotation from the artist proclaims that the aim of his realistic paintings is "to make any representations of natural forms even more clearly definitive than photographs themselves." Encouraged, I note that in drypoint sketches, such as *Hopkins Landing, Howe Sound* (1935), and *Tree Study* (1935), at the base of the trees are shrubs with definite ovate leaves (figures 20, 21). These, to my eye, are still visible when ink drawing becomes painting in 1952 — an exaggerated, cartoon-like salal represented by a few studied leaves.

figure 21
E. J. Hughes
Tree Study, 1935
intaglio on paper

Collection of the
Vancouver Art Gallery,
Vancouver Art Gallery
Acquisition Fund

Photo: Trevor Mills,
Vancouver Art Gallery

VAG 89.36

But artists rarely pay meticulous attention to foliage. Six months after seeing Hughes's leaves, in the room devoted to "The Aesthetic Movement" at the Museum of Fine Arts in Boston, I am impressed that in fabric inspired by William Morris designs four or five nuances of colour and texture are sometimes woven into one leaf. And in the stained glass or frontispieces on furniture, the artist individuates by showing corners of leaves, or holes, eaten out by insects. But in the work of the Hudson River School, or in the landscapes of John Constable, we have vista with background, even if it's in the foreground; by the time of Camille Pissarro's *Sunlight on the Road, Pontoise* (1874), the leaves of trees and shrubs are daubs of paint, fingertip size. As Impressionism takes hold, dots and dashes in the same painter's *Spring Pasture* (1889) fail to distinguish grass, hedge, and tree. Foliage is not specific shapes or veinings, but a melding of a thousand points of light, or a score of colours. Even the most meticulous botanical artists trust to convention to catch a leaf.

Salal-seeing in a gallery, or on a forest path, often requires seeing *through* salal — seeing through to the wave on wave of black-green light curling and rolling not toward the viewer but away from her, as in Emily Carr's *A Rushing Sea of Undergrowth* (1935) (figure 22). Something luminous emanates from within the foliage: as Carr writes redundantly, "Air moves between each leaf. Sunlight plays and dances. . . . The silence is full of sound. The green is full of colour." [2]

Watching out for salal in all sorts of situations has made me notice many things I would otherwise have missed: the Indian music on the boom-box as a young woman divides and replants wisps of fern, the surprising and then soon vanished flower girl on the steps of St. Pancras Church, the class system hiding in both experiences. Obviously, too, poems and words have often helped me to "see" salal — to realize that in salal I might detect "some texture reminiscent of parchment" (Bolster 1994, 53), that I might hear, in salal, the stillness of a deer's "soft-step" and link it to the "rhythm of an orca's heart" (Bowling 63), and that I might learn to accept "a trashed car in the salal/rusting in peace" (Baker 23).

Each of these instances points in some small way to that capacity of literature — I'm paraphrasing here from Rilke on trusting in "small

things" — to bring about a "reconciling" in our innermost awareness while still our conscious mind "stays behind, astonished" (Rilke 33–4). We *see* — we're startled and our mind bends to find a meeting of deer step and orca rhythm just as we know such joining is beyond us, or cannot be.

David Wagoner's poem "Lost" — the one that came to mind when I was out picking with Rick Ross — proposes that after all you are only lost if a "tree or bush is lost on you" (182). The seeing I'm after will mean that salal is not lost on us. Somehow we will know a plant; somewhere we will appreciate the plant's point of view; somewhere we can look at a flower before we have a name for it; and we will allow, even within the standardizing forces of a shared language, that a habitat will mean differently to different plants and birds in different seasons, differently observed.

A PAINTED HISTORY

I keep looking for paintings, drawings, representations (on pottery), but in five years of accidental searching, I have only found two "works of art" that designate salal in their titles. One I have only seen on the Web: K. Meeker-Rouhier's *After the Storm — Salal Blossoms,* a work that appears slightly Turneresque, an imitation of nineteenth-century brooding darkscapes with a source of light, in this case highlighting the enduring "fragile little blossoms." The other is Joanna Henderson's *Beach Salal,* seen at the Island Folk Art Gallery in Tofino, BC, and the only painting I know that features salal — almost a salal still life.

Given the invisibility of this evergreen perennial, I am surprised that when he introduces Kitty Harmon's *The Pacific Northwest Landscape: A Painted History,* Jonathan Raban twice mentions salal. In a magazine version of Raban's essay, salal's creeping behaviour is evidence of the Northwest's aggressively proximate wilderness. Plants grow with such speed in this moist fertility that humans are unusually aware of being outgrown and overgrown (2001a, 41). When, near the end of his Introduction, Raban comes to discuss Emily Carr, he imagines the sculptured "undergrowth" of her late paintings to consist of "bracken, blackberry, and salal" (2001b, 22). Raban takes us to the edge of the forest where, he notes, Carr felt the curious observer hesitated, repelled by the "dank" and the "density" (qtd. in Raban 2001b, 22). And, of course, in his association, the salal remains potential and unregarded —a marker of "gross and copious fecundity, where powerful half-seen beings live in the shadows" (22).

At the 2001 version of Artropolis, Vancouver's warehouse-sized exhibition of the visual arts, the largest painting (measuring 12 feet by 12 feet) depicted, in acrylic and oil pastel on plywood, an aerial view of what lies underfoot. The work was untitled. I might have labelled it groundscape or even salalscape. Artist Ian Thomas explained in an exhibition and catalogue note: "Upon walking out of my studio one day, I noticed an old maple branch that had fallen and now lay broken amongst grass and leaves and salal. This patch of ground has obsessed me for the last four years" (123).

SUCKING TIDE

**I find it thrives more luxuriantly
near the ocean than elsewhere.**

· **David Douglas** *Journal*

Despite cultural differences, Doreen Thompson describes the appeal
of salal-picking in terms remarkably similar to the other pickers and
harvesters I have met. Mr. Chuong and his fellow pickers, for example,
each day bring down to Victoria from Jordan River, along with their
bales of salal, a love of working in the forest, a respect for the beauty
of the unregarded, a lively sensitivity to weather, and pride that links
birth home to new home. But I have put Doreen's recollections near the
end of the book, the last of my transcriptions of pickers's ways of knowing, and in imagined dialogue with a poem, to return to the original
inspiration for writing about salal: my former student Anne Rayner's
remark that salal is a particularly interesting plant because it so often
provided a livelihood for women living on the Gulf Islands. No doubt
Doreen values the income that she earned from salal, and is proud of
her hard work, but she also indicates that she appreciated the diversion — getting out of the house — and the adventure of salal-picking,
as well as the combination of female companionship and solitude that
the work allowed.[1]

I interviewed Doreen Thompson by telephone, an inadequate, remote means of visiting Cortes Island, BC, for which Doreen quite rightly scolded me.

❧ I started picking in 1969, or maybe 1970, when the ferry first arrived on Cortes, because that was when we could start taking it out easily — or when we could ship it out easily. They were paying 23 cents, 25 cents a bunch for it, and it was a way for me to make a little money when my children were small, without having a job away from the house. Jobs were pretty scarce in those days anyway. So that's basically why I started and when I started.

When you start you don't make a lot of money, because you have to get fast, and you have to find a good patch that nobody's found before. I don't know what I would have been making in a day — it wouldn't have been much. The fellow who was buying it showed me how to pick it. He was quite willing. His name was George Stephenson. He was buying salal in Campbell River — I think maybe for Callison and maybe Western Evergreens at different times. He'd show you what to pick and how to pick and what to do with it once you had it picked. And he'd come by once a week and take to Campbell River in his truck all the salal you had stored in your yard, along with the salal of every other picker on the island. For a while, he actually had a shed here for sorting the salal, and a couple of local women worked in

it. So at that time we picked the salal and delivered it to the shed down on
Manson's Landing. And we were paid once a week. Always you got a cheque
the week after you took the stuff in.

When the children were small, I just picked when I could. I left the island
for a few years in the early '80s, and when I came back I picked it fairly regularly
— pretty much five days a week. I'd leave the house, be in the patch by nine
for sure, and quit about 3:30–4:00 o'clock, depending upon weather and time
of year, because of the light in the woods. And a very short lunchtime. Salal
pickers get very good at doing everything fast that isn't making them money
while they're in the woods, like eating and things like that.

On Cortes, at the time, maybe twelve people would be picking, of which
half would be doing it sort of full time. Certainly not eight hours a day, five
days a week. But about half would have been working pretty steadily at it.
And the season here on Cortes went from around the first of October through
until about the end of April.

Most of us, other than a fellow who was retired — who of course had a
supplementary income and what have you — most of us were housewives.
I guess you could call us housewives, although I don't really like that word.
We were out there working hard; some of us had spouses that worked all the
time, and some of us had spouses who worked seasonally. Usually loggers or
boommen or something like that. Ferry skippers. We were women who enjoyed

figure 24

*Judy Christensen
and Beth Slater with
all-terrain vehicles,
1986.*

CORTES ISLAND, BC
Photo credit: Doreen
Thompson

the outdoors, the camaraderie of picking together. Generally no more than three people picked together, because it's just that kind of a thing. I also enjoy being out there alone. There was a pension-age woman who picked alone all the time. She just loved to be out there in the woods alone. And for most of us, as well as income, it was something to do. It got us out of our homes. And it sort of became a way of life, you know? You'd look out in the morning on a rainy day and think, "I don't want to go out there," but because Judy had to or Judy was going, you'd go. And when you got out there you thoroughly enjoyed being out there.

figure 25

Volkswagen as salal transporter, 1976.
CORTES ISLAND, BC
Photo credit:
Doreen Thompson

SOLITARY TOGETHER

❧ The solitude is — it just gets to you. You just get out there in the woods, and you're usually not within sight of a second person, if you have one with you. Within shouting distance, though, because a few of us — not myself — got lost if they went around the other side of a tree. So within shouting distance, so that you could holler at lunchtime when everybody packed in to a central point. And then you hollered again at quitting time and we packed in again to a central point. In the '80s, when I was doing it, I was using an ATV, because it had got so that anything near the roads was picked or … Like Harold — he was a pensioner who lived down at Smelt Bay — he had his patches, and we would not go into Harold's patches, and he would not go into ours. Ours tended to be a little bit farther away from the road than his did in many cases.

There were people who would come in from outside and plunder whatever they could. It was very cooperative until someone moved here from somewhere else, in the '80s, and had no regard for where established patches were, and he certainly wasn't welcome.

Has it changed? Yes, it's changed. It's changed in that myself and the woman I picked with were probably the last of the really heavy pickers, along with Harold. My picking partner passed away much too early, and I got other things going in my life, and my willingness to be out there in all kinds of weather died off. So I wasn't picking steadily. When Harold became too old — about 87 or something — and stopped, the buyer stopped coming. It wasn't worth his while, because he didn't know whether there would be a full load every week.

I picked longs. Already in wire or elastic — not loose. When I stopped picking in the '80s the price for a hand of salal was starting at a dollar, in the fall, and then moving up over the winter, but I don't think I ever got more than $1.65.

Mavis Jones's "Shallal" is the only poem I know devoted — in title and sustained contemplation — to *Gaultheria shallon*. Two things to note: first, "Shallal" is autobiography focusing on family relations, maybe especially on daughter to father as mediated by mother — and so, scarcely about, or *in*, a language of salal; second, the poem's title and spelling give primary attention to shallal and its language. Each turn of stanza recognizes shallal transformed by language, or into what poet Stephanie

Bolster terms "the language you used to speak" (1995, 8). In stanza 1, salal is habitat for a small creature. In the second stanza, salal was a better garden than the cultivated. And so on. But primarily, Jones listens to plant, speaking through the word into which we reduce it.

At some level, Jones's poem attempts to think like a plant, and so it follows in a well-established romantic tradition. Apostrophe, as Don McKay argues, is the literary device that compactly expresses its origin. "O salal" is a form of celebration (2001b, 66–67). As Tim Lilburn notes, "we become what we attend to" (96). But the process of thinking, as it were, *inside* a plant goes well beyond "pensive mood" and a "heart ... danc[ing] with the daffodils."

❧ My sense of the plant is that basically it is an invasive weed. It's beautiful, especially when it's in bloom, though it only blooms out where there's lots of light. Now, I do a lot of hiking and stuff, and when I come to a patch of salal I think to myself, "I used to love to find this stuff! Now I hate it because it's so hard to walk through!" Try walking — "sucking tide," we always called it — through salal, when you're going downhill and it's all pointing upwards, growing up the hill. I still think, though, that it's very beautiful and I love it. It's a love-hate relationship.

SHALLAL

I gather memories like seashells
and set them in a box of scented cedar
wood. My fingers stain with berries
as I work. I hold my breath
and listen to the night.
Small creatures rustle under the shallal.

When my father was away at night
my mother told us stories. Like berries
they fell onto our plate. Cedar
logs cracked softly. Smoke like breath
drifted among the trees. Shallal
instead of garden, and seashells:

For six days my father cut shallal,
my mother said. Her hands were stained with cedar.
As she swelled with my new self her breath
was sweet and soft as berries.
She listened in the night
to sea rhythms. Seashells

marked her garden paths. Seashells
shone between the cosmos and shallal.
My father cleared the cedar
bush to build a house. His breath
came hard with pick and axe. Nights
and quiet rest, a rosary of berries.

The wood stove was good for pies. Blackberry
was his pleasure. Through shallal
my gentle mother carried water. Cedar
kindling and her breath
created fire. At night the sea shelled
dreams, the honest, well-earned night.

For a babe there is no break of night
from day. I slept within the cedar-
smelling house. No need for me to bury
memory now, it is soft breath,
love which shimmers like seashells,
a garden under moon and dark shallal.

So I will praise red berries and shallal,
a quiet house sleeping, cedar
smoke hallowing the night. (Jones 48–49)

TONGUE TWISTER

A lot of people say that salal is hard to walk through. Especially when salal occurs in fiction and in poetry, it most often occurs as a barrier, an impediment — it's often described as a jungle. The very thing that makes it marketable — its toughness and so on — is also what makes it so hard to get through. So Mavis Jones is unusual in taking something of a child's eye view. Salal as tongue-twister — hard to talk through. You might think of Jones's "Shallal" as language-centred botanics — that is, it takes the name, and learns the plant through repeating its name. Jones's title announces this interest. In emphasizing the Chinookan pronunciation with an uncommon spelling, she invites us to understand the shrub's native status. In writing in the twelfth-century, and intricately playful, form of the sestina, she sings with the troubador's common touch. Salal is an eco-network of sixes: seashells-cedar-berries-breath-night-shallal. The poem is a narrative of memory, anchored in a mother's stories for her daughter, backed up to a mother's personal story (in stanzas three and four), then expressed directly (stanza five) — and then allowed to breathe. The poem, that is, works through transpiration to a sacred apostrophe to salal's own inherent salal-ness.

The model of the sestina is fairly closely matched in sustaining the same end words through each stanza, though not according to the traditional rigid patterning. The end-word "berries" in the first four stanzas sidesteps to the singular "blackberry" in stanza 5, and puns as "bury" in stanza 6. This example signals Jones's impulse for half-rhymes, near-rhymes, assonance, and consonance. Shallal's soundscape is foregrounded as the rustle of *ssss* and *eehh* and *thth* and *shsh*. The poem is surely a riff on the child's tongue-twister "Sally sells seashells by the seashore." It uses language, that is, to approach some pre-linguistic state of awareness.

❧ There *is* a living in it. If you want to be out there, and take the attitude that "this is my job," there's definitely a living in it. I mean, if you're in a decent patch, you can pick 10 handfuls an hour. However, the next day you may be in a poor patch, and get eight or maybe even seven. But it's eventually going to even itself out.

The fellow who moved in here went into patches and picked it too hard. We knew how to manage it so that we could pick it every other year, if not every year. And he came in and he didn't care about local stuff — he was only a renter, he was going to move on — and he picked it until he actually spoiled some patches that we could have gotten a few more years out of. They were beginning to get canopied, but if you picked them gently you could pick them every year. However, if you went in and picked it too thoroughly, or picked too much of it, it would die off, because it couldn't come back under the canopy.

That will happen, but all in all, you can't kill the damn stuff! As a resource, those areas that you can kill easily by over-picking are going to be gone in a few years anyway just because of the forest canopy. And areas that you don't kill by overpicking, but overpick to the point where you're not going to pick it next year, are going to come back the year after that. Or it may take two years, but there's just no keeping it down.

I was speaking to someone yesterday who picked salal fairly consistently a few years ago. She goes out, if she's going to town, once in a while and picks a bale and takes it with her. She's well into her 60s now, but very active and able. And she said, "If I hear in town about people who are going to come over here and pick, I always tell them, 'No. The salal on Cortes is picked by Cortes Islanders. Stay away.'"

A research site on salal near Shawnigan Lake is now being abandoned because of overharvesting by pickers....

The salal research plots near Shawnigan were posted with signs in nine languages advising that research was underway and prohibiting picking. The signs, unfortunately, disappeared....

"It's a tough one," said [Brian] Titus. "The irony here is the difficulty of communicating with the people you want to help."

Titus said he hoped to show that through proper thinning, the salal values could be more than doubled.

Bill Cleverly
"Salal Pickers Put Forestry Research at Risk"
Victoria Times–Colonist **3 May 2004**

I met Doreen Thompson at the suggestion of Brian Titus of the Pacific Forestry Centre. When I asked Doreen how they knew one another, I discovered that she had babysat him when he was a child, and that they'd kept in touch ever since. When my research collaborator Maia Joseph heard this, she enthused about yet another rhizomatic branching: "Now, that's a salal connection if there ever was one."

Maybe some sestina-like symmetry can be discovered here — that Titus, the professional enabler of pickers, discovered an avocation from a woman with a disposition to be a picker, and that Doreen's conviction that the thoroughly local resource belongs to the locals morphs into Brian's finding ways for migrating forest peoples to reconnect to the local.

DOREEN'S WORKWORLD

As Jones's poem tangles shells and shallal, it also learns a conceptual rhyme. Work, although the word is not repeated, recurs as an idea in every stanza as a tribute to physical effort not always evident to the child, and as a recovery of the range of women's work.

❧ I loved being out there. I loved the solitude. I loved watching the changing of the seasons in the woods: the first croak of the frogs in the spring and the first song of those little house wrens — those little brown devils. I always call them "jenny wrens." It's out there that you realize that hemlock trees *flower*. And pine trees have the wonderful candles with the flower on top. I can remember one February in particular here when everything was frozen solid — there was no snow, but everything was frozen — creeks had big icicles hanging in them. And Judy and I went out, and we cut trails into a new place where we could get salal. We took chainsaws and our ATVs, and now we had a new place to adventure in. So it was the adventure and the soul satisfaction. And you were out there, and you were making money. But money wasn't the whole thing.

When Maia listened to this interview, she was reading Jack Hodgins's novel *The Invention of the World*, and there she discovered Doreen's ebullient fictional counterpart: "I can't help sensing a little bit of Maggie Kyle in her."

"Doreen's story," Maia elaborated, "evokes some of those generally positive stereotypes that we tend to associate with women's work — the importance of a communal, social dimension, and the fact that, when necessary, the work fits around duties of home and family. But I also like how her account of wintertime trailblazing — riding ATVs and operating chainsaws — literally slashes through stereotype."

The Doreen-Maggie entrepreneur, in love with solitude yet within shouting distance of her friends, also exceeds the gender-specific elements of her story as she connects with a motif central to much nature writing: physical work out of doors enables a deep and last-ing understanding of the other-than-human world. Mavis Jones, poet, celebrates salal by alluding to stained fingers and strained muscles as if kinesis is essential to recognizing beauty. Doreen Thompson, picker, recounting the details of her work, turns poetic, listening for the songs that ride the wind, noticing the light within a flower.

salalman@hotmail.com

Other things go on. Like salal.
· Ernie Myer

Doreen Thompson, and Chuong Chau, and Jim Freed, and Cindy Prescott, and many of the others whose stories sustain this book, are versions of a figure I have come to think of as "salalman." Salalman has within him something of the caring of Superman — that concern to do good, to go where he's needed. But salalman especially looks out for the ground, the forest, the things that grow in it. His world is "'the plant Earth'" (Stafford 1986, 19).[1] She or he (there are female and male versions) is dedicated to dirt. And if we ask, more than a little awed, "Who is that masked man?" "What is his kryptonite?" "Where is her phone booth?" we'll find no answers, because salalman then and now is always the mild-mannered reporter.

Tom Wilkins is the founding owner of Wilkins Nursery, a complex of greenhouses on Vashon Island, Washington, that specializes — or did until very recently — in Northwest native ground covers. Tom Wilkins's email address is salalman@hotmail.com. When I first heard that, I knew the surprise might bring this small book to a close.

You might have never had a chance to meet salalman face-to-face. You might not recognize him in your community, or on the streets of your neighbourhood. But you can find him in cyberspace. Not that the process of growth and sustained change in all those "-ing" words stops. But the possibility of reaching salalman from your desk via Hotmail did seem to rewrite those gerunds in my Table of Contents. I don't have the techno-confidence to say much about salal and hyperreality, but I know that Tom's story, like his email address, makes a turn worth considering.

Tom lives at the end of a narrow gravel road on Vashon Island. Salal-man seems as hidden as salal is invisible. On a mid-March morning, early, I cross Dales Passage, between Point Defiance and Vashon. The ferry is the *MV Quinault.* Translations of Quinault are provided: "river with a lake in the middle," reads one; another, in the onboard notes about the vessel, proposes "people of the big and little water." I take these as omens, as promising the fluidity of a watery tautology.

We talk over herbal tea at Tom's dining room table, and later in the yard. Weeks later I discover that I have either not pushed the record button, or somehow erased our conversation. And so we recreate the interview by telephone later in the year. What follows then is, in a sense, an electronic conversation.

❧ So how did I get into the nursery business? Boy, it's amazing. Now that I'm so deeply ensconced in my studies as a nurse practitioner, it seems all of a sudden like ancient history. Basically, it comes down to a curiosity about the natural world, and also a desire to have a hands-on, get-my-hands-dirty kind of approach to life. I like to get into things, as opposed to just studying up on them. My original business — until the nursery got established — was landscaping. I was a designer and contractor. My motto in business — and it continues to be my motto — is "I don't want to be rich; I just want to be filthy." By which I meant I didn't want just to make a living. I wanted to get my hands into the stuff of matter. To work in the practical sense. I always thought of myself as an applied scientist.

I have a bachelor's degree in Zoology. And then I decided to get into teaching, and I went to Stanford and got a Master's in Science Education, in teaching at the secondary level. I taught originally for three years down in California in the early '70s, then for three years up at Vashon High School in the early '80s. In between those two times, I got into the nursery business, maybe because in the early '70s there was a lot of interest in house plants — everyone was getting into plants. It's something that branched off from the environmental movement.

I started taking classes at a community college, and went to work in a local nursery, and started absorbing material. My vocational route was to become a California-certified nurseryman. It took me until 1985 to actually significantly start a nursery. When I moved up to Washington from California, I went to work out at another greenhouse for a couple of years — you know, sort of getting more up on Northwest plants. Then I became a landscape contractor for about five years. And then I started thinking about establishing a wholesale growing operation.

At that time a teaching job on Vashon opened up, and I took it, thinking I'd have time during the summers to work on getting the nursery established. It didn't work out because I found the teaching was so demanding that it didn't leave me the time. I eventually quit teaching, and realized that maybe if I grew a relatively short turnover crop — nothing romantic like Japanese maples or dogwoods — but if I grew ground covers, I could make a living until such time as I could grow those other things. And so salal was sort of an unromantic, unexciting piece of that. But I discovered in a really short time that I loved growing ground covers, and that it was a viable crop, not only economically in terms of the size of the investment I had to make and how quickly I started getting a return on the investment, but also because it turned out that I liked doing it. It just started working for me.

At the time I was conceptualizing the nursery, I made a long-term business plan predicting cash flow over a five-year period, and I pretty much held to my plan. Why I consider myself to have been reasonably successful — I made a good living growing ground covers — can be partly attributed to discipline. You know, doing what I set out to do, and not just going halfcocked on life. Really thinking out how it was going to work economically.

Salal became one of the top sellers. In '85, when I started with ground covers, I would say it was a minor part of the mix. I'm not sure exactly when it started happening — maybe around the early '90s — but more and more I started developing a greater emphasis on natives. I'd always loved salal and wanted to grow it, but I'd had other things that I was growing. Eventually, though, these other things, like English ivy — the dreaded English ivy — started falling out of favour.

I got pretty adept at growing salal. I did it all from my own seed. I did some experiments: I took berries and I dried them. I'd originally assumed that they had to be fresh, but I took some berries I had dried until they were almost mummified, and I put them in the blender just for a short time, and it kind of shakes the seed out from the dried skin. So as long as you don't run it too long, and don't powder the dried berry itself, you get a pretty clean batch of seed really quickly — it's a much easier way to do it.

"So you were prospering selling salal and other ground covers, and selling more this year than the year before, and then somewhere along the line you decided to change careers?" I ask.

❧ Wilkins Nursery went from 1985 to 2004, so 19 years. And maybe in the late '90s I just started getting a little burnt out. The nursery industry has plenty of challenges — whenever you're dealing with learning about the natural world it's challenging. But the kinds of challenges that I was having to deal with more and more were business challenges, because of competition — there was more and more competition. It was increasingly a buyer's market — price became the big thing. While I was able to continue doing reasonably well, I had to work much harder for it, and I was lowering my prices every year. So I was making less and less, and working harder, and dealing with people that I felt didn't ... It was more about the price, not about the quality of the plants and the service. The quality of my relations with people was the most important thing to me, and it just wasn't there like it used to be. Certainly there were exceptions. Like, for example, my business relations with Ingrid Wachtler at Woodbrook Nursery: she's a wonderful human being. That kind of interaction is what sustained me. There were several landscapers that I really loved working with, and most of those people continued to be there. But more and more it was about negotiating over price.

I was mentioning before that I think of myself as an applied scientist. I like working in the field. I like doing *real* things. Something that feels immediate to me, where I can make a difference. And, of course, one of the things I missed the most toward the end of my nursery career was interacting with people. Nursing — and actually what I want to be is a nurse practitioner — involves working with people. It's work that there's a huge need for anywhere in the world. And it has much more flexibility than having a nursery where it's not 9 to 5, five days a week. With a nursery, you have to be involved seven days a week, and being the bottom-line person, the responsibility was wearing on me.

Sometimes it scares me that I'm as old as I am and I'm starting this new thing, and I think I'm a little crazy. But mostly I don't think I'm crazy. I feel pretty good about it.

Tom Wilkins claims an identity as salalman. He intends to keep the name now as he turns toward a new career. So, as we part, I ask about his email address: "Was that planned?" and "How did it come about?"

❧ Well, I started growing more and more salal. And, along with "We don't want to be rich; we want to be filthy," I had another slogan for my nursery: "We want to be your Northwest kinnikinnick connection." I thought, I've got to give salal some sort of time here. Salal is really important to me, so I'll make my email address "salal." And I liked the sound of "salalman" — I liked the feel of it. And by that time — it was in the last couple of years — salal was my biggest crop. I don't have those numbers at my fingertips, but I'm guessing that I probably made as much on salal as I did on kinnikinnick. And, well, it was salal's turn.

Salal's turn. The "turn" of salal. I suspect "salalman" is, or was, good marketing. An address which has such a likeable "sound" and "feel" is easy to remember. Having a botanic mnemonic would be especially valuable to Tom, who, in his modest disarming way, does not carry business cards.

Salalman, crossing a vocation nurturing native ground covers with an avocation, comforting and healing people, might seem the antithesis of a microserf. Yet connecting to him through Hotmail™ connects to hi-tech, however virtually. The landscapers at Microsoft headquarters in Redmond, Washington, have made extensive use of native plants, including lots of salal as ground cover. Even the ultimate global corporation boasts its local connection. The frenetically observant Douglas Coupland notices in his novel *Microserfs* that the "winding path" across the "Campus" in Redmond speaks of "Wookiees and Smurfs amid the salal, ornamental plums, rhododendrons, Japanese maple, arbutus, huckleberry, hemlock, cedars, and firs" (27). Bug, one of Coupland's most stressed-out programmers, chooses *not* to follow this path in order to demonstrate his suitability for Microsoft. When he crosses the campus he takes the most direct route, through the undergrowth, in heavy rain — defying, presumably, the thicket and tangle of salal: "Bug believes that Bill [Gates] keeps note of who avoids the paths and uses the fastest routes to get him from A to B, and that Bill rewards these devil-may-care trailblazers with promotions and stock in the belief that their code will be just as innovative and dashing" (27).

The path meanders. Tom's career of caring for plants morphs into a new career as nurse practitioner, caring for people. Salalman's story tells of leaving a life raising native ground covers. It seems like an oddly paradoxical gap in which to leave a book about salal.

But, like Tom, I liked the sound of it, and it felt right. And I was pleased that the sound of an email address confirmed the idea that the word *salal* is a micro-poem. So I asked my research collaborator Maia Joseph to explain why it felt right. After some mulling, she noted that Tom's story of salal certainly fits with the notion of an understory. Tom gets interested in salal because it might be economically viable. Usually when the unnoticed salal gets any attention, it's because it can be sold. And for Tom, Maia reminds me, "the ever-unassuming salal even plays second fiddle to kinnikinnick." "I like," she writes, putting words in my mouth, "how salal's modest practicality invites a sustainable, long-term relationship between plant and nursery worker."

Salalman at Hotmail returns us to notions of "web" and "net"

and connection. Part of the web lies in the several identities of salalman. "Tom Wilkins seems so multi-faceted," Maia enthused after listening to the interview. "He's the practical, get-your-hands-dirty worker; the disciplined businessman; the well-educated teacher; and the nurturing caregiver."

Travelling with salal, both moving through space and across the page with eye or pen, I have been always surprised at the connections a little-known shrub initiates. A hand-carved café sign in Port Townsend; a berry-rake manufactured in Sweden; a residential development in Port Moody, BC (figure 26). Seedman to picker to winemaker. Such connections, and the apparent loss of their quality and integrity, motivate salalman. "Tom moves away from salal, and from the nursery business more generally, because he feels like he's not making as many significant connections anymore," Maia reminds me. "The salal business has gotten too big — the understory industry he once thrived in has become too competitive." At least for Tom, this is the big story that comes up on him from behind.

Tom Wilkins leaves the ground cover business, but as he does so he realizes that a big part of his identity continues to reside in salal. I have discovered that, in a sense, I had to leave literature in order to find my way back to it. I have learned that salal does a kind of writing on the landscape. It highlights the edges, marks the shade, insulates the base of Douglas-firs. Then there are "the other animals and the plants [that] once shared a common language with human beings" (Abram 146), and the writing in the leaf veins, the growth patterns, the underground rhizomatics.

Kim Stafford suggests that place might be understood as the accumulation of fine details. My travels to locate these details have not so much been home and away, or exotic and mundane, but another accumulation: for miles and for years. That salal has continued to shift and slip means I can no more track every consequence or surprise in the salal-cedar-hemlock biome than every word-shape in Timothy

Taylor's novel *Stanley Park*. So, I have accepted the randomness of travel, and trusted the rhizomatic happenstance of accumulation.

I have also, often, paused to listen. I have tried to allow that this and that matters, even if I cannot always know how it matters. I have sought to cultivate a form of attentiveness that poet and essayist Don McKay describes as a "hearkening both within and beyond language," sustained through pondering, ruminating, mulling (2001b, 66). Listening for the Northwest understory involves deference and absence in the presence of those who are custodians of the story. The "Understory," Sue Wheeler proposes in her poem of that title, is infinitive:

> To walk out of the field guide
> and listen. To wait
> for the world to approach with its dapple and hands.
> ...
> There's an understory here, shades
> of meaning ...
>
> To open the grammar of being seen
> and let the creatures name you. (11)

We won't be home until we listen
        low to the earth

· Kim Stafford

If place really is a meeting place then "the lived reality
of our daily lives" is far from being localised — in
its connections, its sources and resources, and in its
repercussions, that "daily life" spreads much wider....
[Consider] the commodity chains through which our
lives are sustained. What we are showing when we
research and teach such things is not that local places are
not grounded, real, etc., but that global spaces *are so too.*

· Doreen Massey "Globalisation"

NOTES

LISTENING: A PREFACE

[1] In the case of salal, the berry is not, strictly speaking, a "fruit" or "berry," but a "persistent ... calyx" (Hitchcock 343). The botanical term for the outermost layer of the fruit is "pericarp."

[2] Don Gayton describes the West Kootenay "coastal refugium" of salal in his book *Kokanee: The Redfish and the Kootenay Bioregion*, and in a personal communication he shared the refugium's precise location on Kootenay Lake's east shore.

MULLING: AN INTRODUCTION

[1] John Cody's joining of "musquash" and "guib" with the colloquial "thingamajig" tempts the reader to think of all three as nonsense terms, but realizing that they are dialect, localized terms to describe particular species — muskrat and antelope — intensifies the irony of his urging.

[2] My earlier mulling a possible book on salal may be found in "The Salal File" of *The Arbutus/Madrone Files: Reading the Pacific Northwest* (80–84). Other aspects of the telling of salal are included there, although some short sections appear in modified form in this book.

[3] Pyle's *Wintergreen* will remind that wintergreen is occasionally a popular name assigned to *Gaultheria shallon*, although it much more

commonly designates another species — not native to the Pacific Northwest and less durable when picked, but also a reliable ground cover — *Gaultheria procumbens.*

[4] Other recent books focusing on a genus include Anna Pavord's *Tulip* (1999) and Jane Brown's *Tales of the Rose Tree: Ravishing Rhododendrons and their Travels around the World* (2004).

NAMING

[1] Barton's titles are italicized where they refer to the title of a Carr painting. In this case, two Carr paintings are titled *Wood Interior.* Doris Shadbolt differentiates the two with parenthetic descriptors: the 1929–30 version, is "formalized," and the 1932–35 version (figure 4), is "painterly" (Shadbolt 166, 206, 240).

[2] One of the odd byways of the salal lexicon, an analogue with no apparent or recorded linguistic connection, is the name of the island in Edgar Allan Poe's *The Narrative of Arthur Gordon Pym of Nantucket.* Tsalal is an island near Cape Horn, where everything is black (and with attendant racist overtones). A Hebrew word, *tsalal* means "to be dark." The name is pronounced, Pym tells us, "with a prolonged hissing sound" (236). At least one poet has written *Gaultheria* in such sibilant but far more benign darkness:

> Salal grows in the darker places,
> like love, and, like love,
> takes hold in the shadows. (Anon. "Salal")

[3] On a tape loop in the Southeast Alaska Discovery Building, Ketchikan, Alaska, you can listen to Annabelle Peele, Haida Elder of the Raven Clan, describe preparations for a potlatch. Among the six berries she mentions is salal, which she distinctly pronounces *sh*alal.

[4] In scientific writing, "rhizomatous" and "rhizomatously" are the preferred adjectival and adverbial forms; however, "rhizomatic" and "rhizomatically" are more common in literary and philosophical discourse. In the spirit of cross-pollination, I use both. When discussing the ecology of salal, I favour "rhizomatous," while I like "rhizomatic" where it connects to a slightly broader range of often cross-disciplinary contexts.

⁵ Salal is not only *rooted* linguistically, but also continues to proliferate, to spread: a catalogue of contemporary salal-related names would take up several pages. For example, the newsletter of the Greater Vancouver Orienteering Club is called *Salal Days*. The Salal Chapter of the Washington Native Plant Society is centred in the Skagit Valley. In addition to The Salal, a condominium built in 2005 by the Polygon corporation (figure 26), Port Moody, BC, is also home to the Salal Housing Coop. In 1996, the City of Vancouver named a new street in the Kitsilano neighbourhood Salal Drive; the city clerk described it to council as a "hockey stick-shaped road." Lower Columbia College in Longview, Washington, publishes *The Salal Review: An Arts and Literary Journal*, asserting on its website that "[t]he arts are like the salal — often overlooked, but vital to our quality of life." The Salal Press in Victoria, BC, has a growing list of regionally relevant titles.

⁶ John Asher Dunn lists *dza'west* ("laughing berries") as a name for salal in *Sm'algyax: A Reference Dictionary and Grammar of the Coast Tsimshian Language* (14). Coast Tsimshian belongs to the Tsimshianic language family (along with Southern Tsimshian, Gitksan, and Nisga'a), and is spoken by the Coast Tsimshian people of the central and northern BC coast. Plant names and information about aboriginal uses of plants, however I have documented them here, originate with the communities themselves, with elders, and with generations of storytellers — all incompletely and inadequately acknowledged in this book. For some sense of salal as ecological marker, along with its "untold" understandings, I recommend Philip Kevin Paul's *Taking the Names Down from the Hill*.

⁷ In *Plants of Haida Gwaii*, Nancy J. Turner compiles salal words in the two dialects of the Haida language, Skidegate and Masset, including the Skidegate word *hlk'waakuusda* — "to pick a whole cluster of salalberries" (120). Erna Gunther compiles names for salal in the Qwiqwidicciat (Makah), Quileute, Quinault, Klallam, Samish, Skagit, Skokomish, Snohomish, and Swinomish languages in *Ethnobotany of Western Washington: The Knowledge and Use of Indigenous Plants by Native Americans* (43).

⁸ The Hanaksiala people amalgamated with the Haisla in 1947, but do maintain a somewhat distinct identity. Originally from the Kitlope

Valley, the Hanaksiala now share with the Haisla the settlement of Kitamaat Village, which is located at the head of the Douglas Channel (traditional Haisla territory extends along the channel, well beyond Kitamaat Village). The main settlement of the Oweekeno people, speakers of Oweekyala, is situated on the north side of the Whannock River in Rivers Inlet. The Hanaksiala, Haisla, and Oweekyala languages belong to the Wakashan language family. Originally from Kitasu Bay, the Kitasoo now have their main settlement at Klemtu, also on the BC coast. Southern Tsimshian (of the Tsimshianic language family) is the language of the Kitasoo people, but most Kitasoo who now speak a native language speak the Wakashan language Heiltsuk.

[9] Compton notes that in Hanaksiala and Haisla, the food called *nk̓ʷɬ* (salal berry) is attached to the supporting plant *nk̓ʷlas* (240). In Southern Tsimshian, there is a prefix, *sXán*, to affix to trees and bushes that "bear items of economic, utilitarian or some other cultural interest" (456). So, we have the *sXántsawós*, salal berry bush (457).

[10] SENĆOŦEN, spoken by the Saanich people, is a dialect of the North Straits Salish language. The Saanich homeland is on southeastern Vancouver Island, BC.

NURTURING

[1] The Woodbrook Nursery site is at 5919 78th Avenue NW, Gig Harbour, Washington. In June 2003, a four-inch container of salal was selling for $2.20 US; a gallon container was $5.50 US.

[2] Many of the companies listing on the Florida Fern Growers website include salal as a "crop." They are evidently marketing "quality cut foliage," but, despite the term "crop," it appears they do not have plantations, or salal growing in nurseries.

DEPENDING

[1] A study in 1990 leaves open the question of whether there are "allelopathic chemicals in extracts of salal foliage and litter" (Haeussler 100).

[2] The list of birds and animals that feed on salal is compiled from

works by C. S. Schopmeyer (422–23), Ian McTaggart Cowan (116–29), William R. Van Dersal (135), and Mark C. Drever and Alton S. Harestad (676). In contrast to this list, I note that Russell Link's *Landscaping for Wildlife in the Pacific Northwest* categorizes salal among landscaping plants that are "deer-proof (or close to it)" (65).

[3] Animals depending on salal flowers and berries would probably not be affected by over-harvesting, as blossoms and fruit are not present in the semi-shaded conditions ideal for commercial salal.

ARRANGING

[1] In a column titled "The Indigenous Gardener" in *Wingspan,* the magazine of the Wild Bird Trust of British Columbia, Rosalind Thorp, declaring that "salal is of good structure and pleasing habit," notes that *Gaultheria shallon* "tops many a rotting structure like the cap of a large green mushroom: an umbrella of leathery leaves." As if endorsing the sculpture at Open Studio, she concludes that "[t]he concept of salal in an old stump is worth consideration."

PICKING

[1] Several of the articles in *Nontimber Forest Products in the United States* (Jones *et al.*) mention the demographics of pickers, and the linguistic and cultural barriers to collecting accurate information. Of particular interest is Edmund Clay Goodman's account of off-reservation gathering rights for Native Americans (278–80) and articles by Eric T. Jones and Kathryn Lynch, and Richard Hansis.

[2] In December 2004, Rick Ross writes that "the area where we picked has been included in the City of Courtenay and is slated for major development in the New Year — golf course, shopping centre, and lots of housing." In 2006, Rick Ross sold Western Evergreens.

[3] Weather data from Environment Canada's online National Climate Archive.

[4] Jean Howarth presents a two-page guide to "picking greenery" — quite different from my account — in *Treasure Island,* a collection of her newspaper columns (23–24).

[1] The earliest dated sample has the source "Columbia," collected by "[John] Scouler"; the final numeral in the date is difficult to read, but is presumably 1825 (Folder 22). The same folder has a sample labelled simply "Menzies" (presumably 1793) from the "Herb.[arium] Forsyth," and was "Purchased 1835," leaving me to wonder how this item connects to the sample held by the Academy of Natural Sciences, Philadelphia (Specimen 61, Menzies Collection). There is a photo of the Lewis and Clark specimen (Folder 37, Specimen 74, Lewis and Clark Herbarium). Two items are signed or designated "Douglas" and "Douglas Oregon"; the second only is dated "June 4 1834" and oddly spelled "*Gualtheria sallal*" (sic). One sample has a date as recent as July 1958.

[2] The samples collected in Ketchikan, Alaska; the "Redwood forest" near Crescent City, California; and from "slightly shady places in Muskeg" are filed in Folder 35. Those labelled "Oregon Boundary Commission 1858" and "California Academy of Sciences" are filed in Folders 11 and 15 respectively.

[3] The sample labelled "plants very plentiful" is filed in Folder 4.

[4] I learn later from Sven Landrein of Kew that the herbarium holds 48 samples of Oregon-grape and 36 samples of salmonberry.

[5] The Kew website (www.rbgkew.org.uk) also provides material on the history of Kew, and a Plant Information Centre to assist with locating specimens, including seven of *Gaultheria shallon* in the Living Collection.

[6] The two specimens of *Gaultheria shallon* in the Economic Botany Collection are catalogue number 51227, described as a "cake of compressed fruits," and number 51228, the leaves and fruit preserved in alcohol. Many of the coastal aboriginal peoples prepared cakes from boiled or mashed salal berries to preserve them for winter use. Ethnobotanist Nancy Turner describes the process in some detail in *Food Plants of the First Coastal Peoples* (77–78). The assumption is that the Kew sample was acquired from an aboriginal community, but little documentary evidence is available. This first specimen is intriguing for its note that the common (aboriginal) name for salal, presumably provided by "the Indians at the North End of Vancouver Island," is "Broo." The note continues, with question mark included, "Procured by Mr. Sand?"

— a connection I have not been able to trace.

[7] The Latin binomial *Gaultheria shallon* connects a version of the plant name often used by first peoples of the North Pacific Coast to Quebec, France, and Sweden. Jean-François Gaultier (1708–1756), king's physician in Quebec from 1742, was an ardent naturalist and corresponding member of the Académie Royale des Sciences. (Various spellings of his name may be found, but according to *The Dictionary of Canadian Biography* Vol. 3, he signed Jean-François Gaultier.) Pehr Kalm (1716–1779), botanist and student of Carolus Linnaeus, came to North America to collect seeds and plants under the auspices of the Royal Swedish Academy of Sciences in 1747; Gaultier served as Kalm's guide when he visited Quebec in 1749. In recognition of Gaultier's hospitality and botanical knowledge, Kalm named the genus *Gaultheria*, some 150 species, after him (Boivin).

GETTING NATIVE

[1] While Jim Freed and other voices in this book provide considerable insight into the harvest of non-timber forest products in the Pacific Northwest, the Web is an excellent resource for information related to this work. Detailed materials on sustainable harvesting (e.g. no more than 25 percent foliage to be removed in any one year), habitat and marketing are available at various Washington State University websites. The US Department of Agriculture (USDA) offers a comprehensive bulletin on "Income Opportunities in Special Forest Products," written by Margaret G. Thomas and David R. Schumann (www.fpl.fs.fed.us/documnts/usda/agib666/agib666.htm). Another USDA report, "Access, Labor, and Wild Floral Greens Management in Western Washington's Forests," by Kathryn A. Lynch and Rebecca J. McLain (http://www.fs.fed.us/pnw/pubs/gtr585.pdf), examines the management of floral greens on Washington's Olympic Peninsula between 1994 and 2002. Information on the scope of management challenges is also available in an article by Beth Baker published by the American Institute of Biological Sciences (www.aibs.org/washingtonwatch/washington_watch_1998_09.html). The website of the Centre for Non-Timber Resources at Royal Roads University offers a searchable bibliography, a Canadian directory of individuals and organizations

involved in the field, and links to case studies (www.royalroads.ca/Channels/for+learners/divisions+centres+and+schools/centre+for+non-timber+resources/default.htm). As for hard copy materials, a good place to begin is a handbook by Nan C. Vance *et al.* titled *Special Forest Products*, which includes a 12-page bibliography. See also Richard Miller's more general book on foraging, and articles by Richard Hansis and Jim Freed.

[2] According to the USDA report by Lynch and McLain cited in the endnote above, in 2002 the Makah initiated a "five-year demonstration project aimed at fostering a culture of forest resource stewardship, developing sustainable forest resource management practices, and creating sustainable forestry-based livelihoods, focusing primarily on nontimber forest products.... In this project, they are seeking to work with tribal carvers, basket weavers, and artists and are exploring ways to develop a limited number of selected value-added products made from floral greens, mushrooms, and edible plants such as berries, for the local and Olympic Peninsula markets" (2003, 45).

Further information on the harvesting rights and practices of the Native American tribes of the Olympic Peninsula is available in the report.

GATHERING

[1] The cover photograph of *During My Time* shows a grinning Florence Davidson preparing salal berry jam. The passage is reprinted in Nancy Turner's *Plants of Haida Gwaii* with Haida plant names interpolated (45).

WORKING

[1] I have followed the usage of Wendy Cocksedge and Brian Titus in referring to Chuong, Khim and Kosal as Mr., a form I understand as an honorific, paying respect. Chuong Chau also sometimes goes by the name Chuong Nguyen.

SOURCING

[1] Also used in Sourcing Northwest's potpourri mixture is white pearly everlasting (*Anaphalis margaritacea*), another commonplace native

species. Its habitat includes "rocky slopes, open forests, clearings, meadows, fields, pastures, roadsides" (Pojar and McKinnon 304).

CONTAINERING

[1] I have searched extensively, and do not think that a book specifically devoted to salal exists. Bill seems to have in mind a guide to wildcrafting in general.

[2] Presumably the Japanese market for "shorts" is consistent with a general cultural preference for delicate simplicity and minimalist composition. One guide to Japanese flower arrangement urges removing all but a few leaves from greenery and flowers (Teshigawara 32). Foliage might be spare in order to enhance space and colour: "Depth is achieved through choice of material, stem placement, elimination of nonessentials and careful use of space within and around an arrangement" (Quinn 7). An arrangement in Lee Early Quinn's *Japanese Free Style Flower Arrangement* shows a single yellow Fuji chrysanthemum floating in a large flat dish with three salal leaves to one side, and two on the other (76).

RAMBLING

[1] In Stephanie Quainton Steel's version of the story, Salal Joe might have escaped from Russia and may still be alive in California.

[2] "Oasis" refers to the moisture-retaining floral foam — similar to Styrofoam and usually green — used by florists to hold and keep cut flowers fresh.

BOTANIZING

[1] Detail on the cultural and scientific fusion shaping global botanizing can be found in *Visions of Empire*, edited by David Philip Miller and Peter Hanns Reill. Miller develops Bruno Latour's concept of "centers of calculation" to describe the accumulation and systematization of information — in this case, the botanical collections assembled by Joseph Banks — that would in turn provide for intellectual control of remote lands.

[2] Major events related to the European "discovery" of salal include: Archibald Menzies's notation on salal dated December 21, 1792; he

gathers dried samples on this voyage. The first reference to *Shele wele* (salal) by Lewis and Clark is dated December 8, 1805, with detailed description of Shallon (salal) on February 8, 1806. Frederick Pursh lists salal in his *Flora Americae Septentrionalis*, published in 1814. Thomas Nuttall's *The Genera of North American Plants* (1818) lists *G. shallon* as "apparently an arbutus" (263). David Douglas describes salal in April 1825, and it is introduced into cultivation the following year.

Spanish botanists Martín de Sessé, José Mariano Mociño, Juan Castillo, and Jaime Senseve may have collected specimens of salal during the Royal Botanical Expedition to New Spain (1781–1803), which included a stop at the Spanish port of Nootka Bay on Vancouver Island. However, Paloma Blanco Fernández de Caleya, the curator of the Herbarium of Sessé and Mociño at the Royal Botanic Garden in Madrid, reports that the herbarium's collection does not include any specimens of *Gaultheria shallon*. Likewise, the Hunt Institute for Botanical Documentation at Carnegie Mellon University, Pittsburgh, which holds the Torner Collection of Sessé and Mociño Biological Illustrations (containing approximately 1,800 illustrations of botanical subjects), does not include any images of salal from this early botanical expedition to the Pacific Northwest.

[3] Dr. John Scouler, Douglas's good friend and companion, records the encounter with the "charming *Gaultheria shallon*" on April 9, 1825 (Douglas himself records April 8, 1825): "On leaping from the boat, the first object which attracted our notice, was the *Gua ltheria shallon* [*sic*] growing in abundance among the rocks, and covered with its beautiful roseate flowers" (qtd. in McKelvey 286).

[4] David Douglas apparently sent his specimens to the Royal Horticultural Society (RHS), which was founded by Joseph Banks. Banks died in 1820; Douglas collected in northwestern North America during the 1820s, while the society was in a period of transition. Diana Miller of the RHS Herbarium reports in 2005 that all of the society's "early specimens were sold during the mid-1800s together with the library when the society was short of money. Although I have looked in the past, there are no records in our archives as to where the specimens went when they were sold by Sothebys." According to Serena Marner of the Fielding-Druce Herbarium at Oxford University, some of Douglas's

collections were bought by the botanist Henry Borron Fielding (1805–1851), who left his collections to Oxford. The Fielding-Druce Herbarium holds two specimens of *Gaultheria shallon* collected by Douglas. Gina Murrell informs that the Cambridge University Herbarium also holds a Douglas *Gaultheria shallon* specimen. Vicki Noble reports that the British Natural History Museum, which now houses Joseph Banks's personal herbarium collection, does not hold any *Gaultheria shallon* specimens collected by Douglas.

[5] For a recent sample of the obsession with Lewis and Clark, with its own nationalist blinkers and some moving critical reflection, see Dayton Duncan's *Out West: American Journey along the Lewis and Clark Trail* (1987).

[6] Elizabeth Heckendorn Cook's challenging commentary on flowers and cultural assumptions about female sexuality and femininity includes a careful reading of Erasmus Darwin's poem *The Loves of the Plants* (1789). For an extended study of the female and botanizing, see Ann Shteir's *Cultivating Women, Cultivating Science*. Landry's *The Invention of the Countryside: Hunting, Walking, and Ecology in English Literature, 1671–1831*, also occasionally discusses gender and the shifting role of women as botanizers.

[7] In her intriguing intellectual history of perambulating as alternative to hunting, Landry embraces the intricate and ambiguous relations among hunting, botanizing, and poetry. Kevin Hutchings takes a complementary approach to Landry's in his book *Imagining Nature: Blake's Environmental Poetics.* His commentary on "green romanticism" traces the complex of late eighteenth-century ideas linking Enlightenment science, the fashionable taste for botany, Romanticism, bioregion and the early ecology implicit in the concept of "nature's economy." Hutchings also reminds us of William Blake's alertness to "the workers' sympathetic identification with the land" (31), an identification central to many of the interviews in this book.

[8] Wilderness, albeit subject to geometric control, is integral to gardening even in the seventeenth century (Hunt 27–8, 92, 166). For a history and cultural analysis of the Victorian "wild garden" movement, see Anne Helmreich's article on *The Wild Garden* (1870) by William Robinson. In present-day England, a how-to gardening book urging the revival of Victorian gardens even in the smallest urban lots lists *Gaultheria*

shallon among its recommended plantings (Highstone 169).

[9] The suitability and increased planting of salal do not necessarily breed familiarity abroad: Graham Stuart Thomas, described as "the greatest gardener of the second half of the twentieth century," reports fleetingly and with a hint of bafflement seeing "huge hummocks" of the unfamiliar plant in a garden in Munstead in 1931 (Wallinger 73).

BROWSING

[1] The tasters in November 2000 were Theresa Scott, Grzegorz Danowski, Monika Karpinska, Gillian Gausboel, Tobias Vanveen, Diana Stech, Colleen Derkatch, Crystal Leung, Pam McMartin, Jacky Shin, Heather Pokotylo, Alexis Harrington, Eugene Khaskin, Christie Hurrell, and Pam Hooper.

STORYING

[1] The Shallon Winery's website explains that "we cannot make wine from [salal berries], because it needs to be diluted with water, and the government wouldn't let us add that much water to a wine." Paul van der Veldt has advised me that it's possible to make a very good salal wine, just not within government guidelines. The Shallon Winery website gives different versions of the stories I have reported.

GLEANING

[1] Forest Shomer later reports that the Swedish berry rake, manufactured by Brod. Berglund, is now out of production, and he will have to rely on a poor plastic substitute.

[2] Described as the grandfather of ecoforestry, Vancouver Island resident Merv Wilkinson has operated Wildwood Forest Farm, a sustainable commercial woodlot, for over 50 years (Timmer 25).

[3] Fodor's *Seattle and Vancouver* notes the entrées at Port Townsend's Salal Café — "tofu Stroganoff, mushroom risotto with oysters" — and urges: "Try to get a table in the glassed-in back room, which faces a plant-filled courtyard" (82).

SALAL-SEEING

[1] Ian Thom's sumptuous catalogue for the E. J. Hughes exhibition lists only two retrospectives: at the Vancouver Art Gallery in 1967, and at the Surrey Art Gallery in 1983 (224).

[2] Emily Carr's comment is excerpted from a Vancouver Art Gallery display card (13 January 2004) — no original source given.

SUCKING TIDE

[1] Doreen Thompson died in an automobile accident 1 August 2006.

salalman@hotmail.com

[1] Kim Stafford explains that he discovered "the plant Earth" in a perceptive child's misspelling (1986, 19).

BIBLIOGRAPHY

"2 Arrested in Alleged Scheme to Ship Marijuana from Canada." KIROTV. com. 3 February 2004. 9 February 2004 <http://www.kirotv.com/ print/2813693/detail.html>.

Abram, David. "Panel Discussion." *Canadian Journal of Environmental Education* 7.1 (Spring 2002): 291–93.

Abram, David. *The Spell of the Sensuous: Perception and Language in a More-Than-Human World.* New York: Vintage, 1997.

Adaptation. Dir. Spike Jonze. Perf. Nicolas Cage, Meryl Streep, Chris Cooper, Tilda Swinton, Cara Seymour, Brian Cox, Judy Greer, Maggie Gyllenhaal. Culver City, CA: Columbia TriStar, 2002.

Anderson, Lorraine. *Sisters of the Earth: Women's Prose and Poetry About Nature.* New York: Vintage, 2003.

Anderson, M. Kat, Michael G. Barbour, and Valerie Whitworth. "A World of Balance and Plenty: Land, Plants, Animals, and Humans in a Pre-European California." *California History* 76.2–3 (Summer-Fall 1997): 12–47.

Anderson-Dargatz, Gail. *The Cure for Death by Lightning.* Toronto: Vintage Canada, 1996.

Armstrong, Jeannette. "Words." *Telling It: Women and Language Across Cultures.* Ed. The Telling It Book Collective (Sky Lee, Lee Maracle, Daphne Marlatt, Betsy Warland). Vancouver: Press Gang, 1990. 23–29.

Armstrong, Margaret. *Field Book of Western Wild Flowers.* New York: C. P. Putnam's Sons, 1915.

Atkinson, Scott. *Wild Plants of the San Juan Islands.* Seattle: The Mountaineers, 1985.

Babineau, Guy. "Cubes." *The Church Wellesley Review* (Winter 1998). <http://collection.nlc-bnc.ca/100/202/300/church_wellesley/2000/00-october/w98/babineau.htm>.

Baker, Beth. "Growing Interest in Special Forest Products Yields New Management Challenges." *Washington Watch* (September 1998). <www.aibs.org/washington-watch/washington_watch_1998_09.html>.

Baker, Winona. *Thin Smoke of the Heart: Haiku of the West Coast.* Gabriola, BC: Reflections, 1992.

Ballard, Heidi. "Impacts of Harvesting Salal (*Gaultheria shallon*) on the Olympic Peninsula, Washington: Harvester Knowledge, Science, and Participation." PhD Dissertation. Berkeley, CA: University of California, 2004.

Barton, John. *West of Darkness: A Portrait of Emily Carr.* Kapuskasing, ON: Penumbra, 1987.

Bean, W. J. *Trees and Shrubs Hardy in the British Isles.* 8th ed. Vol. 2. 1914. London: John Murray, 1973.

Bennett, Jennifer N., Brent M. Lapthorne, Leandra L. Blevins, and Cindy E.

Prescott. "Response of *Gaultheria shallon* and *Epilobium angustifolium* to Large Additions of Nitrogen and Phosphorus Fertilizer." *Canadian Journal of Forest Research* 34 (2004): 502–06.

Bennett, Jennifer N., Leandra L. Blevins, John E. Barker, David P. Blevins, and Cindy E. Prescott. "Increases in Tree Growth and Nutrient Supply Still Apparent 10 to 13 Years following Fertilization and Vegetation Control of Salal-Dominated Cedar-Hemlock Stands on Vancouver Island." *Canadian Journal of Forest Research* 33 (2003): 1516–24.

Berry, Don. *Trask: The Coast of Oregon, 1848.* 1960. Sausalito, CA: Comstock Editions, 1984.

"Berry Picker." Equipment, Inside Passage Seeds and Native Plant Services. 26 July 2004 <www.insidepassageseeds.com/Equipment.htm>.

Berry, Wendell. "The Regional Motive." *A Continuous Harmony: Essays Cultural and Agricultural.* New York: Harcourt Brace, 1972. 63–70.

"Birds: A Virtual Exhibition." Royal British Columbia Museum. 2 February 2005 <www.royalbcmuseum.bc.ca/nh_papers/gracebell/english>.

Blackman, M. B. *During My Time: Florence Edenshaw Davidson, a Haida Woman.* Seattle: U Washington P, 1982.

Blackwell, Laird R. *Wildflowers of Mount Rainier.* Edmonton, AB: Lone Pine, 2000.

Blevins, Leandra L., Cindy E. Prescott, and Annette Van Niejenhuis. "The Roles of Nitrogen and Phosphorus in Increasing Productivity of Western Hemlock and Western Redcedar Plantations on Northern Vancouver Island." *Forest Ecology and Management* 234. 1–3 (1 October 2006): 116–22.

Boateng, Jacob O., and Phil Comeau. *Salal Complex.* Victoria, BC: Ministry of Forests/Forest Renewal BC, 2002.

Boivin, Bernard. "Jean-François Gaultier." *Dictionary of Canadian Biography.* Volume 3. CD-ROM. Ed. Ramsay Cook. Toronto: U of Toronto P, 2000.

Bolster, Stephanie. "Vancouver, November." *BC Studies* 124 (Winter 1999–2000): 144.

"*Boschniakia hookeri* Walpers." Washington Department of Natural Resources, Washington Natural Heritage Program and the USDI Bureau of Land Management, 2003. 16 July 2005 <www.dnr.wa.gov/nhp/refdesk/fguide/pdf/boshoo.pdf>.

Bolster, Stephanie. "In which Alice visits Pacific Rim National Park." *Canadian Literature* 141 (Summer 1994): 53–54.

Bolster, Stephanie. "Many Have Written Poems about Blackberries." *Breathing Fire: Canada's New Poets.* Ed. Lorna Crozier and Patrick Lane. Madeira Park, BC: Harbour, 1995. 8–9.

Bowering, George. *Burning Water.* 1980. Toronto: General, 1983.

Bowling, Tim. *Thin Smoke of the Heart.* Montreal/Kingston: McGill-Queen's UP, 2000.

Brett, Brian. *Coyote: A Mystery.* Saskatoon: Thistledown, 2003.

Bringhurst, Robert, *et al. Carving the Elements: A Companion to the Fragments of Parmenides.* Berkeley, CA: Editions Koch, 2004.

Bringhurst, Robert, ed. and trans. *Being in Being: The Collected Works of Skaay of the Qquuna Qiighawaay.* Vancouver/Toronto: Douglas & McIntyre, 2001.

Brockman, C. Frank. *Flora of Mount Rainier National Park.* Washington, DC: United States Government Printing Office, 1947.

Brown, Jane. *Tales of the Rose Tree: Ravishing Rhododendrons and their Travels Around the World.* London: HarperCollins, 2004.

Brown, Robert L., and A.L. Hafenrichter. "Stabilizing Sand Dunes on the Pacific Coast with Woody Plants." Miscellaneous Publication No. 892. United States Department of Agriculture Soil Conservation Service, February 1962: 1–17.

"Brushpicker Arrested on Outstanding Warrants." *The Sun* (Bremerton, WA) 13 October 1999. 9 January 2002 <http://www.thesunlink.com/news/99october/daily/1013code.html>.

Buckingham, Nelsa M., and Edward L. Tisch. *Vascular Plants of the Olympic Peninsula, Washington.* Seattle: University of Washington Cooperative Park Studies Unit, 1979.

"Bust Plant Poachers." *National Geographic* 206.1 (July 2004): np.

Campbell, R. Wayne, *et al. The Birds of British Columbia.* Victoria, BC: Royal British Columbia Museum, 1990–2001.

Carr, Emily. *Klee Wyck.* 1941. Toronto: Irwin, 1965.

"Centre for Non-Timber Resources." Royal Roads University, 2005. 27 June 2005 <www.royalroads.ca/Channels/for+learners/divisions+centres +and+schools/centre+for+non-timber+resources/default.htm>.

Chipman, Art. *Wildflower Trails of the Pacific Northwest.* Medford, OR: Pine Cone, 1970.

City Clerk, as Chair of Street Naming Committee. "New Street Name in Kitsilano — Salal Drive." Administrative Report. Vancouver City Council, 17 July 1996: 5527–3. 19 July 2000 <http://city.vancouver.bc.ca/ctyclerk/cclerk/960730/a16.htm>.

Clark, Lewis J. *Wild Flowers of the Pacific Northwest from Alaska to Northern California.* Sidney, BC: Gray's, 1976.

Clark, Lewis J. *Lewis Clark's Field Guide to Wild Flowers of Forest and Woodland in the Pacific Northwest.* Vancouver: Evergreen, 1974.

Clements, Edith S. *Flowers of Coast and Sierra.* New York: H. W. Wilson Company, 1928.

Cleverly, Bill. "Salal Pickers Put Forestry Research at Risk." *Victoria Times-Colonist* 3 May 2004: B1.

Cocksedge, Wendy. "The Role of Co-operatives in the Non-Timber Forest Product Industry: Exploring Issues and Options Using the Case Study of Salal (*Gaultheria shallon*; Ericaceae)." Occasional Paper. BC Institute for Co-operative Studies, 2001. 15 June 2004 <http://web.uvic.ca/bcics/research/pdf/pub-2-12Apr01.pdf>.

Cody, John. *Wings of Paradise: The Great Saturniid Moths.* Chapel Hill, NC: U North Carolina P, 1996.

Cohen, Michael. *Garden of Bristlecones: Tales of Change in the Great Basin.* Reno: U Nevada P, 1998.

Compton, Brian Douglas. "Upper North Wakashan and Southern Tsimshian Ethnobotany: The Knowledge and Use of Plants and Fungi Among the Oweekeno, Hanaksiala (Kitlope and Kemano), Haisla (Kitamaat) and Kitasoo Peoples of the Central and North Coasts of British Columbia." PhD Thesis. University of British Columbia, 1982.

Cook, Elizabeth Heckendorn. "'Perfect' Flowers, Monstrous Women: Eighteenth-Century Botany and the Modern Gendered Subject." *Defects: Engendering the Modern Body.* Ed. Helen Deutsch and Felicity Nussbaum. Ann Arbor: U Michigan P, 2000. 252–79.

Coupland, Douglas. *Microserfs.* Toronto: HarperCollins, 1995.

Coupland, Douglas. *Life After God.* New York: Pocket Books, 1994.

"Daily Data Report for October 2003, Courtenay Puntledge, British

Columbia." Climate Data Online, National Climate Archive, Environment Canada. 2 January 2005 <http://www.climate. weatheroffice.ec.gc.ca>.

Dash, Mike. *TulipoMania: The Story of the World's Most Coveted Flower and the Extraordinary Passions It Aroused.* New York: Crown Publishers, 1999.

Davey, Lorna. "Clean and Bright." *Discovery Magazine* (May 1996). <http:// www.royalbcmuseum.bc.ca/discover/ds24596/cleanbri.html>.

Davis, H. L. *Honey in the Horn.* New York: Avon Books, 1962.

Davis, Wade. *The Clouded Leopard: Travels to Landscapes of Spirit and Desire.* Vancouver: Douglas & McIntyre, 1998.

Dean Moore, Kathleen. "Writing the Northwest, II." Plenary. The Sixth Biennial Conference of the Association for the Study of Literature and the Environment: "Being in the World, Living with the Land." University of Oregon, Eugene, OR. 22 June 2005.

Deleuze, Gilles, and Félix Guattari. *On the Line.* Trans. John Johnston. New York: Semiotext(e), 1983.

Deming, Alison. *Science and Other Poems.* Baton Rouge: Louisiana State UP, 1994.

Dirks-Edmunds, Jane C. *Not Just Trees: The Legacy of a Douglas-Fir Forest.* Pullman: Washington State UP, 1999.

Dirks-Edmunds, Jane C. "A Comparison of Biotic Communities of the Cedar-Hemlock and Oak-Hickory Associations." *Ecological Monographs* 17.3 (July 1947): 235–60.

Doig, Ivan. *The Sea Runners.* New York: Atheneum, 1982.

Doig, Ivan. *Winter Brothers: A Season at the Edge of America.* New York: Harcourt Brace Jovanovich, 1980.

Doss, Diane. Listserv communication (Washington Native Plant Society [WNPS] Listserv). 6 June 2006.

Douglas, David. *Journal Kept by David Douglas During His Travels in North America 1823–1827.* New York: Royal Horticultural Society/Antiquarian, 1959.

Drever, Mark C., and Alton S. Harestad. "Diets of Norway Rats, *Rattus norvegicus,* on Langara Island, Queen Charlotte Islands, British Columbia: Implications for Conservation of Breeding Seabirds." *The Canadian Field Naturalist* 112.4 (October–December 1998): 676–83.

Duncan, David James. *My Story as Told by Water.* San Francisco: Sierra Club, 2002.

Duncan, Dayton. *Out West: American Journey along the Lewis and Clark Trail.* New York: Viking, 1987.

Dunn, John Asher, comp. and ed. *Sm'algyax: A Reference Dictionary and Grammar of the Coast Tsimshian Language.* 1978/1979. Seattle/London: U Washington P, and Juneau, AK: Sealaska Heritage Foundation, 1995.

Eberhardt, Tom. "Let Salal Hedges Grow in the Wild." Letter to the editor. *Victoria Times-Colonist* 14 December 2003: D3.

Efron, Sarah. "Marketing of Forest Floor Has Consequences." *The Georgia Straight* 9–16 December 2004: 59.

Enari, Leonid. *Plants of the Pacific Northwest: 663 Selected Northwest Wild Flowers, Shrubs, Trees and Weeds.* Portland, OR: Binfords & Mort, 1956.

Evernden, Neil. "Beyond Ecology: Self, Place, and the Pathetic Fallacy." *The Ecocriticism Reader: Landmarks in Literary Ecology.* Ed. Cheryll Glotfelty and Harold Fromm. Athens: U Georgia P, 1996. 92–104.

Evernden, Neil. *The Social Creation of Nature.* Baltimore: Johns Hopkins UP, 1992.

Faludy, George. *Notes from the Rainforest.* Willowdale ON: Hounslow Press, 1988.

"Floral and Greenery Products." Ministry of Forests, Government of British Columbia. 23 July 2001 <www.for.gov.bc.ca/hfp/botan/ chapt.2.htm>.

"Florida's Fern Capital of the World: Directory of Growers and Shippers of the World's Finest Live Cut Foliage." Florida Fern Growers Association. 21 July 2004 <http://www.pvns.net/fern/growers.htm>.

Fodor's Seattle and Vancouver. New York: Fodor's Travel Publications/Random House, 1999.

Forrest, Mary, comp. *Trees and Shrubs Cultivated in Ireland.* Ed. E. C. Nelson/ Heritage Gardens Committee. Dublin: Boethius, 1985.

Foster, David. "Brush Rustling: An Underground Economy Worth Millions Feeds Yuppie Sensibilities, Desperation in the Forests of the Northwest." *Idaho News* 22 February 1998. 1 July 2000 <http://www. idahonews.com/022298/a_sectio/14281.htm>.

Freed, Jim. "The Future of the Special Forest Products Industry." *Western Forester* 42.6 (September 1997): 6–7.

Freed, Jim. "Integrating Timber and SPF in a Plan." *Western Forester* 42.6 (September 1997): 13.

Frye, T. C., and George Rigg. *Elementary Flora of the Northwest.* New York: American Book Company, 1914.

Gallagher, Tess. "He Would Have." *Moon Crossing Bridge.* Saint Paul, MN: Graywolf, 1992. 26.

Gallagher, Tess. "Simple Sonatina." *Amplitude: New and Selected Poems.* Saint Paul, MN: Graywolf, 1987. 180.

"Gaultheria." The New Encyclopedia Britannica. 15th ed. Vol. 5. Chicago: Encyclopedia Britannica Inc., 2005. 150–51.

Gayton, Don. *Kokanee: The Redfish and the Kootenay Bioregion.* Vancouver: Transmontanus/New Star, 2002.

Gayton, Don. Personal communication (email). 3 December 2002.

Genthe, Henry. "The Sargasso Sea." *Smithsonian Magazine* (November 1998). 6 February 2003 <www.smithsonianmag.si.edu/smithsonian/issues98/nov98/sargasso.html>.

Gilkey, Helen. *Handbook of Northwest Flowering Plants.* 2nd ed. Portland, OR: Binfords & Mort, 1961.

Gloss, Molly. *Wild Life.* 2000. New York: Houghton Mifflin, 2001.

Goodman, Edmund Clay. "Indian Reserved Rights." *Nontimber Forest Products in the United States.* Ed. Eric T. Jones *et al.* Lawrence, KS: UP Kansas, 2002. 273–81.

Gould, Stephen Jay. "An Evolutionary Perspective on Strengths, Fallacies, and Confusions in the Concept of Native Plants." *Nature and Ideology.* Ed. Joachim Wolschke-Bulmahn. Washington, DC: Dumbarton Oaks Research Library and Collection, 1997. 11–19.

Green, Jeff, and Anne Huang. "Brown Elfin." Natural History Research Paper. Royal British Columbia Museum, 1998. 5 January 2000 <www.royalbcmuseum.bc.ca/hn_papers/anneh/text/brownelf.html>.

Griffith, Thomas. "The Pacific Northwest." *Atlantic Monthly* 237 (April 1976): 47–93.

Gulyás, Lee. "North Coast Meditation." *Jeopardy Magazine* (Western Washington U). 37 (Fall 2001): 19.

Gulyás, Lee. "North Coast Meditation (revised 2003)." Unpublished. Personal communication (email). 22 May 2003.

Gunther, Erna. *Ethnobotany of Western Washington.* 1945. Seattle: U Washington P, 1973.

Guppy, Crispin S., and Jon H. Shepard. *Butterflies of British Columbia.* Vancouver: U British Columbia P, 2001.

Guterson, David. *Our Lady of the Forest.* New York: Alfred A. Knopf, 2003.

Guterson, David. *Snow Falling on Cedars.* New York: Vintage, 1995.

Haeussler, S., D. Coates, and J. Mather. *Autoecology of Common Plants in British Columbia: A Literature Review.* FRDA Report 158. Victoria, BC: Forestry Canada and the British Columbia Ministry of Forests, 1990. 15 June 2004 <http://www.for.gov.bc.ca/hfd/pubs/Docs/Frr/Frr158.pdf>.

Hale, Amanda. *Sounding the Blood.* Vancouver: Raincoast, 2001.

Hamilton, Gordon. "BC's Other Forest Industry." *The Vancouver Sun* 3 August 2004: F1.

Hamilton, Robert. "There was nothing so adventurous, nothing so free and unstuffy as the impending meal under the sky." *Western Living* June 2001: 46, 48.

Hansis, Richard. "Workers in the Woods: Confronting Rapid Change." *Nontimber Forest Products in the United States.* Ed. Eric T. Jones *et al.* Lawrence, KS: UP Kansas, 2002. 52–56.

Hansis, Richard. "A Political Ecology of Picking: Non-Timber Forest Products in the Pacific Northwest." *Human Ecology* 26.1 (1998): 67–86.

Harris, Barbara, and Leopoldina Hrubant. "Plant and animal names of Indian origin in British Columbia." *Syesis* 4: 1/2 (December 1971): 223–25.

Harris, James G., and Melinda Woolf Harris. *Plant Identification: An Illustrated Glossary.* 2nd ed. 1994. Spring Lake, VT: Spring Lake, 2001.

Harvey, Athelstan George. *Douglas of the Fir: A Biography of David Douglas, Botanist.* Cambridge: Harvard UP, 1947.

Harvey, Brian. "Why the World Needs Wetlands." *Waters* (Vancouver Aquarium and Marine Science Centre). (Summer 2000): 20–22.

Harvey, Graham. *The Forgiveness of Nature: The Story of Grass.* London: Jonathan Cape, 2001.

Haskin, Leslie L. *Wild Flowers of the Pacific Coast.* 2nd ed. Portland, OR: Binfords & Mort, 1967.

Healey, Derek. "Salal: An Idyll for Orchestra, opus 71." Unpublished score. Canadian Music Centre. Vancouver, BC.

Heckman, Hazel. *Island in the Sound.* Seattle: U Washington P, 1967.

Heffernan, Helen. "A Clear-cut Equation." *Word Works.* Vancouver: Federation of BC Writers, 2003.

Helmreich, Anne L. "Re-presenting Nature: Ideology, Art, and Science in William Robinson's 'Wild Garden.'" *Nature and Ideology.* Ed. Joachim Wolschke-Bulmahn. Washington, DC: Dumbarton Oaks Research Library and Collection, 1997. 81–111.

"Herbarium Collections." Royal Botanic Gardens, Kew. London, England. 26 September 2004 <http://www.kew.org/collections/herbcol.html>.

Highstone, John. *Victorian Gardens.* San Francisco: Harper & Row, 1982.

Hilbert, Vi (told by). *Coyote and Rock, and Other Lushootseed Stories.* Audio recording. New York: HarperCollins, 1992.

Hill, Clara Chapman. *Spring Flowers of the Lower Columbia Valley.* Seattle: U Washington P, 1958.

Hitchcock, Charles Leo, and Arthur Cronquist. *Flora of the Pacific Northwest.* Seattle: U Washington P, 1973.

Hobhouse, Penelope. *A Book of Gardening: A Practical Guide.* The National Trust (Great Britain). Boston and Toronto: Little, Brown & Co., 1986.

Hodgins, Jack. *The Macken Charm.* Toronto: McClelland & Stewart, 1995.

Hodgins, Jack. *Broken Ground.* Toronto: McClelland & Stewart, 1998.

Hodgins, Jack. *The Invention of the World.* 1977. Scarborough, ON: Signet, 1978.

Holm, Bill. *Northwest Coast Indian Art: An Analysis of Form.* 1965. Seattle/London: U Washington P, 1978.

Howarth, Jean. *Treasure Island.* Toronto: Dorset, 1979.

Huffman, David W., John C. Tappeiner II, and John C. Zasada. "Regeneration of Salal (*Gaultheria shallon*) in the Central Coast Range Forests of Oregon." *Canadian Journal of Botany* 72 (1994): 39–51.

Huffman, David W., John C. Zasada, and John C. Tappeiner II. "Growth and Morphology of Rhizome Cuttings and Seedlings of Salal (*Gaultheria shallon*): Effects of Four Light Intensities." *Canadian Journal of Botany* 72 (1994): 1702–1708.

Hugo, Richard. *Making Certain It Goes On: The Collected Poems of Richard Hugo.* New York: W. W. Norton, 1984.

"Humble Salal Bush Praised As Saviour Of Timber In BC." *The Daily Province* 14 May 1935: 7.

Hunt, John Dixon. *The Figure in the Landscape.* Baltimore, MD: The Johns Hopkins UP, 1976.

Hutchings, Kevin. *Imagining Nature: Blake's Environmental Poetics.* Montreal/Kingston: McGill-Queen's UP, 2002.

Jarvis, P. J. "Plant Introduction to England and Their Role in Horticultural and Sylvicultural Innovation, 1500–1900." *Change in the Countryside: Essays on Rural England, 1500–1900.* Ed. H. S. A. Fox and R. A. Cutlin. London: Institute of British Geographers, 1979. 145–64.

Johnston, La Rea J. Dennis, Alfred M. Wiedemann, and Frank H. Smith. *Plants of the Oregon Coastal Dunes.* Corvallis, OR: Oregon State UP, 1999.

Jolley, Russ. *Wildflowers of the Columbia Gorge.* Portland, OR: Oregon Historical Society, 1988.

Jones, Eric T., and Kathryn Lynch. "The Relevance of Sociocultural Variables to Nontimber Forest Product Research, Policy, and Management." *Nontimber Forest Products in the United States.* Ed. Eric T. Jones *et al.* Lawrence, KS: UP Kansas, 2002. 26–51.

Jones, Eric T., Rebecca J. McLain and James Weigand, eds. *Nontimber Forest Products in the United States.* Lawrence, KS: UP Kansas, 2002.

Jones, Mavis. *Her Festival Clothes.* Montreal/Kingston: McGill-Queen's UP, 2001.

Justice, Clive. *Mr. Menzies' Garden Legacy: Plant Collecting on the Northwest Coast.* Delta, BC: Cavendish, 2000.

Kevin Paul, Philip. "The Sweetly Neglected." Plenary. 12th Annual Stabilizing Indigenous Languages Symposium: "Weaving Language and Culture Together." Saanich Tribal School, Brentwood Bay, BC. 4 June 2005.

Kevin Paul, Philip. "The Sweetly Neglected." *Spilled.* Ed. Melanie O'Brian *et al.* Vancouver: Artspeak, 2004. 13–16.

Kevin Paul, Philip. *Taking the Names Down from the Hill.* Roberts Creek, BC: Nightwood, 2003.

Kimmerer, Robin Wall. *Gathering Moss: A Natural and Cultural History of Mosses.* Corvallis, OR: Oregon State UP, 2003.

Kruckeberg, Arthur R. *Gardening with Native Plants of the Pacific Northwest: An Illustrated Guide.* 1982. Seattle/London: U Washington P, 1993.

Landry, Donna. *The Inventory of the Countryside: Hunting, Walking, and Ecology in English Literature, 1671–1831.* New York: Palgrave, 2001.

Leeson, Ted. *The Habit of Rivers: Reflections on Trout Streams and Fly Fishing.* New York: Penguin, 1994.

Leopold, Aldo. *A Sand County Almanac: With Other Essays on Conservation from Round River.* 1949. New York: Ballantine, 1970.

Lewis, Meriwether, and William Clark. (*Herbarium of the Lewis & Clark Expedition The Journals of the Lewis & Clark Expedition.* Vol. 12). Ed. Gary E. Moulton. Lincoln: U Nebraska P, 1999.

Lewis, Meriwether, and William Clark. *The Journals of the Lewis & Clark Expedition.* Vol. 7. Ed. Gary E. Moulton. Lincoln, U Nebraska P, 1991.

Lewis, Meriwether, and William Clark. *The Journals of the Lewis & Clark Expedition.* Vol. 6. Ed. Gary E. Moulton. Lincoln: U Nebraska P, 1990.

Lilburn, Tim. "Philosophical *Apokatastasis:* On Writing and Return." *Thinking and Singing: Poetry and the Practice of Philosophy.* Ed. Tim Lilburn. Toronto: Cormorant, 2002. 95–119.

Link, Russell. *Landscaping for Wildlife in the Pacific Northwest.* Seattle: U Washington P, 1999.

Lippard, Lucy R. *The Lure of the Local: Senses of Place in a Multicentered Society.* New York: New Press, 1997.

Lowther, Christine. *New Power.* Fredericton: Broken Jaw, 1999.

Lynch, Kathryn A., and Rebecca J. McLain. "Access, Labor, and Wild Floral Greens Management in Western Washington's Forests." General Technical

Report PNW-GTR-585. Portland, OR: US Department of Agriculture, 2003. 9 December 2006 <http://www.fs.fed.us/pnw/pubs/gtr585.pdf>.

Lyons, C. P., and Bill Merilees. *Trees, Shrubs and Flowers to Know in British Columbia and Washington.* Vancouver: C. P. Lyons Lone Pine, 1995.

MacDonald, Betty. *The Egg and I.* 1945. Philadelphia/New York: J. B. Lippincott Company, 1973.

MacKay, David. "Agents of Empire." *Visions of Empire: Voyages, Botany and Representations of Nature.* Ed. David Philip Miller and Peter Hanns Reill. Cambridge: Cambridge UP, 1996. 38–57.

Macnair, Peter L., and Alan L. Hoover. *The Magic Leaves: A History of Haida Argillite Carving.* 1984. Victoria, BC: Royal British Columbia Museum, 2002.

Malamud, Bernard. *A New Life.* 1961. New York: Pocket, 1973.

Manguel, Alberto. *A History of Reading.* Toronto: Alfred A. Knopf, 1996.

Marlatt, Daphne. *Steveston.* Photographs by Robert Minden. 1974. Vancouver: Ronsdale, 2001.

Marlatt, Daphne. *Ana Historic.* Toronto: Coach House, 1988.

Marner, Serena K. Personal communication (email). 30 June 2005.

Marriott, Anne. "Underbrush." *D'Sonoqua: An Anthology of Women Poets of British Columbia, Vol. 2.* Vancouver: Intermedia, 1979.

Massey, Doreen. "Globalisation." *Geography* (October 2002): 293–96.

McClure, Robert. "Bouquets May Hold Ill-Gotten Greens." *Seattle Post- Intelligencer* 14 February 2002. 13 February 2004 <http://seattlepi. nwsource.com/local/58249_greens14.shtml>.

McConnaughey, Bayard H., and Evelyn McConnaughey. *The Audubon Society Nature Guides: Pacific Coast.* New York: Alfred A. Knopf, 1985.

McKay, Don. "The Bushtits' Nest." *Vis à Vis: Field Notes on Poetry and Wilderness.* Wolfville, NS: Gaspereau, 2001. 83–106.

McKay, Don. "Remembering Apparatus: Poetry and the Visibility of Tools." *Vis à Vis: Field Notes on Poetry and Wilderness.* Wolfville, NS: Gaspereau, 2001. 51–73.

McKelvey, Susan Delano. *Botanical Exploration of the Trans-Mississippi West 1790–1850.* 1956. Corvallis, OR: Oregon State UP, 1991.

McTaggart-Cowan, Ian. "The Ecological Relationships of the Food of the Columbian Black-tailed Deer, *Odocoileus hemionus columbianus* (Richardson), in the Coast Forest Region of Southern Vancouver Island, British Columbia." *Ecological Monographs* 15.2 (April 1945): 110–39.

McWhirter, George. *A Staircase for All Souls: The British Columbia Suite.* Lantzville: Oolichan, 1993.

McWhirter, George. "To the Salal (*Gaultheria shallon*) Berry: An Apologia." Unpublished.

Meeker-Rouhier, K. *After the Storm — Salal Blossoms.* Scappoose, OR: Melton Publishing, 2000. 26 September 2004 <http://www.meltonpub.com/Gallery/salal.html>.

Messier, Christian, and James B. Kimmins. "Above-and-Below-Ground Vegetation Recovery in Recently Clear Cut and Burned Sites Dominated by *Gaultheria shallon* in Coastal British Columbia." *Forest Ecology and Management* 76 (1991): 275–94.

Miller, David Philip. "Joseph Banks' Empire, and 'Centers of Calculation' in Late Hanoverian London." *Visions of Empire: Voyages, Botany and Representations of Nature.* Ed. David Philip Miller and Hanns Reill.

Cambridge: U Cambridge P, 1996. 21–37.

Miller, David Philip, and Peter Hanns Reill, eds. *Visions of Empire: Voyages, Botany and Representations of Nature.* Cambridge: U Cambridge P, 1996.

Miller, Diana. Personal communication (email). 7 January 2005.

Miller, Richard Alan. *Native Plants of Commercial Importance: The Nomadic Life of the Professional Forager.* Metairie, LA: Acres USA, 1988.

Moulton, Gary E. "Introduction to Volume 12." *The Journals of the Lewis & Clark Expedition.* Vol. 12 (*Herbarium of the Lewis & Clark Expedition*). By Meriwether Lewis and William Clark. Ed. Gary E. Moulton. Lincoln: U Nebraska P, 1999. 1–10.

Murphy, Alexandra. *Graced by Pines: The Ponderosa Pine in the American West.* Missoula, MT: Mountain, 1994.

Murrell, Gina. Personal communication (email). 30 June 2005.

Nafar, F., and S. M. Berch. "Traditional Isolation and Molecular Methods: Which Works Best for Identification of Ericoid Mycorrhizal Fungi of Salal." 19 July 2000 <http://otaku.unbc.ca/nfrep/abstract_soils5.html>.

Newitt, Angela. "Some Childhood Memories of Clo'oose." *Raincoast Chronicles: Eleven Up.* Collector's Edition III. Ed. Howard White. Madeira Park, BC: Harbour, 1994. 24–32.

Noble, Vicki. Personal communication (email). 10 January 2005.

Nuttall, Thomas. *The Genera of North American Plants, and a Catalogue of the Species, to the Year 1817.* Philadelphia: np, 1918.

Nuxalk Food and Nutrition Handbook: A Practical Guide to Family Foods and Nutrition Using Native Foods. The Nuxalk Food and Nutrition Program. Vancouver:

School of Family and Nutritional Sciences, University of British
Columbia, and Bella Coola: Nuxalk Health Clinic, 1984.

Orlean, Susan. *The Orchid Thief.* 1998. New York: Ballantine, 2000.

Osborn, A. *Shrubs and Trees for the Garden.* London: Ward, Lock & Co., 1933.

Parish, Roberta, Ray Coupé, and Dennis Lloyd. *Plants of Southern Interior
British Columbia and the Inland Northwest.* Vancouver: BC Ministry of Forests
and Lone Pine, 1996.

Pavord, Anna. *The Naming of Names: The Search for Order in the World of Plants.*
London: Bloomsbury Publishing, 2005.

Pavord, Anna. *The Tulip: The Story of a Flower That Has Made Men Mad.* London:
Bloomsbury Publishing, 1999.

Penn, Briony. *A Year on the Wild Side.* Victoria, BC: Horsdal & Schubart, 1999.

Poe, Edgar Allan. *The Narrative of Arthur Gordon Pym of Nantucket.* Ed. Harold
Beaver. 1838. Harmondsworth: Penguin, 1975.

Pojar, Jim, and Andy McKinnon, eds. *Plants of Coastal British Columbia including
Washington, Oregon and Alaska.* Vancouver: Lone Pine, 1994.

Pollan, Michael. *The Botany of Desire: A Plant's-Eye View of the World.* New York:
Random House, 2001.

"Population Update." *The Blackfish Sounder* 11 (2003): 7.

Prescott, Cindy E., and Leandra L. Blevins. "The Salal Cedar Hemlock
Integrated Research Program (SCHIRP): Management through
Understanding." *The Forestry Chronicle* 75.3 (May/June 1999): 447–51.

Purdy, Al. *Beyond Remembering: The Collected Poems of Al Purdy.* Madeira Park,
BC: Harbour, 2000.

Pyle, Robert Michael. *The Audubon Society Handbook for Butterfly Watchers*. Ill. Sarah Anne Hughes. New York: Charles Scribner's Sons, 1984.

Pyle, Robert Michael. *The Butterflies of Cascadia: A Field Guide to All the Species of Washington, Oregon, and Surrounding Territories*. Seattle: Seattle Audubon Society, 2002.

Pyle, Robert Michael. *Wintergreen: Rambles in a Ravaged Land*. 1986. Seattle: Sasquatch, 2001.

Pyle, Robert Michael. *Watching Washington Butterflies*. Seattle: The Seattle Audubon Society, 1974.

Pyper, Charles V., and R. Kent Beattie. *Flora of the Northwest Coast*. Lancaster, PA: New Era, 1915.

Quinn, Lee Early. *Japanese Free Style Flower Arrangement*. Princeton, NJ: D. van Nostrand, 1964.

Raban, Jonathan. *Waxwings*. New York: Pantheon, 2003.

Raban, Jonathan. "Battleground of the Eye." *Atlantic Monthly* 287.3 (March 2001): 40–52.

Raban, Jonathan. Introduction. *The Pacific Northwest Landscape: A Painted History*. Ed. Kitty Harmon. Seattle: Sasquatch, 2001.

Ramsey, Jarold. *Love in an Earthquake*. Seattle: U Washington P, 1973.

The Random House College Dictionary, Revised Edition. New York: Random House, 1975.

Rehder, Alfred. *Manual of Cultivated Trees and Shrubs Hardy in North America*. 1927. New York: Macmillan, 1967.

"Research Shorts." *University Affairs* (November 2002): 7.

Ricou, Laurie. *The Arbutus/Madrone Files: Reading the Pacific Northwest.*
Edmonton, AB: NeWest, 2002.

Rilke, Rainer Maria. *Letters to a Young Poet.* Trans. Stephen Mitchell. New
York: Vintage, 1986.

Robinson, William. *The Wild Garden: or, our groves and gardens made beautiful by the
naturalisation of hardy exotic plants; being one way onwards from the dark ages of flower
gardening, with suggestions for the regeneration of the bare borders of the London Parks.*
London: The Garden Office, 1881.

Rosowski, Susan J. *Birthing a Nation: Gender, Creativity, and the West in American
Literature.* Lincoln: U Nebraska P, 1999.

Ross, Rick. Personal communication (email). 20 December 2004.

Ruffner, W. H. *A Report on Washington Territory.* New York: Seattle, Lake
Shore and Eastern Railway, 1889.

"Salal." Botany Loop Trail (virtual tour), Donald F. Samuelson Model
Watershed, Grays Harbor College, Aberdeen, WA. 18 June 2001 <http://
ghc.ctc.edu/mwp/tours/botany>.

"Salal." Sinister Designs. 30 March 2005 <http://www.sinister-designs.
com/poetry/nh/salal.html>.

"Salal." Slugs and Salal Plant Directory. Ed. Louise Lungle. 2004. 4 October
2004 <http://www.slugsandsalal.com/plantdb/shrubs/salal.html>.

"Salal and Huckleberry Creates New Industry." *West Coast Advocate* 2
February 1956: 6.

The Salal Review: An Arts and Literary Journal. Lower Columbia College,
Longview, WA. 18 June 2001 <http://lcc.ctc.edu/departments/salal/>.

Schopmeyer, C. S., comp. *Seeds of Woody Plants in the United States.* Agricultural

Handbook No. 450. Washington, DC: US Department of Agriculture, 1974.

Shadbolt, Doris. *Emily Carr.* Vancouver: Douglas & McIntyre, 1990.

Shields, Carol. *Unless.* Toronto: Vintage Canada, 2003.

Shomer, Forest. Personal communication (email). 17 December 2004.

Shteir, Ann. *Cultivating Women, Cultivating Science: Flora's Daughters and Botany in England, 1760–1860.* Baltimore: Johns Hopkins UP, 1996.

Simpson, Brennan M. *Flower at My Feet: Western Wildflowers in Legend, Literature and Lore.* Surrey, BC: Hancock House, 1996.

Singer, Natalia Rachel. *Scraping By in the Big Eighties.* Lincoln/London: U Nebraska P, 2004.

Smith, Alisa. "Cabin Fever." *Western Living* Vancouver edition (June 2003): 22–26.

Smith, Bruce. "Salal Harvest Isn't Clearcutting." Letter to the editor. *Victoria Times-Colonist* 18 December 2003: A13.

Smith, Kathleen M., Nancy J. Anderson, and Katherine I. Beamish, eds. *Nature West Coast: A Study of Plants, Insects, Birds, Mammals and Marine Life as Seen in Lighthouse Park.* Comp. and ill. by members of the Vancouver Natural History Society. Victoria, BC: Sono Nis, 1988.

Snowden, Mary Ann. *Island Paddling: A Paddler's Guide to the Gulf Islands and Barkley Sound.* 1990. Victoria, BC: Orca, 1997.

Snyder, Gary. *The Practice of the Wild.* San Francisco: North Point, 1990.

Snyder, Gary. "Interview." *At the Field's End: Interviews with Twenty Pacific Northwest Writers.* Ed. Nicholas O'Connell. Seattle: Madrona, 1989. 307–22.

"Special Forest Products." Washington State University. 7 January

2002 <http://thurston.wsu.edu/Forest%20Products/SFP%20
Articles/sfp.salal.htm>.

St. John, Harold, and Edith Hardin. *Flora of Mt. Baker.* Portland, OR: Mrs. C.
S. English, 1929.

Stafford, Kim. *The Muses Among Us: Eloquent Listening and Other Pleasures of the
Writer's Craft.* Athens: U Georgia P, 2003.

Stafford, Kim. *An Intricacy of Simple Means.* Deer Isle, ME: Haystack Mountain
School of Crafts, 2002.

Stafford, Kim. *Lochsa Road: A Pilgrim in the West.* Lewiston, ID: Confluence, 1991.

Stafford, Kim. *Places and Stories.* Pittsburgh: Carnegie Mellon UP, 1987.

Stafford, Kim. *Having Everything Right: Essays of Place.* Lewiston, ID: Confluence,
1986.

Steel, Stephanie Quainton. "Salal Joe's Garden." *Living in Harmony: Nature
Writing by Women in Canada.* Ed. Andrea Pinto Lebowitz. Victoria, BC:
Orca, 1996. 188–98.

Steel, Stephanie Quainton. "Salal Joe's Garden." *Harvest of Light: An Artist's
Journey.* Victoria, BC: Orca, 1991. 63–75.

Sterling, Shirley. "Yaya' and the Firbough: A Philosophy of Respect."
Canadian Journal of Environmental Education 7.1 (Spring 2002): 43–53.

Stewart, Hilary. *Cedar.* Vancouver: U British Columbia P, 1992.

Stoutenberg, Adrien, and Laura Nelson Baker. *Wild Treasure: The Story of
David Douglas.* New York: Charles Scribner's Sons, 1958.

Stuart, John D., and John O. Sawyer. *Trees and Shrubs of California.* Berkeley,
CA: U California P, 2001.

"Sudden Oak Death — *Phytophthora ramorum.*" Canadian Food Inspection
Agency, Government of Canada, 4 May 2006. 18 August 2006 <http://
www.inspection.gc.ca/english/plaveg/protect/pestrava/sodmsc/
sodmsce.shtml>.

Sund, Robert. *Ish River.* San Francisco: North Point, 1983.

Sunde, Scott. "Cracking Down on Forest Poachers." *Seattle Post-Intelligencer*
30 March 1999. 3 March 2000 <http://seattlepi.nwsource.com/local/
brus30.shtml>.

Swann, Brian. "Plant Mind." *ISLE* 9.2 (Summer 2002): 259.

Szczawinski, Adam F. *The Heather Family (Ericaceae) of British Columbia.*
Victoria, BC: A. Sutton, 1962.

Taylor, Ronald J., and George W. Douglas. *Mountain Plants of the Pacific
Northwest: A Field Guide to Washington, Western British Columbia, and Southeastern
Alaska.* Missoula, MT: Mountain, 1995.

Taylor, Timothy. *Stanley Park.* Toronto: Alfred A. Knopf, 2001.

Teshigawara, Kasumi. *Space and Colour in Japanese Flower Arrangement.* London:
George Newnes, 1965.

Thom, Ian. *E. J. Hughes.* Vancouver: Douglas & McIntyre/Vancouver Art
Gallery, 2002.

Thomas, Audrey. "Kill Day on the Government Wharf." *West by Northwest:
British Columbia Short Stories.* Ed. David Stouck and Miler Wilkinson.
Victoria, BC: Polestar, 1998. 127–35.

Thomas, Ian. "Untitled." *Artropolis 2001.* Ed. Briana Doyle and Lynne
Melcombe. Vancouver: A. T. Eight Artropolis Society, 2001.

Thomas, Jack Ward, as cited in Roosevelt IV, Theodore. "The Business

of Building Sustainable Communities: Rewriting these United States."
Open Spaces 6.1 (2003): 31–35.

Thomas, Margaret G., and David R. Schumann. "Income Opportunities
in Special Forest Products — Self-Help Suggestions for Rural
Entrepreneurs." Agriculture Information Bulletin AIB-666. Washington,
DC: US Department of Agriculture, 1993. 28 June 2005 <http://www.fpl.
fs.fed.us/documnts/usda/agib666/agib666.htm>.

Thoreau, Henry D. *The Annotated Walden.* Ed. Philip van Doren Stern. New
York: Potter, 1970.

Thoreau, Henry D. *The Journal of Henry D. Thoreau 1855–1861.* Ed. Bradford
Torrey and Francis H. Hallen. New York: Dover, 1962.

Thorp, Rosalind. "The Indigenous Gardener: Salal on a Stump." *Wingspan*
(Wild Bird Trust of British Columbia) (Spring 1999): np.

Timmer, Dagmar. "Grandfather to a New Generation of Foresters." *World
Conservation* 3–4 (1999): 25–26.

Titus, Brian. Personal communication (email). 11 January 2007.

Turner, Nancy J. *The Earth's Blanket: Traditional Teachings for Sustainable Living.*
Vancouver/Toronto: Douglas & McIntyre, 2005.

Turner, Nancy J. *Plants of Haida Gwaii.* Winlaw, BC: Sono Nis, 2004.

Turner, Nancy J. *Food Plants of Coastal First Peoples.* 1995. Vancouver: U British
Columbia P, 1997.

Turner, Nancy J. *Ethnobotany of the Nitinaht Indians of Vancouver Island.* Occasional
Papers of the BC Provincial Museum No. 24. Victoria, BC: Ministry of
Provincial Secretary and Government Services/Parks Canada, 1983.

Tweit, Susan J. *Seasons on the Pacific Coast: A Naturalist's Notebook.* San Francisco:

BIBLIOGRAPHY · 247

Chronicle, 1999.

Underhill, J. E. *Northwestern Wild Berries.* Saanichton, BC: Hancock House, 1980.

Vales, D. G. *Functional Relationship Between Salal Understory and Forest Overstory.* MSC Thesis, University of British Columbia. Victoria, BC: Research Branch, Ministry of Forests and Lands/Wildlife Branch, Ministry of Environment and Parks, 1986.

Van Dersal, William R. *Native Woody Plants of the United States: Their Erosion-Control and Wildlife Values.* Miscellaneous Publication No. 303. United States Department of Agriculture. Washington, DC: United States Government Printing Office, 1938.

Vance, Nan C., Melissa Borsting, David Pilz, and Jim Freed. *Special Forest Products: Species Information Guide for the Pacific Northwest.* Portland, OR: US Department of Agriculture, Forest Service, Pacific Northwest Research Station, 2001.

Varner, Collin. *Plants of the Gulf and San Juan Islands and Southern Vancouver Island.* Vancouver: Raincoast, 2002.

Wagoner, David. *Traveling Light: Collected and New Poems.* Urbana/Chicago: U Illinois P, 1999.

Wagoner, David. *In Broken Country: Poems.* Boston/Toronto: Little, Brown and Co., 1979.

Wagoner, David. "Lost." *Collected Poems 1956–1976.* 1976. Bloomington: Indiana UP, 1978. 182.

Wagoner, David. *The Nesting Ground: A Book of Poems.* Bloomington: Indiana UP, 1963.

Wallinger, Rosamund. *Gertrude Jekyll's Lost Garden: The Restoration of an Edwardian Masterpiece.* The Antique Collector's Club. Woodbridge,

Suffolk: Garden Art, 2000.

Washington State: Contrast in Nature. Pamphlet. Olympia, WA: Washington State
Parks and Recreation Commission, 1996.

Welch, Craig. "A War in the Woods." *The Seattle Times* 6 June 2006. 18 August
2006 <http://seattletimes.nwsource.com/html/localnews/2003042206_
salal06m.html>.

Wheeler, Sue. *Habitat.* London, ON: Brick Books, 2005.

White, Richard. *Land Use, Environment, and Social Change: The Shaping of Island
County, Washington.* Seattle: U Washington P, 1980.

Whitehead, F. H. "The Relationship Between Light Intensity and
Reproductive Capacity." *Plant Response to Climatic Factors: Prod. Uppsala Symp.
1970.* Paris: Unesco, 1973. 73–75.

Williams, Richard L. *et al. The Northwest Coast.* New York: Time-Life Books,
1973.

Williams, William Carlos. *Paterson (Book One).* New York: New Directions,
1946.

Windley, Carol. *Visible Light.* Lantzville, BC: Oolichan, 1993.

Wordsworth, William. *"Lyrical Ballads" and Other Poems, 1797–1800.* Ed.
James Butler and Karen Green. Ithaca: Cornell UP, 1992.

Xiao, Guoping, and Shannon M. Berch. "Ericoid Mycorrhizal Fungi of
Gaultheria Shallon." *Mycologia* 84.3 (1992): 470–71.

Zeigler, Anna. Personal communication (email). 16 March 2000.

Zwinger, Susan. *The Last Wild Edge: One Woman's Journey from the Arctic Circle to
the Olympic Rain Forest.* Boulder, CO: Johnson, 1999.

INDEX

A

A Rushing Sea of Undergrowth (Carr) 182, *183*
A Year on the Wild Side (Penn) 90
Abram, David 1, 2, 12—13, 17, 154, 205
Adams, Vanessa 37—39, 43
Adaptation (Kaufman) 13
After the Storm — Salal Blossoms (Meeker-Rouhier) 184
Ana Historic (Marlatt) 61
Anderson, Angela 39—43
Anderson, Lorraine 145
Anderson-Dargatz, Gail 161
Armstrong, Jeannette 28
As For Me and My House (Ross) 81
Astoria, OR 3, 4, 166—67

B

Babineau, Guy 160
Bainbridge Island, WA *33, 34, 43*
Ballard, Heidi 92, 94
Baranof Springs, AL 5

Barton, Benjamin Smith 149
Barton, John 24
Beach Salal (Henderson) 184
Bean, W. J. 151
Bellingham, WA *120*
Berry, Wendell 69
Birds of British Columbia, The (Campbell *et al.*) 53
Boas, Franz 30
Boateng, Jacob O. 47, 55, 56
Bolster, Stephanie 65, 182, 192
Botany of Desire, The (Pollan) 13, 56, 59, 61
Bowering, George 155
Bowling, Tim 182
Bown, Alan 55
Brar, Parminder 41
Brett, Brian 5
Bringhurst, Robert 101, 119
Brock University 55
Broken Ground (Hodgins) 23
Brown, Robert L. 57
Burning Water (Bowering) 155

Burns Bog, BC 48

C

Camosun Bog, BC 48
Campbell, R. Wayne 53
Campbell River 71, 125, *126*, 132, *140*, 188
Cape Creek, OR 52
Carr, Emily 24–25, *25*, 154, 182, *183*,
    184–85
Carver, Raymond 61–62
Carving the Elements (Bringhurst) 119
Christensen, Judy *189*
Chuong Chau 104–14
CIDA (Canadian International
    Development Agency) 36, 142
Clark, William *149*, 149–50
Cleverly, Bill 195
Cocksedge, Wendy 57, 103, 104, 106,
    110, 114
Cody, John 9
Cohen, Michael 13
Collins, Don 93, 95
Collis, Christie 161, 163–64
Colombia, salal shipments to 36–37
Comeau, Phil 47, 55, 56
Compton, Brian 29–30
Cook, Elizabeth 151
Cook, James 146
Cortes Island, BC 188–90, *188*, *189*,
    190, 195
Coupland, Douglas 77, 203–204
Courtenay, BC 71, 125–32, *134*, 136
Coyote: A Mystery (Brett) 5
Coyote and Rock, and Other Lushootseed Stories
    (Hilbert) 28
Cronquist, Arthur 155

Cure for Death by Lightning, The (Anderson-
    Dargatz) 161
Curtis's Botanical Magazine 151, 152

D

Davey, Lorna 121
Davidson, Florence Edenshaw 100
Davis, H. L. 115–16
de Kok, Rogier P. J. 81, 83
Dean Moore, Kathleen 6–7
Deleuze, Gilles 49–50
Dirks-Edmund, Jane C. 55
Doig, Ivan 16, 22
Doss, Diane 57
Douglas, David 121, 147–48, 150–51,
    169, 187
Duncan, David James 38, 89, 115
*During My Time: Florence Edenshaw Davidson,
    a Haida Woman* (Davidson) 100

E

Eberhardt, Tom 95
Efron, Sarah 71
Egg and I, The (MacDonald) 51
Erlich, Gretel 145
Evernden, Neil 26–27, 58–59

F

Flora of the Pacific Northwest (Hitchcock
    and Cronquist) 155–56
Florida, salal shipments to 36–37
Food Plants of the Coastal First Peoples
    (Turner) 35
Forest Renewal, BC 56
Forrest, Mary 153
Forgiveness of Nature: The Story of Grass, The

(Harvey) 13

Foster, David 70

Freed, Jim 56, 89–97, 99, 151

G

Gallagher, Tess 4, 61–62

Garden of Bristlecones, A (Cohen) 13

Gardiner, Anne 120

*Gathering Moss: A Natural and Cultural
    History of Mosses* (Kimmerer) 13

Gaultheria procumbens 42

Gaultheria shallon 10, 26, 82, 147 *see* salal

Gayton, Don 5

Gibbs, Donna 86

Gloss, Molly 125

Gould, Stephen Jay 97

Great Marpole Midden, The (Dikeakos) 27

Griffith, Thomas 103

Green, Jeff 54

Guattari, Felix 49–50

guidebooks, genre of 19–22

Guppy, Crispin S. 54

Guterson, David 54, 79, 80

H

Hafenrichter, A.L. 57

Haida 28, 100–101

Haisla 29, 30

Hale, Amanda 54

Hamilton, Robert 161

Hansis, Richard 70

Hanaksiala (Henaaksiala) 29

Harvey, Athelstan George 148

Having Everything Right (Stafford) 133, 135

Heffernan, Helen 78

Hilbert, Vi 28

Hitchcock, C. Leo 155

Hodgins, Jack 10, 23, 80, 180, 196–97

Holm, Bill 99, 101

Honey in the Horn (Davis) 115–16

Hoover, Alan 100, 113

Hopkins Landing, Howe Sound (Hughes)
    181, 181

Howarth, Jean 74

Hoyt Arboretum 65–67

Huang, Anne 54

Huffman, David 48–49, 50, 51, 52

Hughes, E. J. 179–82, *180, 181*

Hugo, Richard 22, 63–64

Hutton, Tom 159, 161

I

In Broken Country (Wagoner) 12

Inside Passage Seeds 169–77

interviews, methodology of 3, 16–17

Invention of the World, The (Hodgins) 180,
    196–97

J

Jarvis, P.J. 151

Jones, Mavis 23, 191–94, 196-97

Joseph, Maia 195, 196, 204–205

Justice, Clive 151

K

Ketchikan, AL 3, 5, 83–101

Kevin Paul, Philip 10, 30–32, 100

Kew Gardens 81–87

Khaley, Manju 42

Khim, Mean A. L. 104–14

Kimmerer, Robin 13

Kitasoo 29

Kroetsch, Bob 11, 137

L

Landry, Donna 151
Last Wild Edge, The (Zwinger) 29
Latino immigrant harvesters 70—71,
    92—94, 96, 97
Latta, Bill 11
Leopold, Aldo 33
Lewis, Meriwether 148—50, 161
Lewis and Clark Herbarium 83
LI-COR Biosciences Corporation 52
Life After God (Coupland) 77
Lilburn, Tim 192
Linnaeus, Carl 146
Lippard, Lucy 2
Lochsa Road (Stafford) 15, 133
Lowry, Malcolm 22
Lowther, Christine 179
Lunn, Corry 62

M

MacDonald, Betty 51
Macnair, Peter 100, 113
Magic Leaves, The (Macnair and Hoover)
    100, 101
Makah 28, 94, 96
marijuana, smuggling of (in salal) 71
Marlatt, Daphne 22, 61, 135
Marriott, Anne 48
Massey, Doreen 207
Mayhew, Margaret 163
McClure, Robert 70
McConnaughey, Bayard H. 55
McDonald, Bob 119
McGill, Chris 159

McKay, Don 20, 192, 206
McKelvey, Susan Delano 147
McWhirter, George 162—63
Mail, Mike 71
Massey, Doreen 207
Mayne Island, BC 10
Meeker-Rouhier, K. 184
Menjivar, Alfredo 70—71
Menzies, Archibald 146—48, 150, 151
Messier, Christian 51
Microserfs (Coupland) 203—204
Mill, John 40
Moeller, Dan 65—67
Moulton, Gary E. 148, 149
Muses Among Us, The (Stafford) 16
MV Quinault 200
My Story as Told by Water (Duncan) 38,
    89, 115
Myer, Ernie 17, 136—44, 199
Myer Floral 137

N

Nataros, Rod 35—37
"native," as concept 89—90, 97, 99
NATS Nursery 35—43, 36, 39
Nautilus Explorer 47, 86—87
Nelson, Laura Baker 148
Nesting Ground, The (Wagoner) 19
New, Bill 25
Newitt, Angela 161, 167
Nigei Island, BC 4
Nontimber Forest Products in the United States
    70
Northwest Coast Indian Art: An Analysis of
    Form (Holm) 99, 101
Northwestern Researchers and

Harvesters Association 93
nurseries 33–43, 48, 55, 139, 151,
    199–205
Nygaard, Darrel 62–63

O

October Ferry to Gabriola (Lowry) 22
On the Line (Deleuze and Guattari)
    49–50
Orchid Thief, The (Orlean) 13
Oregon State Health Center 96
Oregon State University 48, 49, 50
Orlean, Susan 13
Our Lady of the Forest (Guterson) 54,
    79–80
Oweekeno 29

P

Pacific Forestry Centre 57, 103
Pacific Northwest Landscape: A Painted
    History, The (Harmon) 184
Paterson (Williams) 81
Penn, Briony 86, 90, 161
Peterman, Mike 166
Pfeiffer Big Sur State Park 5
Pissaro, Camille 182
Plant Identification Terminology: An Illustrated
    Glossary (Harris) 20
Pollan, Michael 13, 56, 59, 61
Port Townsend, WA 4, 5, 169, 176, 205
Portland, OR 3, 65–66, 96
Practice of the Wild, The (Snyder) 159, 165
Prescott, Cindy 45–49, 53–54, 58–60, 96
PRT Reid Collins Nursery 40, 41
Purdy, Al 26
Pyle, Robert Michael 10–12, 20, 54–55

Q

Quileute 28–29

R

Raban, Jonathan 5–6, 184–85
Ramsey, Jarold 21
Rayner, Anne 23–24, 187
Reflections of Early Vancouver in My Childhood,
    1893–1912 (Schwesinger) 160
Rehder, Alfred 151
Rilke, Rainer Maria 182–84
Ross, Dick 77
Ross, Rick 51, 71–77, 80, 125–34, 126,
    135
Ross, Sinclair 81
Royal Roads University 57, 94, 103

S

salal 10, 21, 116, 149, 152
    arranging 61–64
    botanizing of 145–54
    description of 1, 11, 20, 55–56, 66–
        67, 149, 155–57
    ecology of 45–58
    export of 125–34
    First Nations/Native American uses
        of 26, 29–30, 31–32, 94, 96,
        99–101, 160, 167
    growing of 33–43, 201–202, 203
    harvesting ("picking") of 56–58,
        69–80, 89–97, 103–14, 132,
        187–91, 196–97 see also wildcrafting
    naming of 23–32, 27, 147, 194
    Native American uses, see First Nations
    parasites 55–56
    propagators 37–43

represented in art 99—101, 179—85

rhizomes 47—51, 50, 53, 57

seeds and harvest of 34, 35—36, 37, 38, 39—42, 49, 126, 145, 163, 169—77, 174, 202

wildcrafting 69, 70—76

wine 167—68

women and 30—32, 96, 100—101, 161, 167, 187—97

salal berries

   eating of 1, 31—32, 159—64

   harvesting of 171—72

Salal Café 5, 176

Salal Cedar Hemlock Integrated Research Program 45—46

Salal Complex (Forest Renewal BC) 56—57

Salal Joe, legend of 136

Sand County Almanac (Leopold) 33

Saturna Island, BC 4, 119

Savary Island, BC *21*

Sea Runners, The (Doig) 16

Seattle Post-Intelligencer 70, 71

Scraping By in the Big Eighties (Singer) 57

Shallon Winery 166—68

Shepard Jon S. 54

Shields, Carol 38

Shomer, Forest 97, 119, 169—77

Singer, Natalie Rachel 57

Sitka, AL 5

Slater, Beth *188, 189*

Smith, Bruce 95

Snow Falling On Cedars (Guterson) 80

Snowden, Mary Ann 136

Snyder, Gary 15, 159, 165, 168, 198

Social Creation of Nature, The (Evernden) 26—27

Sok Kosal 104—14

Sounding the Blood (Hale) 54

Sourcing Northwest *120*, 121—23

South Puget Sound Community College 57

Southeast Asian immigrant harvesters 70, 91, 93, 97, 104—14

Spell of the Sensuous, The (Abram) 1, 12—13

Stafford, Kim 15, 16, 30, 133, 135, 151, 199, 205, 207

Stagner, Rod 167—68

Stanley Park (Taylor) 10, 117—18, 162

Steel, Stephanie Quainton 136

Stephenson, George 188

Sterling, Shirley 6

Steveston (Marlatt) 22

Stewart, Ann 121—23

Stoutenberg, Adrien 148

Sunde, Scott 71

Surrey, BC 3, 35

Swan, James 101

Swann, Brian 145

Swanton, John 101

T

Tacoma, WA 4, 131

Taking the Names Down from the Hill (Kevin Paul) 30—31

Tappeiner, John 49, *50*

Taylor, Timothy 10, 117—18, 162

Telling It: Woman and Language Across Cultures (Armstrong) 28

Thacker, Bob 166

Thomas, Audrey 165—66

Thomas, Ian 185

Thomas, Jack Ward 45

Thompson, Doreen 187–97
Thoreau, Henry David 99, 162
Titus, Brian 57, 103–107, 110, 113, 195–96
Tofino, BC *116*, 160, 184
Traveling Light (Wagoner) 12
Tree Study (Hughes) *181, 181*
Turner, Nancy 35, 100, 177
Turtle Bay, BC 136

U

Union Bay, BC 62
University of British Columbia 45, 159
University of Lethbridge 11
Unless (Shields) 38

V

Vales, D.G. 53
van der Veldt, Paul 167
Van Dersal, William R. 47
Vancouver Aquarium 86
Vancouver Island, BC 3, 5, 45, 94, 130, 131, 136, 139, 140, 141, 154, 161, 175
Vance Nan C. 55
Vashon Island, WA 199–200

W

Wachtler, Ingrid 33–34, *139*
Wagoner, David 12, 19, 22, 72, 184
Walden (Thoreau) 99
Walsh, Charles 122
Washington State University 89
Waxwings (Raban) 5–6
West of Darkness (Barton) 24
West Kootenays, BC 5

Western Evergreens 71, 77, *77, 126,* 125–34, *134,* 188
Wheeler, Sue 206
White, Richard 160
Wickaninnish Inn 160
Wild Life (Gloss) 79, 125
Wilkins, Tom *34,* 34, 139, 199–206
Wilkins Nursery 199, 202–203
Wilkowski, Joe 136, *see* Salal Joe
Willapa Hills, WA 10
Williams, Richard L. 54
Williams, William Carlos L. 81
Windley, Carol 153–54
Wings of Paradise (Cody) 9
Winter Brothers (Doig) 22
Wintergreen: Rambles in a Ravaged Land (Pyle) 10–12, 20
Wood Interior (Carr) 25
Woodbrook Nursery 33–34, *43*

Z

Zeigler, Anna 153
Zwicky, Jan 180
Zwinger, Susan 29

ACKNOWLEDGEMENTS

Anne Rayner was the first to make me look at salal and to suggest —
maybe unwittingly — that in that looking might be a book.

Bill New, as he has for 30 years, kept listening, advising, encouraging, and editing.

Rosemary Leach is a gardener and a lover of plants who gave hundreds of hours to putting this material into publishable form.

Jennifer Yong found salal berry vinaigrette in Tofino. Joel Martineau
and Jan Kelly found salal jam on Vancouver Island. Erin Peters introduced me to Salal Joe. Janet Giltrow brought me photographs of the
salal forest on Savary Island. Mary Bryson provided a salal jelly recipe.
Margaret Butschler was always on the lookout for pictures. Longtime
friend Joan Sherritt drew salal for me in pen and ink; her drawing
forms the basis for the printer's devices in this book.

I am grateful to Ken MacCrimmon, founding director of the Peter
Wall Institute for Advanced Studies at the University of British
Columbia: my associate residency there provided some quiet, and stim-
ulating conversation to get me started. Mike Healey convinced me that
a scientist could be interested in a plant book by an English professor.
Laurie McNeill and Shane Plante provided early help with the research. And Shasta Grenier discovered her own enthusiasm, both for

blackberry and the black berry of salal — enthusiasm that moved her work as research assistant beyond thorough to the imaginative and evocative. Maia Joseph extended Shasta's work on the project as far as the Library of the Royal Horticultural Society, then edited with enthusiastic interest and empathy. Maia contributed both scrupulous care and cultural vision to this storying of a species; I have frequently relied on her judgement and drawn on her suggestions.

Maybe half the names mentioned in these pages of thanks are students who have taken one or several courses with me. In this crucial network, I must also mention Christie Hurrell, Lisa Szabo, Yael Katz, Bob Kull, Anna Ziegler, Susan Beckett, Travis Mason, Theresa Scott, Gary Lewis, Angela Waldie, Myra Wright, Jacky Shin, and Colleen Derkatch. These will stand for the many more who, especially in various courses in "habitat studies," have tolerated or embraced my obsession with *Gaultheria shallon*.

David Brownstein sent me a salal reference every ten days or so. Cindy Prescott was my generous guide in the field of professional forestry research. Rhoda and Glen Love welcomed me into their home, and then filled my day and night with salal facts and stories. An anonymous reviewer provided very helpful advice. For various forms of help, support, and encouragement, I would also like to thank Michael Cohen, John and Judy Berezowskyj, Ken and Sharon Rooke, Herbert Rosengarten, Coni O'Neill, Anne Kaufmann, Brenda Peterson, Richard Mackie, Nancy Pagh, Cheryll Glotfelty, Paul Tennant, Mary Berbee, John McLean, Fran Kaye, Lee Gulyás, Kali Robson, Katie Eliot, Michael Peterman, Margaret Murdoch, Pattie and Kieran Kealy, Mary Brown, George McWhirter, Marney Ward, Kim Stafford, Mavis Jones, Peggy Acott, Bob Thacker, Sherry Mitchell, and Theresa Kishkan.

Liz Gilbert answered questions about the David Douglas material in the Royal Horticultural Society (RHS) Archives, while Diana Miller at the RHS, Serena Marner at Oxford University's Fielding-Druce Herbarium, Gina Murrell at the Cambridge University Herbarium, and Vicki Noble at the General Herbarium of the British Natural History Museum helped locate some of Douglas's *Gaultheria shallon* specimens. Serena Marner also provided access to images of Douglas's specimens. Michèle Losse, Rogier de Kok, and Julia Steele smoothed my visit to Kew Gardens, and Sven Landrein at Kew answered later questions about salmonberry and Oregon-grape. Adrienne Aikins told me about the use of salal at the Royal British Columbia Museum. Jeff Jewell helped me in the archives at the Whatcom Museum. Rick McCourt arranged for my visit to the Academy of Natural Sciences in Philadelphia; Alfred E. (Ernie) Schuyler and James Macklin generously guided me through the herbarium there. Christos Dikeakos kindly accommodated my request for a specific detail from his artwork. Danielle Currie of the Vancouver Art Gallery, Duane Sneddeker of the Missouri Historical Society, and Patricia Gow of Polygon Realty Ltd. also helped me access images for the book.

Wendy Cocksedge is coordinator of Research and Extension at Royal Roads University's Centre for Non-Timber Resources. Dr. Brian Titus is research scientist at the Pacific Forestry Centre in Victoria. Both have a huge fund of knowledge about special forest products, which I could not even begin to represent adequately in these pages. I am grateful for their generous help and, even more so, for the inspiration of their work toward a future of sustainable community-based forestry.

Among the fine staff of the English Department at the University of British Columbia, I'd especially like to thank Tim Conklin, who kept passing me salal bits, including the story of the blue bear scat, and Carol Wong, who writes and draws plants with great sensitivity. Dominique Yupangco helped me prepare many of the illustrations.

In editing the manuscript, Smaro Kamboureli nicely fused scepticism and enthusiasm. More important, she encouraged the whole project in her long willingness to believe there could be some hybrid text imagined as a horticultural-literary ethnography.

NeWest Press, its Board and cheerful, dedicated staff, continue to redefine the idea of region, and to find new regions in the West. To them, and to Treva and our precious family, go my ultimate thanks.

This book incorporates the voices and salutes the knowledge of many people who agreed to be interviewed. Their tape-recorded comments will be deposited in the University of British Columbia Archives.

Vanessa Adams. NATS Nursery, Surrey, BC. 29 July 2003.

Angela Anderson with Rod Nataros. NATS Nursery, Langley, BC. 8 September 2004.

Chuong Chau, Mean A. L. Khim, and Sok Kosal, with Wendy Cocksedge and Brian Titus. Pacific Forestry Centre, Victoria, BC. 26 August 2004.

Jim Freed. Applebee's Restaurant, Olympia, WA. 17 March 2004.

David E. Hibbs. Oregon State University, Corvallis, OR. 18 March 2004.

Dan Moeller. Hoyt Arboretum, Portland, OR. 21 November 2003.

Ernie Myer. The Myer Floral Company, Inc., Vancouver, BC. 14 July 2003.

Rod Nataros. NATS Nursery, Surrey, BC. 7 July 2003.

Cindy Prescott. University of British Columbia, Vancouver, BC. 8 May 2006.

Rick Ross. Western Evergreens, Courtenay, BC. 15 August 2003.

———. Western Evergreens and field, Courtenay, BC. 21 October 2003.

Forest Shomer. Inside Passage Seeds, Port Townsend, WA. June 2003.

John Tappeiner. Oregon State University, Corvallis, OR. 18 March 2004.

Doreen Thompson. Cortes Island, BC (by telephone). 28 January 2005.

Ingrid Wachtler. Woodbrook Nursery, Gig Harbor, WA. 9 June 2003.

Tom Wilkins. Vashon Island, WA (by telephone). 1 November 2004.

PERMISSIONS

The author and NeWest Press gratefully acknowledge permissions from publishers to quote from works published by them.

"Shallal" by Mavis Jones, from *Her Festival Clothes*, © 2001. Reprinted by permission of McGill-Queens University Press. Excerpt from "Sweetly Neglected" by Philip Kevin Paul, from Melanie O'Brian *et al.*, eds. *Spilled*, © 2004. Reprinted by permission of Artspeak. Excerpt from "What We Call Life" by Philip Kevin Paul, from *Taking the Names Down from the Hill*, © 2003. Reprinted by permission of Nightwood Editions. Excerpt from "Understory" by Sue Wheeler, from *Habitat*, © 2005. Reprinted by permission of Brick Books. Excerpt from "To the Salal (*Gaultheria shallon*) Berry: An Apologia" by George McWhirter, from an unpublished manuscript titled *The Incorrection.* Reprinted by permission of the author.

Laurie Ricou is a Professor of English at the University of British Columbia. He is a former president of the Western Literature Association, and former Editor of the journal *Canadian Literature.* His previous publications include *Vertical Man/Horizontal World: Man and Landscape in Canadian Prairie Fiction, A Field Guide to "A Guide to Dungeness Spit,"* and *The Arbutus/ Madrone Files: Reading the Pacific Northwest.* He currently lives in Vancouver, BC.

The first page of an eight-page score.

This work was inspired by the chance discovery of a
Salal shrub at the Savill Gardens, Windsor, England.
The Salal is an evergreen shrub common to the
Pacific Coast of Canada and the Northwestern United
States — an area in which I spent some ten years.
This piece is based on Salish and Kwakiutl melodies,
as well as motives from my opera, "Seabird Island."

· Derek Healey (Composer's Note 30 March 1990)

figure 27

"Salal: An Idyll for Orchestra, opus 71."
by Derek Healey